Charles Nebeker Thompson

**A Treatise on Building Associations**

Adapted to the use of Lawyers and Officers

Charles Nebeker Thompson

**A Treatise on Building Associations**
*Adapted to the use of Lawyers and Officers*

ISBN/EAN: 9783337401795

Printed in Europe, USA, Canada, Australia, Japan

Cover: Foto ©Suzi / pixelio.de

More available books at **www.hansebooks.com**

# A TREATISE

ON

# BUILDING ASSOCIATIONS.

ADAPTED TO THE USE OF

## LAWYERS AND OFFICERS.

———·———

## WITH COMPLETE SET OF FORMS.

———

By CHARLES N. THOMPSON.

———

CHICAGO:
CALLAGHAN & COMPANY.
1892.

# PREFACE.

My purpose is to give an authoritative exposition of the law of building associations, in such concise and clear form as to be available in the hands of both lawyers and persons interested in the subject matter. Considering it as the most logical and satisfactory method, I have started with the building association in its preliminary organization, and examined its career through to final settlement and dissolution, from both legal and practical standpoints. It is my intention that the unprofessional reader may disregard the notes, while the lawyer may examine the authorities therein referred to as supporting any given proposition. It is believed that any work citing the law, to acquire the confidence of the reader, must also refer to the authorities supporting the propositions. The only law book in the United States on the subject, was written ten years ago, and since then, statutory enactments of the different states have made such changes as to justify a new treatment.

A purpose auxiliary to the chief one has been to simplify the legal status of a building association, and to avoid the application of some more or less complicated doctrines maintained by some courts. In sustaining this purpose, parts of the book will appear elementary to the lawyer.

Some years' connection with building associations, in different capacities, has given me an opportunity to observe their practical workings. Suggestions of remedies for their needs, are, therefore, the outgrowth of these observations.

No attempt has been made to give tables for apportioning or declaring dividends. It is mathematics, as in any other calculation, and while there have been many ingenious labor saving tables invented, there is no unanimity as to their perfect accuracy. Each secretary, generally, has his own method, borrowing some, perhaps, from other systems and adding his own notions, and the variation in the results obtained is but slight. The forms have been prepared after examining those in use in the different states. I desire to acknowledge the kindly assistance of Mr. Charles E. Holloway, of Indianapolis, in securing those forms.

C. N. T.

INDIANAPOLIS,
August 1st, 1892.

# TABLE OF CONTENTS.

## CHAPTER I.

### INTRODUCTION.

Section 1. Origin of Building Associations.............................

Section 2. Definition of Building Associations.........................

Section 3. General Scheme.............................................

Section 4. Different Types...........................................

## CHAPTER II.

### PRELIMINARY ORGANIZATION.

Section 1. Preliminary Agreements....................................

Section 2. Agreements Legally Considered.............................

Section 3. Articles of Incorporation.................................

Section 4. Corporate Name............................................

Section 5. Preparation of Corporate Articles.........................

Section 6. Conformity with Creative Law..............................

Section 7. Procedure after Registration..............................

## CHAPTER III.

### CHARTER.

Section 1. Importance of Charter.....................................

Section 2. Must generally adhere to Statute..........................

Section 3. What Constitutes Charter and its Legal Effect.............

Section 4. Effect of Failure to Observe Statute......................

Section 5. Construction..............................................

Section 6. Amendment.................................................

Section 7. Corporate Seal............................................

V

# CHAPTER IV.

## MEMBERS.

Section  1.  Effect of Incorporation............................
Section  2.  Membership Qualifications..........................
Section  3.  Purposes of Membership.............................
Section  4.  Purpose not Material...............................
Section  5.  Right to Borrow....................................
Section  6.  Right to Withdraw..................................
Section  7.  Certificate of Stock and Pass-books...............
Section  8.  Member Estopped to deny Incorporation.............
Section  9.  Illegal to invest Funds in Other Corporations.....
Section 10.  Death of Stockholder..............................

# CHAPTER V.

## BY-LAWS.

Section  1.  Framing and Adoption...............................
Section  2.  Definition.  Power to Enact and Amend..............
Section  3.  Notice of Amendment................................
Section  4.  Character of By-Laws...............................
Section  5.  Construction of By-Laws............................
Section  6.  Amendment of By-Laws...............................
Section  7.  Resolutions and Amendment..........................
Section  8.  Mode of Amendment..................................
Section  9.  Provisions of By-Laws..............................

# CHAPTER VI.

## GOVERNMENT AND OFFICERS.

Section  1.  Officers and Election..............................
Section  2.  Pass-books and Dues................................
Section  3.  General Meetings...................................
Section  4.  Special Meetings...................................
Section  5.  Quorum, Voting and Proxies.........................
Section  6.  Objects of General Meetings........................
Section  7.  Character, Duty and Liability of Directors.........
Section  8.  General Guidance for Directors.....................
Section  9.  Minutes of Meetings................................
Section 10.  Powers of Directors................................
Section 11.  Term of Election of Directors......................
Section 12.  Duties of President................................

Section 13. Duties of Vice-President.............................
Section 14. Duties of Secretary.................................
Section 15. Duties of Treasurer................................
Section 16. Duties of Attorney.................................
Section 17. Appraising Committee..............................
Section 18. Percentage of Value to be loaned....................
Section 19. Executive Committee...............................
Section 20. Auditing Committee............................
Section 21. Officers' Bonds................................
Section 22. Sureties on Official Bonds.........................
Section 23. Resignation and Removal of Directors................
Section 24. Officers' Relations and Responsibilities to the Association.

# CHAPTER VII.

## POWERS.

Section 1. General Powers.................................
Section 2. Implied Powers............................
Section 3. Powers of Agents................................
Section 4. Power to Sue..................................
Section 5. Power to Compromise with Shareholders..............
Section 6. Power to Loan Money..............................
Section 7. Power to hold Real Estate........................
Section 8. Power to issue Stock to Another Corporation.

# CHAPTER VIII.

## RIGHTS OF MEMBERS.

Section 1. Legal Status of Members..........................
Section 2. Preferential Stock.........................
Section 3. Paid Up Stock...........................
Section 4. Members and Officers must observe Rules..............
Section 5. Member's Right to Inspect Books.................
Section 6. Member as an Investor...........................
Section 7. Payments.................................
Section 8. Right of Withdrawal.............................
Section 9. Manner of Withdrawal.........................
Section 10. Legal Status of Withdrawing Member................
Section 11. Liability of Withdrawing Members...................
Section 12. Rights of Withdrawing Members of Insolvent Associa-
tion.....................................
Section 13. Right to Withdraw Limited to Present Funds...........
Section 14. Stock Pledged Cannot be Withdrawn.................

Section 15.  Amount Withdrawable............................................
Section 16.  Construction of By-Laws Concerning Withdrawals......
Section 17.  Transfer of Shares........ ................................
Section 18.  Forfeitures....................................................
Section 19.  The Legal Status of Member as Borrower................
Section 20.  Duty of Association to Loan its Money................ ......
Section 21.  Selection of Borrower................... ....................
Section 22.  Methods of Premium Charges.............................
Section 23.  Auction Premiums............................................
Section 24.  Premium Fixed, Unchangeable..........................
Section 25.  Premiums Chargeable to Maturity Only.................
Section 26.  Formal Application for Loan...............................
Section 27.  Appraisement................................... ........-....
Section 28.  Abstract of Title.............. ..........................
Section 29.  Interest Not Collectible on Interest and Premium.......
Section 30.  Payment of Instalments.....................................
Section 31.  Provisions of Note or Bond...............................
Section 32.  Provisions of Mortgage....................................
Section 33.  Complaint upon Bond or Mortgage.....................
Section 34.  Loans to Outsiders..........................................
Section 35.  Loans to Married Women...................................
Section 36.  Mortgage Covenants........................................
Section 37.  Application of Payments....................................
Section 38.  Assignment of Shares as Collateral Security...........
Section 39.  Payments on Stock not *ipso facto* payments on loan....
Section 40.  Payments on Re-assigned Stock..........................
Section 41.  Assigned Shares Cannot be Credited....................
Section 42.  Liability of Borrower under his Mortgage for Losses....
Section 43.  Acknowledgment of Mortgage............................
Section 44.  Leases by the Association..................................
Section 45.  Satisfaction of Mortgages........ .....................
Section 46.  Borrower Entitled to Set Off..............................
Section 47.  Amount Payable Upon Foreclosure....... .............
Section 48.  The English Rule.............................................
Section 49.  Rule Laid Down Upon Voluntary Re-payment............
Section 50.  Uncertainty of the Foregoing Rules......................
Section 51.  The Natural and Logical Rule.............. ............
Section 52.  By-Laws should Provide for Record Cancellations.......

## CHAPTER IX.

### FINES.

Section 1.  Necessity of Fines...........................................
Section 2.  Must be Reasonable..........................................
Section 3.  Stop After Foreclosure......................................
Section 4.  No Interest on Fines.........................................
Section 5.  Are Lien on Stock............................................

# CHAPTER X.

## USURY.

Section 1. Definition.....................................................
Section 2. Premium not Usurious as Formerly.......................
Section 3. Premiums Authorized by Statute..........................
Section 4. When Interest is not Usurious............................
Section 5. Illegal Interest not Recoverable by Association..........
Section 6. May be Recovered Back by the Borrower.................
Section 7. A Personal Defense........................................
Section 8. Rule for Officers...........................................

# CHAPTER XI.

## POWER OF THE ASSOCIATION TO BORROW MONEY.

Section 1. A Practical Aspect.........................................
Section 2. English Authorities........................................
Section 3. American Authorities......................................
Section 4. Weight of American Authorities..........................
Section 5. Implied Power to Borrow..................................
Section 6. Overdrawing Bank Account is Borrowing...............
Section 7. Resolution to Borrow......................................
Section 8. The Effect of Assigning Mortgages.......................
Section 9. No Power to Sell Its Mortgages..........................

# CHAPTER XII.

## DISSOLUTION AND SETTLEMENT.

Section 1. Dissolution when all Stock is Matured..................
Section 2. Other Methods of Dissolution............................
Section 3. What Acts Will Not Dissolve.............................
Section 4. Dissolution by Unanimous Agreement...................
Section 5. Effect of Appointment of a Receiver....................
Section 6. Final Settlement with Members and Creditors..........
Section 7. Settlement Before Maturity...............................
Section 8. Assignment for Creditors .................................
Section 9. Appointment of Receiver amd Winding Up............
Section 10. Marshalling of Assets....................................
Section 11. Liability of Stockholders.................................

Section 12.  Liability of Borrowers for Debts............................
Section 13.  No Liability for Losses under the Mortgages............
Section 14.  Liability of Withdrawing Member....................
Section 15.  Assets to be Distributed among Borrowers and Non-Borrowers alike......................................................
Section 16.  Consolidation of Associations.............................

# CHAPTER XIII.

## PRACTICAL RESULTS.

Section  1.  The Character of a Building Association.................
Section  2.  Method of Loans.......................................
Section  3.  Some Results.........................................

# APPENDIX.

## STATUTES AND CONSTRUCTION.

FORMS OF
        Agreement for Incorporation...........................
        Application for Membership............................
        Articles of Association................................
        Act of Incorporation..................................
        Stock Certificate.....................................
        Assignment............................................
        By-Laws...............................................
        Application for a Loan................................
        Appraisers' Report....................................
        Rules.................................................
        Mortgage Note.........................................
        Bond..................................................
        Mortgage..............................................
        Transfer for Loans....................................
        Note..................................................
        Trust Deed............................................
        Insurance Clause......................................
        Bond..................................................
        Bond Used by Pennsylvania Associations................
        Mortgage Used by Pennsylvania Associations............
        Bond Used by New Jersey Associations..................
        Mortgage Used by New Jersey Associations..............
        Mortgage Used by the Mutual Home Saving and Loan
            Association of Dayton, Ohio.......................
        Bank Mortgage Used in Massachusetts...................

FORMS OF

Stock Register........................................
Warrant.............................................
Bank Check..........................................
Building Agreement...................................
Building Specifications...............................
Indemnifying Bond Against Liens.......................
Contractor's Waiver of Liens..........................
Sub-Contractor's Waiver.... ........................
Bond for Secretary...................................
Bond for Treasurer...................................

# TABLE OF CASES.

## A

| | Page. |
|---|---|
| Abbott v Building Association, 1 Del., 397 | 156 |
| Albright v Building Association, 102 Pa. St., 411 | 17-52 |
| Allemania, etc., Association v Mueller, 8 Bull, 97 | 93 |
| Allen v Curtis, 26 Conn., 456 | 38 |
| Anderson v Cleburne, etc., Association, 16 S. W. Rep., 298 | 17 |
| Archer v Harrison, 3 Jur., N. S., 194 | 94 |
| Armitage v Walker, 2 Jur., N. S., 13 | 67 |
| Ashland, etc., Co. v Centralia, etc., Association, 9 Luz. Leg., Reg., 41 (Pa.,) | 44 |
| Association v Commonwealth, 2 Chest., 546 | 156 |
| Association v Bollinger, 12 Rich., Eq., 124 | 102-103 |
| Association v George, 3 W. N. C., 239 | 105 |
| Association v Kribs, 7 Leg & Ins. Rep., (Pa.,) 21 | 63 |
| Association v Neurath, 2 W. N. C., 95 | 105 |
| Association v Steele, 11 W. N. C., 204 | 83 |
| Association v Wall, 7 Phila., 189 | 125 |
| Athol, etc., Co. v Carey, 116 Mass., 471 | 11 |
| Atkinson v Bradford, etc., Society, L. R., 25 Q. B. Div., 377 | 69 |
| Atwood v Dumas, 149 Mass., 167 | 2-64 |
| Auld v Glasgow, etc., Society, 12 App. Cas., 197 | 31 |

## B

| | |
|---|---|
| Babcock v Middlesex, etc., Bank, 28 Conn., 302 | 87-153 |
| Baltimore, etc., Society v Taylor, 41 Md., 409 | 81-103-104-106 |
| Bank v Porter, 2 Watts, 141 | 91 |
| Bank, etc., v St. John, 25 Ala., 566-611 | 39 |
| Bank of Commerce's Appeal, 73 Pa. St., 59 | 70 |
| Barker v Bigelow, 15 Gray, 130 | 86-87 |
| Barndt v Gruel, 4 Leg. Gaz., 388 | 54 |
| Barton v Enterprise, etc, Association, 114 Ind., 226 | 116-129 |
| Bates v Peoples', etc., Association, 42 Ohio St., 655 | 25-103-156 |
| Bauer v Samson Lodge, 102 Ind., 262 | 29 |
| Baxter v McIntyre, 13 Gray, 168 | 2-98-154 |
| Bechtold v Brehm, 26 Pa. St., 269 | 71-77 |
| Becket v Building Association, 88 Pa. St., 211 | 157 |

Page.

Bergman v St. Paul, etc., Association, 29 Minn., 275............15-29-68
Bexar, etc., Association v Robinson, 78 Tex., 163...................105
Bibb Co., etc., Association v Richards, 21 Ga., 592...........2 13-77-103
Birmingham v Maryland, etc., Association, 45 Md., 541.........52-81-105
Blackburn, etc., Society, v Cunliffe, 20 Ch. D., 902................111
Blake v Buffalo Creek R. R. Company, 56 N. Y., 485.................42
Blake v Wheeler, 18 Hun., 496......................................48
Booz's Appeal, 16 W. N. C., 365...................................128
Booz's Appeal, 109 Pa. St., 594....................................69
Borchus v Huntington, etc., Association, 97 Ind., 180..............82
Border State, etc., Association v Hayes, 61 Md., 597............96 154
Border State, etc., Association v Hilleary, 68 Md., 52............105
Boston, etc., Company v Langdon, 24 Pick, 49......................119
Bowker v Mill River, etc., Association, 7 Allen, 100.....103-120-124
Brooks v Blackburn, etc., Society, L. R. 9 App., Cas., 857........114
Brownlie v Russell, L. R., 8 App. Cas., 235.......................128
Bryant v Cowart, 21 Ala., 92.......................................91
Bucklee v Lordonny, 56 L. J. Ch., 437.............................128
Buffalo, etc., Company v Gifford, 87 N. Y., 294....................11
Building Association's Appeal, 33 P. L. J., 324...................122
Building Association's Estate, 12 W. N. C., 207....................65
Building Association v Arbeiter Bund, 6 Bull, 823...............25-62
Building Association v Bayley, 1 Kulp, 215.........................88
Building Association v Building Association, 100 Pa. St., 191.....156
Building Association v Coleman, 89 Pa. St., 428...................157
Building Association v Commonwealth, 98 Pa. St., 54..............156
Building Association v Egger, 5 Bull, 752.......................93-97
Building Association v Eshelback, 7 Phila., 189...........88-125-156
Building Association v Gallagher, 3 L. T. N S., 101................87
Building Association v George, 3 W. N. C., 239.....................86
Building Association v Groesbeck, 41 L. I., Pa., 16............87-101
Building Association v Hanlen, 7 Luz. L. Reg., 165...............157
Building Association v Henderson, 3 Bull, 386......................70
Building Association v Hetzel, 103 Pa. St., 507....................82
Building Association v Hoary, 8 Luz. L. Reg., 180.................157
Building Association v Hungerbuehler, 93 Pa. St., 258..............88
Building Association v Goldbeck, 13 W. N. C., 24...................42
Building Association v Jones, 2 L. T. N. S., Pa., 17...............29
Building Association v Kelley, 1 Kulp, 9..........................119
Building Association v Leyden, 1 Bull, 126.........................93
Building Association v Lyons, 2 Kulp, 409......................82 104
Building Association v Mangan, 2 Kulp, 210.........................88
Building Association v McDermott, 2 Kulp, 203......................83
Building Association v Mixell, 84 Pa., St., 313....................83
Building Association v Minnick, 1 Kulp, 513........................62
Building Association v Morgan, 2 Kulp, 19..........................87

Page.

Building Association v Morganthal, 2 Pears, 343.................17

Building Association v Raber, 11 Phila., 546.................86

Building Association v Rice, 8 W. N. C., 12.................83

Building Association v Roan, 9 W. N. C., 15.................86

Building Association v Robinson, 46 L. I., Pa., 5.........22-30-82-156

Building Association v Rood, 2 Kulp, Pa., 246.........87-93

Building Association v Rowe, 15 L. I., 45.................88

Building Association v Schuller, 3 W. N. C., Pa., 431.........81-100

Building Association v Semiller, 35 Pa. St., 225.........50-156

Building Association v Silverman, 85 Pa. St., 394.........65

Building Association v Sperring, 106 Pa. St., 334.........66-69

Building Association v Taylor, 13 W. N. C., 13.................85

Building Association v Timmins, 3 Phila., 209.................77

Burbridge v Cotton, 8 Eng. L. & Eq. R., 57.........76-103

Burke v Home, etc., Association, 7 Bull, 114.................79

Burlington, etc., Association v Heider, 55 Iowa, 424.........77-106

## C

Callahan's Appeal, 124 Pa. St., 138.................98

Carmody v Powers, 60 Mich., 26.................12

Cason v Seldner, 77 Va., 293.........81-98-128

Central, etc., Association v O'Connor, 5 Bull, 853.................93

Chapleo v Brunswick, etc., Society, L. R., 6 Q. B. D., 696.........109

Cheesebrough v Millard, 1 Johns. Ch., 409.................126

Chester, etc., Company v Dewey, 16 Mass., 94.................24

Chicago, etc., Society v Crowell, 65 Ill., 453.........53-84

Chillicothe, etc., Association v Ruegger, 60 Mo., 218.........53

Christian's Appeal, 102 Pa. St., 184.........123-128

Christie v Northern Counties, etc., Society, L. R., 43 Ch. Div., 62.....31-32

Cincinnati, etc., Association v Flach, 1 Cin., S. C. R., 468.........93

Clarksville, etc., Association v Stephens, 26 N. J. Eq., 351.....77-84-85-100

Citizens', etc., Association v Goriell, 34 N. J., Eq., 383.................39

Citizens', etc., Association v Lyon, 29 N. J. Eq., 110.................39

Citizens', etc., Association v Webster, 25 Barb, 263.........95-103-104

Citizens', etc., Company v Uhler, 48 Md., 455.................76

City Loan, etc., Association v Goodrich, 48 Ga., 445.................120

City, etc., Company v Fatty. 1 Abb. App. Dec., 347.........95-104

Coetnior, etc., Society, 51 L. T. 253.................110

Colonial, etc., Company v Home, etc., Company, Lim., 33 L. J. Ch., 741..12

Columbia, etc., Association v Bollinger, 12 Rich. Eq., 124.................77

Columbia, etc., Association v Dobbins, 15 L. I., 45.................88

Columbia, etc., Association v Crumb, 42 Md., 192.................54

Commonwealth v Association, 2 Chest., 189.................156

Commonwealth v Collen, 13 Pa. St., 133.................119

Concordia, etc., Association v Read, 93 N. Y., 474.........82-84-103

Conklin v People, etc., Association, 41 N. J., 20.................42

Page.

Connolly v Building Association, 6 W. N. C., 176.....123
Conrow v Spring Garden, etc., Association, 21 Leg. Int., 109.....186
Cook v Henderson, 8 Rec. (Ohio,) 429.....38
Cook v Kent, 105 Mass., 246.....120-154
Cooper v Association, 100 Pa. St.,.....402-156
Craig v First Presbyterian Church, 88 Pa. St., 42.....38
Criswell's Appeal, 100 Pa. St., 488.....113-124
Cross v Peach Bottom, etc., Company, 90 Pa. St., 392.....19
Cullerne v London, etc., Society, L. R., 25 Q. B., 485.....39-40
Cunningham v Alabama, etc., Company, 4 Ala., 652.....70
Curry v Bank, 8 Port. Ala., 360.....20

## D

Dartmouth College Case, 4 Wheat, 518.....16
Davies v Creighton, 33 Grat., 696.....157
Davis v West Saratoga, etc., Union, 32 Md., 285.....112
Delano v Wild, 6 Allen, 1.....2-77-103
Delaware, etc., Association v Keller, 2 W. N. C., 29.....86
Delaware R. R. Company v Tharp, 1 Houst. Del., 149.....18
Denny v West Philadelphia, etc., Association, 39 Pa. St., 154.....72
Diemer v Egolf, 1 Chest., 55.....86
Dilzer v Building Association, 103 Pa. St., 86.....22
Dobinson v Hawks, 12 Jur., 10.....37-24
Doe d Morrison v Glover, 15 Q. B., 103.....63

## E

Early's Appeal, 7 W. N. C., 184.....88
Eastern, etc., Company v Vaughan, 14 N. Y., 546.....11
Eaton v American, etc., Association, 49 N. W. R., 865.....25
Economy, etc., Association v Hungerbuepler, 93 Pa. St., 258.....125
Edelin v Pascre, 22 Grat., 326.....80-124-128
European, etc., R. R. Company v Poor, 59 Me., 277.....42
Everham v Oriental, etc., Association, 47 Pa. St., 352.....84
Everman v Schmitt, 24 Bull, 56.....89-128
Eyre v Building Association, 17 L. I., Pa., 148.....32

## F

Farlow v Kemp, 7 Blkf., 544.....11
Farmer v Smith, 4 H. & N.,196.....89 94
Farmers', etc., Bank v Downey, 53 Cal., 466.....42
Faulkner's Appeal, 11 W. N. C., 48.....56

Page.

Fleming v Self, 24 L. T. Rep., 101........................94
Flounders v Hawley, 78 Pa. St., 45.....................79-156
Flynn v Saving Fund, 37 L. I., (Pa.,) 336................86
Folger v Columbian, etc., Company, 96 Am. Dec., 757........119
Forrest City, etc., Association v Gallagher, 25 Ohio St., 208.............
.................................29-80-100-101-103-105-156
Fox v Cottage, etc., Association, 81 Va., 677..............93
Franklin, etc., Association v Marsh, 29 N. J. L., 225........103
Franklin, etc., Association, v Mather 4 Abb., Pa., 274.......81-155
Franklin Avenue, etc., Institution v Board, etc., 75 Mo., 408......53
Frederick v Corcoran, 100 Pa. St., 413.....................156
Freeman v Ottawa, etc. Association, 114 Ill., 182.........71-78-140
Friel v Association, 1 Leg. Rec. Rep., (Pa.,) 217............68
Fuller v Salem, etc., Association, 10 Gray, 94.............69
Fulton v American, etc., Association, 48 N. W. R., 781........25

G

Galbraith v Building Association, 43 N. J. Law., 389..........70
Gerenfield's Estate, 1 Chest., 356.......................86
German, etc., Association v Metzger, 9 W. N. C., Pa., 204......54
Germantown, etc., Association v Sendmeyer, 50 Pa., St., 67.......24
Germantown, etc., Company v Fitler, 60 Pa. St., 124...........71
Glenn v Statler, 42 Iowa, 107...........................48
Glynn v Home, etc., Association, 22 Kans., 746.............95
Goodrich v City, etc., Association, 54 Ga. 98, 122..........124
Gordon v Winchester, etc., Association, 12 Bush., 110......73-77-106
Gouchenour v Sullivan, etc., Association, 119 Ind., 441........100
Grangers', etc., Company v Kamper, 73 Ala., 325.............18
Grimes v Harrison, 28 L. J. Ch., 23.......................862

H

Hagerman v Ohio, etc., Association, 25 Ohio St., 186.............
.......................16-29-30-79-84-93-95-100-101
Haigh v United States, etc., Association, 19 W. Va., 792.......65-98
Hamilton, etc., Association v Reynolds, 5 Duer., 671...........84
Hammerslough v Kansas City, etc., Association, 79 Mo., 80.......105
Hampstead, etc., Association v King, 58 Md., 279.........120-121
Hand v Society, etc., 18 N. Y. Supl., 157..................41
Handley v Farmer, 29 Beav., 362.........................67-89
Hanner v Greensboro, etc., Association, 78 N. C., 188.......77-97
Hanney v Building Association, 16 W. N. C., 450.............67
Hansbury v Pfeifer, 35 L. I., 395.......................156

Page

Hardy v Metropolitan, etc., Company, L. R., 7 Ch. App., 427............57

Harris' Appeal, 18 W. N. C., 14........................................86

Haskett v Flint, 5 Blkf., 69..........................................11

Hawkeye, etc., Association v Blackburn, 48 Iowa, 385..............105-106

Hayes v Brubaker, 65 Ind., 27.........................................41

Hazel, etc., Association v Groesbeck, 41 L. I., 16....................84

Heckman v Building Association, 11 L. Bar., 110......................156

Heggie v Building, etc., Association, 107 N. C., 581.............55-121

Heintzelman v Druids, etc., Association, 36 N. W. Rep., 100..........28

Hekelnkaemper v German, etc., Association, 22 Kan., 549..32-86-93-95-120

Henderson etc., Association v Johnson, 88 Ky., 191..................106

Henderson, etc., Association v Johnson, 10 S. W. Rep., 787...........71

Henninghausen v Tisher, 50 Md., 583..........................60-66-93

Herbert v Kenton, etc., Association, 11 Bush., 296..............77-106

Herbert v Mechanic's, etc., Association, 17 N. J., Eq., 497......86-124-126

Hinman v Ryan, 3 C. C., (Ohio,) 529..................112-120-128

Hoboken, etc., Association v Martin, 13 N. J., Eq., 427..................
....................................................11-59-86-93-95-103-123

Hodges v New England Screw Company, 53 Am., Dec., 637.......28-39-40

Holgate v Shutt, L. R., 27 Ch. D., 111...............................47

Holmes v Smythe, 100 Ill., 413..............................71-78-140

Holyoke, etc., Association v Lewis, 27 Pac. R., 872..................31

Home Association v Boning, 7 Bull, 174..............................76-79

Horton v Building Association, 6 Bull, 141...........................91

Hoskins v Mechanic's, etc., Association, 84 N. C., 838..........77-95

Houser v Herman, etc., Association, 41 Pa. St., 478.................156

Howard, etc., Association v McIntyre, 3 Allen, 571..................25

Howlett's Estate, 2 Chest, 511.................................86-101

Hughes' Appeal, 30 Pa. St., 471.....................................88

Hughes v Edwards, 9 Wheat, 489......................................91

Hughes v Layton, 10 Jur. N. S., 513.................................51

Hughes v Layton, 33 L. J., M. C., 89................................56

Hughes v Littlefield, 18 Me., 400...................................48

Humboldt, etc., Society v Wennerhold, 81 Cal., 528...............30-48

Hunter v Sun, etc., Company, 26 La. Ann., 13........................49

Huntington, etc., Association v Melscheimer, 14 W. N. C., 314........84

Huylar v Craigin, etc., Company, 40 N. J. Eq., 392..................62


I

Illinois, etc., Company v Zimmer, 20 Ill., 654......................19

Ingolby v Riley, 28 L. T. N. S., 55................................101

In re Cefn Cilcen, etc., Company, 38 L. J., Ch., 78................114

In re Blackburn, etc., Society, 24 Ch. D., 421...................66-69

In re Deveaux, 54 Ga., 673.........................................154

In re Doncaster, etc., Society, L. R. Eq., 158......................89

Page.

In re Durham Co., etc., Society, 25 L. T., Rep., N. S.,83................57
In re Durham, etc., Society, L. R., 12 Eq., 516....................109
In re Estate National Association, 9 W. N. C., 79.....................123
In re German Mining Company, 22 L. J., Ch., 956................114
In re Jreffeison, 3 Kulp, 308...............................86
In re Middlesbrough, etc., Society, 54 L. J. Ch., 592..................101
In re Mutual Society, 24 Ch. D., 425............................69
In re National, etc., Society, ex parte, Williamson, L. R., 5 Ch. App., 309
............................................................109
In re Sunderland, etc., Society, 24 Q. B. Div., 394.  ...............68
In re Victoria, etc., Society, L. R., 9 Eq., 605....................109
In re West Riding Society,  L. R., 43 Ch. Div., 407 ...............128


J

Jackson v Cassidy, 68 Tex., 282............................105
Jackson v Myers, 43 Md., 452...............................112
Jarrett v Cope, 68 Pa. St., 67..........................103-156
Johnson v Elizabeth, etc., Association, 104 Pa. St., 394............83-93
Jones v National, etc., Association, 94 Pa. St., 115............53-112
Jungkuntz v Building Association, 6 Bull, 428................68-140


K

Kansas City, etc., Company v Sauer, 65 Mo., 279................119
Kelly v Accommodation, etc., Association, 2 Phila., 237............88
Kelly v Mobile, etc., Association, 64 Ala., 501...................30
Kilpatrick v Association, 119 Pa. St., 30.....................63
King v Ashwell, 12 East, 22.............................31
Kingsossing, etc., Association v Roan, 9 W. N. C., 15............125
Kisterbock's Appeal, 51 Pa. St, 483........................40
Knoblauck v Building Association, 25 P. L. J,. 39...............68
Knoblauck v Robert Blum, etc., Association, 25 Pitts. L. J., (O. S.,) 39..126
Knox v Childersburg, etc., Company, 86 Ala., 180.............10
Koehler v Black River Falls, etc., Company, 2 Black, 715..........39
Kreamer v Saving Fund, 6 W. N. C., 267....................88
Kreamer v Springfield, etc., Association, 6 W. N. C., 267..........125
Kupfert v Guttenberg, etc., Association, 30 Pa. St., 465............83


L

Laing v Reed, L. R., 5 Ch. App., 4........................109
Lake v Security, etc., Association, 72 Ala., 307................40

Page.

Latham v Washington, etc., Association 77 N. C., 145................77-103
Laurel Run, etc., Association, v Sperring, 3 Kulp., 67...................66
Laurel Run, etc., Association v Sperring, 106 Pa. St., 334................128
Licking Co., etc., Association v Bebout, 29 Ohio St., 252............103-156
Lime City, etc., Association v Wagner, 122 Ind., 78.....................83
Lincoln, etc., Association v Benjamin, 7 Neb., 181.................... 73-77
Lincoln, etc., Association v Graham, 7 Neb., 173............ .......17-77-103
Link v Building Association, 89 Pa. St., 15.................S6-100-125-156
Liquidators of the Blackburn, etc., Society, v Cunliffe 52 L. J. Rep., Ch., 92
........................................................ 110-111-114
Lister v Log Cabin, etc., Association, 38 Md., 115.....73-76-89-95-124-126
Loan Company v Conover, 5 Phila., 18..................................112
Looker v Wrigley, L. R., 39 Q. B. D., 397............................110
Lord v Essex Building Association, 37 Md., 320.........................16
Low Street, etc., Association v Zucker, 48 Md., 448.............81-88-121
Lucas v Greenville, etc., Association, 22 Ohio St., 339..................106
Lynn v Association, 117 Pa. St., 1.................................99-100

# M

Maguire v State, etc., Association, 62 Mo., 344.....................155
Manahan v Varnum, 77 Mass., 405..................................154
Manufacturers, etc., Company v Conover 5 Phila., 18..................55
Marble, etc., Association v Hocker, 3 Phila., 494.....................156
Martin v Nashville, etc., Association, 2 Cold, 418.................73-77-102
Massey v Citizens', etc., Association, 22 Kan., 624..........55-77-81-88-103
Master Stevedore's Association v Walsh, 2 Daly, 14..................71
Matterson v Elderfield, 4 L. R., Ch., 207............................97
McCahan v Columbian, etc., Association, 40 Md., 226............16-30-93-95
McGannon v Central, etc., Association, 19 W. Va., 726............70-100
McGowan v Savannah, etc., Association, 80 Ga., 515..................154
McGrath v Hamilton, etc., Association, 44 Pa. St., 383...........68-89-128
McKenney v Diamond State, etc., Association, 18 Atl. Rep., 905....28-64-67
McKeown v Building Association, 5 Bull, 52....................20-33-122
McLaughlin v Citizens' Association, 62 Ind., 264......................103
McNeall v Florence, etc., Association, 13 Stew., 351.................155
Meal v Hill, 16 Cal., 145...........................................48
Mechanics etc., Association v Conover, 1 McCart, 219 ...........38-86-87
Mechanics, etc., Association v Meriden, etc., Company, 24 Conn., 159..83-105
Mechanics, etc., Association v Wilcox, 24 Conn., 147..............83-103
Melville v American, etc., Association, 33 Barb., 103.................103
Memphis, etc., Company v Woods, 88 Ala., 630..........................25
Merrill v McIntire, 13 Gray, 157................................2-84-103
Metropolitan, etc., Association v Esche, 75 Cal., 513.................48
Michigan, etc., Association v McDevitt, 77 Mich., 1....16-23-38-59-63-74-85

Page.

Miller v Jefferson, etc., Association, 50 Pa. St., 32................................33
Miller's Estate, 2 Pears, 348...........................................157
Mills v Central, etc., Company, 481 N. J. Eq., 1.........................19
Mills v Salisbury, etc., Association, 75 N. C., 292................73-77-103
Minot v Curtis, 7 Mass., 441............................................11
Mobile, etc., Association v Robertson, 65 Ala., 382.....................92
Montgomery, etc., Association v Robinson, 69 Ala., 413.........26-76-103
Monumental, etc., Society v Lewin, 38 Md., 445...................30-100
Morrison v Dorsey, 48 Md., 461...............................11-25-29
Morton, etc., Co. v Wysong, 51 Ind., 4..................................28
Moses v O'Coee Bank, 1 Lea, 398.........................................39
Mosley v Baker, 12 Jur., 551............................................94
Mowbray v Antrim, 123 Ind., 24.........................................44
Moxon v Berkeley, etc., Society, 59 L. J., Ch., 524...................126
Moye v Sparrow, 22 L. T., Rep. N. S., 154.............................109
Murray v Scott, 9 App. Cas., 519......................................111
Muth v Dolfield, 43 Md., 466..........................................112
Mutual, etc., Association v Hammell, 43 N. J. L., 78...................45
Mutual, etc., Association v Meriden, etc., Co., 24 Conn., 159.......26-153
Mutual, etc., Association v Tascott, 28 N. E. Rep., (Ill.,) 801......75-82
Mutual Savings, etc., Association v Wilcox, 24 Conn., 147..........23-153

## N

National, etc., Association v Hubley, 34 Leg. Int., 6..................:68
Neath, etc., Society, v Luce, L. R., 43Ch. D., 158...................111
New Haven, etc., Company v Chapman, 38 Conn., 56......................19
Newman v Ligonier, etc., Association, 97 Ind., 295....................82
Newton Tp., etc., Association v Boyer, 15 Stew., 273.................155
Nicely's Estate, 3 Kulp, 47......................................82-104
North Hudson, etc., Association v First National Bank, 47 N. W. R.
    (Wis.,) 300.....................................................112
North v State, 107 Ind., 356..........................................119
North American, etc., Association, v Sutton 35 Pa. St., 463.....25-86-125

## O

Oak Cottage, etc., Association v Eastman, 31 Md., 556............104-105
Occidental, etc., Association v Sullivan, 62 Cal., 394.................34
Ocmulgee, etc., Association v Thomson, 52 Ga., 427.................95-99
Odd Fellow, etc., Association v Hogan, 28 Ark., 261...................53
Oliver's Estate, 1 Del., 358..........................................86
Orangeville, etc., Association, v Young, 9 W. N. C., 251..............78
O'Rourke v Building Association, 8 W. N. C., 176......................156
Overby v Fayetteville, etc., Association, 81 N. C., 56...........77-95-98
Owen v Roberts, 57 L. T. N. S., 81...................................111

Page.

## P

Paffert v Building Association, 25 P. L. J., 40..........................68
Pangborn v Citizens', etc., Association, 1 Stock, 341....................42
Parker v Butcher, L. R., 3 Eq., 762....................................100
Parker v Fulton, etc., Association, 46 Ga., 166....................77-103
Parker v United States, etc., Association, 19 W. Va., 744.......29-80-100
Patterson v Albany, etc., Association, 63 Ga., 373......................77
Patty v Pease, 8 Paige, 277............................................126
Payette v Free Home, etc., Association, 27 Ill. App., 307...........16-17
People v Lowe, 117 N. Y., 175..........................23-42-60-98-128
People, etc., Association, v Furey, 20 Atl. R., 890.............60-87-155
People, etc., Association v Wroth, 43 N. J. L., 70.................45-48
People's, etc., Bank v Collins, 27 Conn., 142..................86-106
Perrin v Granger, 30 Vt., 595..........................................71
Peters, etc., Association, v Jaecksch, 51 Md., 198....................120
Pfaff v Building Association, 6 W. N. C., 349.........................119
Pfeister v Wheeling, etc., Association, 19 W. Va., 676....73-80-83-100-157
Philadelphia, etc., Association v Moore, 47 Pa. St., 233...............87
Philadelphia, etc., Association v Moore, 21 Leg. Int., 109............156
Philanthrophic, etc., Association v McKnight, 35 Pa. St., 470.........105
Phillips v Columbia City, etc., Association, 53 Iowa, 719.............105
Phillipsburg, etc., Association v Hawk, 27 N. J. Eq., 355..............86
Pooch v Lafayette, etc., Association, 71 Ind., 357.................51-83
Premium Fund Association's Appeal, 26 Pa. St., 156....................71
Provident, etc., Society, v Greenhill, L. R., 9 Ch. D., 122..........101

## Q

Quakertown, etc., Association v Sorver, 33 Leg. Int., (Pa.,) 359......126
Quein v Smith, 108 Pa. St., 325...................................49-113

## R

Red Bank, etc., Association v Patterson, 27 N. J., Eq., 223..73-103-104-125
Redmond v Dickerson, 1 Stock, 507......................................42
Redwine v Gate City, etc., Association, 54 Ga., 474...............13-154
Reeve v Ladies, etc., Association, Ark. Supct. June 25, 1892...........78
Reg. v Registrar of Friendly Society, L. R. Q. B., 741................37
Reg. v Grinishaw, 10 Q. B., 743.......................................37
Reg. v Pratt, 118 Eng. C. L., (6 B. & S. Q. B.,) 672..................37
Reilly v Mayer, 1 Beas., (N. J,) 55..................................126
Reiser v William Tell, etc., Association, 39 Pa. St., 137.............77
Remington v King, 11 Abb. Pr., 278...................................155
Rhoads v. Hoernerstown, etc., Association, 82 Pa. St., 180........56-156
Richards v Bibb Co., etc., Association, 24 Ga., 193...................95

Page

Risk v Delphos, etc., Association, 31 Ohio St., 517..............80-95
Roberts v Price, 16 L. J. C. P., 169...........................48
Robertson v American, etc., Association, 10 Md., 397.......76-83-93-95-103
Robertson v Homestead Association, 69 Am. Dec., 151..................22
Robinson v Smith, 24 Am. Dec., 212...........................39
Rodgers v Building Association, 7 W. N. C., Pa., 95.................29
Rosenback v Salt Spring, etc., Bank, 53 Barb, 506..................71
Rosenberg v Northumberland, etc., Society, L. R., 22 Q. B., 373.......128
Rushville Gas Company v City of Rushville, 121 Ind., 206.............38
Rowland's Estate, 1 Del., 98.................................156

## S

Salem v Mill Dam Co., 6 Pick., 23............................18
Salina, etc., Association v Nelson, 22 Kans., 751..................154
San Buenaventura, etc., Company v Vassault, 50 Cal., 534...........37
Saving Fund v Cake, 2 Leg., Rec., Rep., 172.....................87
Saving Fund v Longshore, 8 Luz. L., Reg., 199.................83-157
Saving Fund v Murray, 14 Leg., Int., 133.......................88
Savings Fund v Young, 9 W. N. C., 251.........................78
Savings Association v Vandervere, 3 Stock, 382...................155
Savings, etc., Association v Stevens, 5 Bull, 113..................79
Schlesinger's Estate, 1 Law Times, N. S., 15.....................85
Schober v Accommodation, etc., Association, 35 Pa. St., 223....50-88-156
Schutte v California, etc., Association, 23 Atl., Rep., 336............63
Seagrave v Pope, 15 Eng. L. & Eq., 477........................76
Seagrave v Pope, 22 L. J. Ch., 258............................94
Second Manhattan, etc., Association v Hayes, 2 Keyes, 192..........155
Security, etc., Association v Lake, 69 Ala., 456..................69-73-76
Seibel v Building Association, 43 Ohio St., 371..............60-98-122-128
Selden v Building Association, 2 W. N. C., 481...................86
Selden v Reliable, etc., Association, 32 P. F. Smith, 336........105-125-157
Shaefer v Amicable, etc., Company, 47 Md., 126..................54
Shaffrey v Workingmen's, etc., Association, 64 Ind., 100.............103
Shannon v Dunn, 43 N. H., 194.............................77-103
Shannon v Howard, etc., Association, 36 Md., 383.........76-81-95-99-100
Sheldon v Mayor, etc., 30 Ala., 540...........................30
Sherman, etc., Association v Rock, 9 Phila., 75...................157
Shibley v Angle, 37 N. Y., 626................................11
Shields v Ohio, 95 U. S., 319.................................18
Shinn v State, 32 Grat., 899..................................49
Siburn v Pearce, L. R., 44 Ch. D., 354..........................66
Silver v Barnes, 6 Bing., N. C., 180.........................76-103
Simpson v Building Association, 38 Ohio St, 349..................17
Skinner's Estate, 4 Phila., 189...............................105
Small v Smith, L. R., 10 App., Cas., 119........................50

Page.

Smith v Los Angeles, etc., Association, 78 Cal., 289.................42
Smith v Mechanics, etc., Association, 73 N. C., 372...........77-81-84
Smith v Pilkington, 4 Jur., N. S., 58.........................94
Smith v Plank Road Co., 30 Ala., 650.........................11
Snider's Estate, 34 Leg., Int, 49............................156
Somerset Co., etc., Association, v Vandervere, 3 Stock, 382.......95
Stile's Appeal, 95 Pa. St., 122..............................78
Sparrow v Farmer, 26 Beav., 511..............................89
Sperring's Appeal, 71 Pa. St., 11............................40
Spinning v Home, etc., Association, 26 Ohio St., 483..........16
Spring Garden Association v Tradesmen's, etc., Association, 46 Pa. St., 493
...................................................... 86-125-156
Springville, etc., Association v Raber, 33 Leg., Int., Pa., 329....87-125-156
State v Bonnell, 35 Ohio St., 10.............................37
State v Building Association, 35 Ohio St., 258..........50-55-112-156
State v Greenville, etc., Association, 29 Ohio St., 92........78
State v McGrath, 95 Mo., 193.............................15-155
State v Oberlin, etc., Association, 35 Ohio St., 258..........88
State v Redwood Falls, etc., Association, 45 Minn., 154.....68-69-155
State v Rohlffs, 19 Atl. R., 1............................99-38
State v Washington, etc., Company, 11 Ohio, 96...............18
State, etc., Association v Kellogg, 63 Mo., 540..............90
Stebbins v Merritt, 10 Cush., 27............................37
Stein v Indianapolis, etc., Association, 18 Ind, 237.......53-106
St. Joseph, etc., Association v Thompson, 19 Kans., 321......83-105
St. Louis, etc., Association v Augustin, 2 Mo. App., 123....103-119
Stohr v San Francisco, etc., Society, 82 Cal., 557...........31
Strohen v Association, 115 Pa. St., 273...................124-128
Sturges v Crowninshield, 4 Wheat, 122.......................19
Stuyvesant v Hone, 1 Sandf., (N. Y.,) 419..................126
Sullivan v Lewiston Institution of Savings, 56 Me., 507......39
Sunbury, etc., Association v Martin, 1 Luz., L. Reg., 147....86
Swentzel v Penn. Bank, 23 Atl. 1 Rep., 405..................39

## T

Tanner's Appeal, 95 Pa. St., 118............................83
Tascott v Mutual, etc., Association, 37 Ill., App., 274.......75
Taylor v Collins, 46 L. T., Rep., N. S., 168................63
Texas, etc., Association v Kerr, 13 S. W. Rep., 1..........20-66
Third Ward, etc., Association v Lotze, 11 Bull., 285..........9
Thompson v Gillison, 28 S. C., 534.........................103
Thompson v Ocmulgee, etc., Association, 56 Ga., 350.........120
Tosh v North British, etc., Society, 11 App., Cas., 489.....128
Twin-Lick Oil Company v Marbury, 91 U. S., 587..............42
Tyrrell, etc., Association v Haley, 20 Atl., R., 1.........63-82

                                                            Page.
Tyrrell, etc., Association v Haley, 139 Pa. St., 476....................92
Tyrrell, etc., Association v Haley, 139 Pa. St., 657....................73


## U

Union, etc., Association v Masonic Hall Association, 2 Stew.,389-54-55-81-101
Uniontown etc., Association's Appeal, 92 Pa. St., 200..................126


## V

Valley Bank, etc., Institution v Savings Society, 28 Kan., 423 .........119
Vann v Fayetteville, etc., Association, 75 N. C., 494.....................77
Vanneman v Swedesboro, etc., Association, 15 Stew., 263...............155
Vermont, etc., Company v Whithed, 49 N. W. Rep., 318...............105
Vos v Cedar Grove, etc., Association, 9 Bull., 194.......................56


## W

Walker v British, etc., Association, 21 L. J. Q. B., 257...................45
Walker v General Mutual, etc., Society, L. R., 36 Ch., Div., 777.....786-66
Walton v Edge, L. R., 10 App. Cas., 33.................................09
Wangerien v Aspell, 47 Ohio St., 250........................18-20-55
Washington, etc., Association v Beaghen, 27 N. J.. Eq., 98......88-125-126
Washington Association v Creveling, 10 Vr., 465.....................155
Waterlow v Sharp, L. R. 8 Eq., 501......................... ...........114
Watkins v Building Association, 97 Pa. St., 514.........................87
Watkins v Workingmen's, etc., Association, 10 W. N. C., 414....:.....87
Watkins v Workingmen's, etc., Association, 97 Pa. St., 514..........95-97
Watson v Aikin, 55 Tex., 536............................................105
Waverly, etc., Association v Buck, 64 Md., 338.....................95-103
Weise v San Francisco, etc., Society, 82 Cal., 646........................31
Weiss' Appeal, 5 W. N. C., (Pa.,) 428.................................125
West Winstead, etc., Association v Ford, 27 Conn., 282...........103-153
Whilden v Broomall, 1 Del., (Pa.,) 142................. ...............86
White v Mechanic's, etc., Association, 22 Grat., 243.........73-85-103-121
Wiggins' Appeal, 100 Pa. St., 158.......................................83
Wilkowski v Hall, 95 Am., Dec., 374.............................91
Wm. Tell, etc., Association, 39 Pa. St., 137............................103
Williamson v Kokomo, etc.. Association, 89 Md., 389..................16-17
Williar v Baltimore, etc., Association, 45 Md., 546.............77-103-105
Wilson v Tucker, 3 Stark., 154..........................................45
Wilson's Case, L. R., 12 Eq., 521......................................110
Winchester, etc, Association, v Gilbert, 23 Grat., 787.........38-73-95-98
Windisch v Korman, 5 Bull., 364.......................................93

Page.

Windhorst v Building Association, 7 Bull., 29.........................156
Winget v Quincy, etc., Association, 128 Ill., 67...............17-25-40-140
Windsor v Bandel, 40 Md., 172.....................................121-128
Winterer v Building Association, 44 L. I., (Pa.,) 122.............33-60-98
Withers v Baird, 32 Am., Dec., 754......................................91
Wittman v Building Association, 7 W. N. C., 80.....................65-128
Wolbach v Lehigh, etc., Association, 84 Pa. St., 211....................83
Wolbach v Lehigh, etc., Association, 4 W. N. C., 157..................156
Wood v Hoskin, 63 Wis., 15............................................158
Wood v Union Gospel, etc., Association, 63 Wis., 9...................158
Woodman v York, etc., R. R. Company, 50 Me., 549....................52
Wright v Deley, 4 H. & C., 209.........................................66

## Z

Zabriskie v Hackensack, etc., Company, 18 N. J., Eq., 178.............19

# INDEX.

**Abstract** of title should be furnished----------------------------81

**Abstracter** may be an officer--------------------------------42

**Acceptance** formal, of resignation of director unnecessary--------48

**Account,** how stated when association in liquidation------------120 n

**Acknowledgment** of mortgage, who may take--------------90, 91

**Actual notice** to association of subsequent incumbrance, effect of 126

**Advancement** on shares is a loan-----------------------76 n, 77 n

**Agents,** directors as--------------------------------------38, 39
   Directors when may delegate to-------------------------------'41
   Contract of, when may be rescinded--------------------------49
   When may be removed---------------------------------------49
   Liability of association for acts of ----------------------------53
   When may delegate powers---------------------------------53 n
   Powers of, should be defined--------------------------------52
   general Powers to bind association--------------------------52, 53
   Special how far may bind association-------------------------52

**Agreement,** see contract.
   Unanimous, stockholders may wind up by---------------------119
   To take shares, nature of------------------------------10, 11
   To take shares, not partnership------------------------------11
   Building form of---------------------------------------------226
   To waive liens form of----------------------------------233, 234

**Amendment,** of charter by legislative authority-----------------18
   When legislature may amend---------------------------------18
   Limits of legislature power to amend--------------------------19
   Mode of amendment-----------------------------------------19
   Of by-laws------------------------------------------31, 32, 33
   Of resolutions----------------------------------------------32

**Amount** payable on foreclosure, natural and logical rule--------96, 97
   Recoverable on foreclosure under the English rule-------------94
   Recoverable on foreclosure under rule of "possible duration"----93
   Recoverable on withdrawal ---------------------------------66
   To be paid on withdrawal ----------------------------------65, 69

**Application** for loan........................................79
    For loan, form of.........................................170
    Of payments..............................................84
    Of stock payments by borrower, effect of..................88
    For membership, form of..................................158

**Appraisers** cannot delegate powers.......................53 n
    Sealed report of.........................................46 n
    Report, form of..........................................184
    May be officers...........................................42

**Appraising** committee..............................3, 46, 80

**Arbitration,** by-laws may provide for.....................29

**Articles** of association, see charter.
    Of incorporation......................................11, 12

**Assessment** on stock.....................................127

**Assets,** what are.....................................89, 126 n
    To be distributed when...................................121
    How distributed..........................................129
    Should be equally distributed.............................60
    Distribution of, upon dissolution........................120

**Assignment** of stock without transfer on books, effect of...70
    Of stock as collateral security...........................85
    Form of..................................................193
    Of shares as collateral security, effect of...............85
    For creditors............................................123
    For creditors does not prevent judgment..................123

**Association** plan of.......................................5

**Assigned,** shares cannot be credited on loan..............88

**Assigning** mortgages, effect of.........................115

**Assignment** of mortgage........................111, 112, 113

**Attorney,** duties of......................................45
    Liability of..............................................45

**Auction** sale of money.................................74, 77

**Auditing Committee,** appointment of......................47
    Character of..............................................47
    Report of impeachable when ...............................47

**Avoiding** usury.  See Usury

**Bailee,** Treasurer is only................................45

**Bank** account, overdrawing..............................114
    Check, form of...........................................225

**Banking,** Association should not engage in................50

**Bidding** ..................................................78
    For preference............................................74

**Bill** to foreclose mortgage, fines do not stop upon filing...101

**Bond,** Secretary and treasurer should give................36, 47
  Duty of directors in regard to......................47
  Sureties responsibility of, how ascertained.............47, 48
  Sureties discharge of............................48
     liability of..............................48
  Effect of failure of surety to read bond..................48
  Form of.........................188, 200, 202, 211, 231, 234, 235
  Not void for uncertainty.........................83
  Provisions of..............................,.......48, 81
  May be deposited as collateral security.................112

**Books,** Inspection of by members........................62

**Borrowing,** Illegal prior to 1874 in English societies without a rule...
  .................................................109, 110
  Unlimited borrowing held ultra vires...................109
  When limit exceeded, directors liable..................109
  For illegitimate purposes not enforceable................109
  For legal liabilities, enforceable.....................109

**Borrowing member** entitled to pro rata part of profits..........60
  Status of..........................71, 72, 73 n
  Selection of................................74

**Borrowing** money by association ...107, 108, 109, 110, 111, 112, 113, 114
  ................................................115

**Borrower,** Member as...............................3
  Liability of....................................90, 127
  Must pay interest during suspension....................120
  Not further obligated if association is unable to perform its contract
  ................................................121
  May set off against his mortgage......................92
  Defaulting, amount to repay ......................96, 97
  Repaying amount of repayment......................96, 97
  Cannot recover on mistake of law.....................98
  Credit entitled to, on application of stock payments...........125
  Withdrawing, credit to be given .....................87
  May pay off loan and retain stock....................87
  Not liable under his mortgage for debts unless so provided..88, 89, 128
  Liability of, for losses...........................89, 90
  Cannot defeat loan as unauthorized...................83

**Borrower's** account when association in liquidation ...........120 n

**Building** agreement, form of .......................226
  Specifications, form of............................227

**Building Association.**
  Origin of....................................1
  Greenwich Union Building Society.....................1
  Brooklyn Building and Mutual Loan Fund Association..........2
  Definition of.................................2

## Building Association.

General scheme of ............................................2

Transfer of stock ............................................3

Maturing of stock ...........................................4

Revenues of .................................................4

Expenses to be incurred ..................................4, 10

Officers to be selected ......................................4

Compensation of officers ....................................4

Serial, plan of .............................................5

Value of shares ............................. ...............5

Permanent, plan of .........................................6

Organization of ............................................9

Agreement, preliminary .....................................10

Contract, preliminary ......................................10

May enforce stock subscriptions .............................10

Use of seal ................................................20

Modified type of corporations ...............................21

Different from ordinary corporations ........................23

Illegal to hold stock in another corporation .................25

Cannot hold stock in another ...............................25

Relation of stockholder to ..................................21

Bound to lend to members ...................................24

Estopped to deny membership ...............................25

Power to enact by-laws .....................................28

Power to amend by-laws ....................................31

Contract of, how signed .....................................41

Relation of officers to ......................................49

General powers of ..........................................50

    to have common seal ..................................50

    to contract .......................................50, 52

    to hold real estate ...............................50, 56

    to sue and be sued ...............................50, 53

    to make by-laws ....................................50

    to compromise debts or remit fines ...............42, 55

    to loan money ......................................55

    to take mortgages ..................................55

    to borrow money .107, 108, 109, 110, 111, 112, 113, 114, 115

Has incidental powers as are necessary .......................50

Should not engage in banking ...............................50

Should not invest in securities not contemplated by statute ......50

Estopped to deny ultra vires acts when .......................51

Not dissolved by ultra vires acts alone ........................51

Contracts through officers and agents ........................52

How far bound by special agent ..........................52, 53

Power of general agent to bind ...........................52, 53

Liability for agent's acts ....................................53

Complaint by, allegations of .............................53, 54

**Building Association.**

Cannot traffic in notes................................55
When may issue stock to another corporation.............56, 57
May sue member for dues.................................63
Should make loans......................................74
May sue upon either bond or mortgage....................82
May borrow for authorized purpose...................109, 114
Must repay unless lender knew purpose was unauthorized..112, 114
No power to sell its mortgages.........................116
Unable to perform contract, borrower not obligated further.....120
When must retire stock.................................121
May sell pledged stock as against purchaser............124
Consolidation of......................................129
Character of..........................................132

**By Bidding** ........................................74

**By-Laws.**

May be amended by directors............................28
Notice of amendments should be given...................28
Character of notice....................................28
Member not bound by, without notice ...................28
Association has power to amend.........................31
Having retroactive effect, apply fully unless vested rights are
    impaired ..........................................32
Mode of amendment, as prescribed must be followed......33
Stockholders adopt.....................................11
Charter should not invade..............................17
Selection of committee to frame........................27
Report of committee, time and place of hearing.........27
Character of, should be well understood................27
Each shareholder should have notice of...............27, 62
Definition of..........................................28
Power of association to enact..........................28
Power to enact resides in stockholders.................28
May provide for amendment by directors.................28
Notice of amendments should be given...................28
Character of notice....................................28
Member not bound by amendments without notice..........28
When acted upon and enforced are binding...............28
Must be reasonable.....................................29
Must not be contrary to public policy .................29
Nor attempt to oust jurisdiction of courts.............29
May provide for arbitration ...........................29
Must be consistent with articles of incorporation and statute.....29
Cannot provide for unreasonable fines..................29
Cannot compel stockholders to offer premium for priority of
    payment after maturity of shares...................29
Member cannot deny signing by-laws after enjoying benefits...29 n

**By-Laws.**

Requiring member to sign an obligation to obey are directory....29

Are part of contract between association and member............30

May be examined to determine when mortgage contract
    terminated...................................................30

Defining duties of secretary, part of surety's contract............30

Construction of, must be fair......................................30

Consisting of several distinct and independent parts, one may
    be void and the others valid...................................30

If waived by association, member violating them cannot com-
    plain...........................................................30

Member holding a greater number of shares than allowed by
    by-laws, but not by statute, cannot defend against a claim
    thereon .................................... ...................30

A loan not in conformity with by-laws, but under an express
    statutory power, is not void...................................30

Association has power to amend....................................31

May be amended so as to affect future benefits but not vested
    claims ........................................................31

Illustrations of rule.....................................31, 32 n

Amendments having retroactive effect, apply fully unless
    vested rights are impaired.....................................32

Resolutions cannot be passed so as to impair vested rights......32

Unwritten regulations when acted on will govern if reasonable..33

Mode of amendment as prescribed must be strictly followed....33

Should not be incorporated in charter............................33

Should be kept distinct from rules...............................33

Provisions of by-laws............................................33

Manner of election of officers and time of holding to be pre-
    scribed by by-laws............................................36

Should fix date of general meetings of stockholders............37

Should provide for call of special meetings......................37

Manner of election of officers as fixed by by-laws to be strictly
    observed......................................................48

Should provide for removal of officers...........................49

Power of association to make.....................................50

May provide for custody of seal..................................51

Member after enjoying benefits cannot question legality of......62

Should provide for liability of withdrawing member.............67

Construction of, concerning withdrawal..........................69

Should provide for penalty for failure to take loan.............74

Should regulate fines........................................101

Form of.........................................................165

**California** Associations.........................................144

**Call** for special meeting........................................37

**Cancelling** stock, effect of......................................121

**Certificate** of stock, form of................................165
    How issued...........................................13, 24, 36
**Cessation** of all corporate acts and enterprises does not dissolve
    the Association.......................................119
**Change** of permanent to serial..............................130
    Serial to permanent.................................130
**Character** of building associations.........................132
**Charter.**
    Preparation of...........................11, 12, 13, 14, 15
    Signing of..............................................12, 13
    Importance of...........................................14
    Legal status of signers.................................14
    Must adhere to statute..................................15
    General adherence to statute sufficient.................15
    Construed by patent intent..............................15
    Corporate objects to be clearly specified...............15
    What constitutes charter................................15, 18
    Charter amendable to the constitution...................15 n
    Relations created by the charter........................15, 16
    Effect of charter exceeding legislative authority.......16
    Effect of failure to strictly comply with statute.......16
    Strict compliance with statute not necessary............16
    Defects in oranization cannot be collaterally attacked.......16, 17
    Effect of defects impairing legality of association......16, 17
    State may withdraw charter for exceeded powers..........16
    When courts may interfere with exceeded powers..........17
    Corporate functions not enlarged by assuming unauthorized
      powers .............................................17
    Charter should not invade by-laws.......................17, 33
    Construction of, is one of intent.......................17
    Amendment by legislative authority......................18
    When legislature may amend..............................18
    Limits of legislative power to amend....................19
    Mode of amendment.......................................19
    Impairment of contract..................................19 n
    Mode of amendment provided in charter must be followed.....20 n
    By issuance of charter, association is a corporation....21
    By-laws must be consistent with.........................29
    Providing for removal of officers.......................48
    When may be annulled....................................51
    Power to forfeit in state...............................119
    Form of, by articles of association.....................159
    Form of, by special enactment...........................162
**Collateral** attack, when acts ultra vires are subject to.........55
**Collateral Security,** assignment of shares as................82
    Form of ................................................193
    Mortgages and bonds may be deposited as................111, 112

**Colorado** Associations............................................143

**Compensation** of officers.............................................4

**Committees**................................................... -- 41, 42, 47

**Complaint** to recover on withdrawal, what must show...............66
   By associations, allegations of............................53, 54, 82
   To foreclose mortgage, fines do not stop upon filing.............101

**Compromise** of debts...............................................42, 55
   Of debts in good faith, will not be set aside.......................55

**Computation** as to amount upon voluntary repayment.............94
   Of amount recoverable on foreclosure under rule of possible
     duration.........................................................93

**Consolidation** of building associations...........................129

**Constitution,** charter amenable to............................15 n

**Construction** of by-laws must be fair.............................30
   By-laws consisting of several distinct and independent parts,
     one may be void and the others valid.........................30
   Of by-law concerning withdrawal..................................69
   Of charter, one of intent.........................................17

**Contingent** fund......................................................7

**Continuous** default, when averred..................................54

**Contract.** To take shares........................................10, 11
   With married women...............................................22
   By-laws are part of, between association and member..............30
   Mortgage contract, by law may be examined to determine when
     terminated .....................................................30
   By laws defining duties of secretary, part of sureties' contract....30
   Of association, how signed.........................................41
   Of agent may be rescinded, when...................................49
   Power of association to make..................................50, 52
   Requiring seal.....................................................52
   Misnomer of association in, effect of ..............................53
   To insure, breach of.............................................84 n

**Co-operative** banks...........................................135, 139
   Form of mortgage of..............................................216

**Corporation.** Relation of stockholders to.........................21
   Association cannot hold stock in another..........................25
   When stock may be issued to..................................56, 57

**Corporate** acts beyond corporate powers, void....................50
   name ........................................................11, 12

**Courts.** By-laws must not attempt to oust jurisdiction of..........29
   Cannot remove officers............................................48
   Will not relieve against authorized forfeiture.....................48
   When may interfere with exceeded powers...........................17

**Covenants** in mortgage..............................................84

**Credit** to be given withdrawing borrower, how ascertained...........87

**Creditors,** assignment for...............................123
 Cannot compel application of stock on loan................86, 125
 Of association must be paid before members.................126
 Members withdrawing are................................65
 Entitled to be paid first................................124
 Members may be.......................................60

**Dayton** Mutual Home Association...................136, 137
 Mortgage of, form of..................................217

**Death** of stockholder......................................26
 Dissolves membership..................................26
 Of stockholder does not dissolve association.................119

**Debtor,** member is to association...........................23 and n, 63

**Debts,** compromise of..............................42, 55
 Liability of borrower for.................................127
 Must be discharged before division.......................121
 Liability of borrower for, under his mortgage............88, 89, 128

**Deed,** Trust, form of......................................194

**Defaulting** borrower amount to repay......................96, 97
 Member may be sued on bond or mortgage.................82
 Member entitled to share in profits......................122
 Member, disposition of..................................71
 Member, tender by......................................54
 Member cannot transfer stock............................70

**Default** of other members does not relieve one..................59

**Deduction** of premium.....................................134

**Defects** impairing legality of association...................16, 17
 In organization cannot be collaterally attacked..............16, 17

**Definition** of building association...........................2
 Of usury...............................................102

**Delaware** associations .....................................140

**Delegation** of duties to agents by directors....................41
 Of powers by appraisers................................53 n

**Delinquent** officers, fines against .............................99

**Deposits** authorized, rights of depositors over members .........113

**Devisees** as members......................................25

**Directors.** To be selected..................................4
 Should keep within corporate powers.....................25
 Illegal action of, may be restrained by stockholders............25
 May amend by-laws, when...............................23
 Cannot defeat supreme powers of stockholders assembled in
  general meeting......................................36
 Should furnish stockholders with copy of report of association...36

**Directors.**
Meetings of.................................................37
Have supervision and management.....................38
As agents and trustees...............................38, 39
Duties of.................................................39
Liability of
    For fraud...........................................89
    For gross negligence................................39
    For ultra vires acts................................39
    For misapplication of funds.........................39
Not liable for acts of co-director when not present.....39, 40
Not liable for mistake in opinion....................39, 40
Rule for guidance of.................................40, 41
Minutes of meetings...................................41
Powers of...............................................41
Contracts of............................................41
Right to delegate to agents...........................41
Personally interested, incompetent to vote .............42
Cannot speculate in funds.............................42
Cannot purchase property for resale to association at a higher
    figure ...........................................42
Cannot make secret agreements for their own profit........42
Duty in granting loans.................................42
May remit fines or compromise debts...................42
Term of election of..................................42, 43
Percentage of value to be loaned in discretion of.........46
May appoint executive committee.......................47
Should require bond, when.............................47
Duty of, in regard to bonds...........................47
Election of, as prescribed by by-laws, to be strictly observed.....48
Resignation of..........................................48
Cannot be removed by stockholders.....................48
Cannot be removed by courts...........................48
May remove agent holding at pleasure ................48, 49
May remove agent under contract, when.................49
Removal of, should be provided for in by-laws.........49
Should understand scheme of association...............51
Should make equal distribution of assets..............60
Liability of, for distributing profits contrary to law........60, 62
Should not invest funds to defeat withdrawals.........68
May give dividends to stockholders shown by the books........70
Grant loans on appraisement...........................80
**Dissolution.** Ultra vires acts alone do not work........51, 56
Rights of withdrawing members on....................68, 69
Dues cease upon.......................................81
Upon maturity of all stock...........................118
Method of.............................................119

**Dissolution.**

Neglect to elect officers does not dissolve association............119
Cessation of all corporate acts and enterprises does not dissolve..119
Non user of franchise does not dissolve.......................119
Insolvency of association does not dissolve ......................119
Death of stockholders does not dissolve.......................119
May be by unanimous agreement..........................119
Agreement of..................................................122
To suspend and close up business is not dissolution............119
Upon agreement must be unanimous.......................119 n
Distribution of assets upon .................................120
Appointment of receiver operates as dissolution as to payments.120
If association is unable longer to perform its contract it is in
    effect dissolved as to borrower.........................121

**Dividends,** How credited.............................121, 122
May be given stockholders shown by books.....................70

**Division** of assets ................................121, 129
of profits...................................................7
of profits in serial........................................122

**Distribution** of assets...............................129
of assets upon dissolution...............................120

**Dues** are partial payments on stock...........................24
Payment of at secretary's place of business when valid..........63
Payment of, to authorized officer...........................63
Suit for, by association....................................63
Cease on appointment of receiver...........................120
Cease if association dissolves before maturity................81
When payable...............................................36
Payable to maturity........................................81
Payable as stipulated......................................81

**Duties** of directors...................................39
of president..............................................43
of vice-president.........................................43
of secretary.............................................43
of treasurer.............................................44
of attorney..............................................45

**Election** of officers, manner of to be strictly observed..........48
of directors, term of..................................42, 43

**Embezzlement,** when secretary or treasurer guilty of............49

**Enabling** statute, powers conferred by.....................83

**English** societies, see borrowing, permanent society..........6
Terminating society..................................6, 118

**Entrance** fee prerequisite to membership...................21

**Estoppel.** Members estopped to deny incorporation................25
    One receiving membership benefits, estopped..................25
    Association estopped to deny membership....................25
    Embezzling officers estopped to deny corporate existence........49
    Association's right to contract...........................51
    Of association to deny its right to make contract.................51
    When member estopped to deny.......................------
    Member when estopped to deny legality of by-laws..............62
    Borrower cannot defeat loan as unauthorized....................83
    Association estopped to allege want of power to borrow for
        legitimate purposes....................................112
    Association cannot defeat recovery of money borrowed as applied to
        unauthorized purposes, unless lender knew of it...........112

**Exclusive** right to name...............................12

**Executive** committee, appointment of.........................47
    Committee, duties of....................................47
    Committee, powers delegated to..........................41

**Expenses** to be incurred..........................4, 10

**Expert** accountants selected as auditors.....................47

**Failure** to transfer stock on books, effect of..................70

**Fees** of appraising committee...............................46 n

**Final** division and settlement, when required..................121

**Fines.** Amount must be reasonable.........................29, 100
    Delinquent cannot be fined twice for same offense.............29
    Must be provided for in unambiguous language...............34 n
    Directors may remit...................................42
    Covenant to pay enforceable........................84, 100
    Necessity of..........................................99
    Against delinquent officer..............................99
    May be recovered as stipulated damages....................99
    Without statutory authority, not enforceable.................100
    Can only be collected from members......................100
    May be charged against land............................101
    Stop after decree of foreclosure.........................101
    Do not stop on filing bill to foreclose.....................101
    No interest on........................................101
    After decree part of principal............................101
    Are lien on stock.....................................101

**Foreclosure of Mortgage.**
    Just computation difficult................................93
    Amount recoverable under the rule of "possible duration".......93
    English rule...........................................94
    American modification..................................94
    Uncertainty of above rules..............................95
    The natural and logical rule.............................96

**Forfeitures.** Must be created by unambiguous language........34
　Should be omitted when..............................................34
　Must be authorized by charter or statute.....................71
　In declaring, law must be strictly complied with..............71
　If authorized, courts will not relieve against...................71
　No notice is necessary unless prescribed.....................71
　Forfeiting membership, effect of...............................71
　Forfeiture of charter, power in state........................119
　Stockholder has no power to sue for forfeiture of charter.......119
　Franchises not forfeited by agreement to suspend and close
　　up business...............................................119

**Forms.**
　Preliminary agreement for incorporation....................158
　Application for membership................................158
　Charter ...................................................159
　Special act of incorporation...............................162
　Of stock certificate .......................................165
　Of by-laws................................................165
　Of application for loan.....................................179
　Of appraiser's report......................................184
　Of rules..................................................185
　Of mortgage note.........................................187
　Of bond.................................188, 200, 202, 211
　Of mortgage..............................189, 206, 213
　Of collateral transfer......................................193
　Of stock note.............................................194
　Of trust deed..............................................194
　Of insurance clause.......................................199
　Of Dayton Mutual Home Association mortgage.................217
　Of co-operative bank mortgage..............................219
　Of stock register..........................................224
　Of warrant................................................225
　Of bank check.............................................225
　Of building agreement.....................................226
　Of building specifications..................................227
　Of indemnifying bond......................................231
　Of waiver of liens......................................233, 234
　Of bond of secretary.......................................234
　Of bond of treasurer.......................................235
　Of resolution to borrow....................................115

**Franchise,** non user of does dissolve........................119
　Not forfeited by agreement to suspend and close up business...119

**Fraud,** liability of director for.........................39, 40

**Fraudulent** satisfaction of mortgage, relief for...............98

**Funds,** misapplication of, liability of directors for............39

**General** agent, powers to bind association........................52, 53

**General Meetings.** Supreme power in management vested in
    stockholders assembled in general meeting...................36
    Directors cannot defeat this power..........................36
    When they should occur......................................36
    Date of, should be fixed by by-laws.........................37
    When shareholder entitled to personal notice.............. ....37
    Unless held pursuant to notice, of no validity..............37
    Must be held in the locality of the shareholders...........37
    Special or unusual matters require notice.................. .37
    Acts of majority present, binding...........................37
    Objects of...................................................38

**Gross** negligence, liability of directors for....................39

**Guidance** for directors......................................40, 41

**Heirs** as members................................................25

**Horizontal** premiums.............................................78

**Idiot** cannot be member..........................................22

**Illegal** action of directors may be restrained by stockholders.........25

**Illinois** associations...........................................140

**Implication,** name acquired by...................................11

**Implied** powers..................................................52
    to borrow money.............................................113
    of association to take mortgage.............................55

**Incapacity** of agent, contract may be rescinded for..............49

**Incidental** powers, association has..........................50, 52

**Incorporation,** averment as to...................................53
    Form of special act for.....................................162
    Form of agreement for.......................................158
    By letters patent...........................................12
    By special legislative act...............................12, 13
    One receiving membership benefits estopped to deny.............25
    Members estopped to deny....................................25
    Right to deny in the state..................................25

**Indemnifying** bond, form of......................................231

**Indiana** Associations............................................144

**Infants** as members..............................................22

**Inspection** of books by members..................................62

**Insolvency** does not dissolve association........................119

**Insolvent** association should have receiver......................123
    Officer of, cannot discharge his indebtedness by his stock.........49
    Rights of withdrawing members of............................67

**Insurance.** Covenant to pay, enforceable.........................84
    Breach of contract to carry.................................84 D

Carrying by borrower...................................................177 n
Clause, form of.......................................................199

**Iowa** Associations..................................................143

**Interest,** None on fines............................................101
Ceases on appointment of receiver..............................120
Charges, how fixed by officers.................................106
Illegal cannot be recovered....................................105
Usurious measure, of damages on recovering back..........105
Usurious, may be recovered back................................105
Usurious, Refunded clears of taint.............................105
·May be charged on the principal without regard to the
    weekly or monthly reductions...............................104
Payable during suspension of business........................120
Should be on the sum advanced ...  .........................104
Payable weekly or monthly not usurious......................104
Not collectible on premium or interest...................80, 105

**Investing** member liability for losses...................89, 90
May be without borrowing.......................................63

**Investor,** liability of...........................................90, 127

**Issue** of stock, see Re-issue of stock.................56, 57

**Judgment** against association binds shareholders...............54

**Junior Incumbrancer** may compel application of stock
    payments on loan...........................86, 88, 124, 125
Must notify association of his claim...........................126

**Kansas** associations...............................................142

**Kentucky,** statutory interest allowed...........................106 n

**Leases,** effect of................................................91, 92

**Legal status** of member...........................................59
of stockholder defined.........................................66

**Legislature** may amend charter.....................................18

**Lenders** to associations entitled to payment over members.........111
Where society exceeds statutory limit, remedy of..............111

**Letters** patent, incorporation by...................................12

**Liability** of attorney.............................................45
Of association for agent's acts................................53
Of directors .....................................................39
Of secretary....................................................44
Of treasurer....................................................45
Of withdrawing member......................................66, 128
On stock, measure of...........................................90
Of borrower for debts of association under his mortgage..88, 89, 128
Of investor.................................................90, 127
Of association must be discharged before division...............121

**Liability.**
Of borrower.............................................90, 127
Of stockholder..........................................90, 127
**Lien** on stock, fines are..................................101
Waiver of, form of...................................233, 234
**Loan.**
Not in conformity with by-laws but under express statutory
    power, not void.......................................30
Duty of directors in granting.............................42
Per centage of value to be loaned........................46
Association has power to make............................55
Duty of association to make..............................74
Advancement on shares is...............................77 n
Application for...........................................80
Note or bond, provisions of..............................81
Mortgage, provisions of..................................81
To outsider not grantable unless authorized..............83
Cannot be defeated by borrower as unauthorized...........83
To married women.........................................83
Shares as collateral security for............85, see form, 193
Payments on stock not ipso facto payments on.............75
Creditor cannot compel application of stock on...........86
Applications of stock payments are compellable by junior
    incumbrancer, or purchaser, or surety............86, 88
Withdrawing borrower may pay off and retain stock........87
Assigned shares cannot be credited on....................88
Leases for...........................................91, 92
Amount payable on foreclosure...............93, 94, 95, 96
Amount payable on voluntary repayment................96, 97
Interest should be charged on the sum advanced..........104
Premium only enforceable against members...............105
Not paid at one time, but receiving legal interest, not usurious..105
Form of application for.................................179
Method of.............................133, 134, 135, 136

**Loans,** character of security for.........................3
    Stock..................................................3
    Mortgage...............................................4

**Losses,** liability of investor and borrower for.......89, 90
    Liability of borrower for............................127

**Maine** Associations..................................141

**Majority** acts of, at meeting, binding...............37

**Making** loans........................................80

**Malfeasance** of agent, contract may be rescinded for...49

**Manner** of withdrawal...............................64

**Married** woman as member........22
  Loans to........83
  Loans enforceable against husband of........83
**Marshalling** of assets........124
  When doctrine of, applies........126
**Maryland** associations........139
**Massachusetts** associations........139
**Matured** value of stock not recoverable on withdrawal........66
**Maturity** of series........121
  Retiring of stock before........68
  Of stock premium chargeable to, only........79
  Of stock in serial........122
  Stockholders may wind up before........119
**Measure** of Damages on recovery of usurious interest........105
  Of liability on stock........90
**Member.** See Stockholders.
  May borrow........3, 23
  May withdraw........3, 8, 24
  May transfer stock........3
  May pledge shares........3
  Pays entrance fees........3, 21
  Should pay additional cost when........6
  How constituted........10
  Relation to corporation........21
  Relation to state........21
  Entrance fee prerequisite of membership........21
  Non compos cannot be a member........22
  Becomes a member by subscribing for stock........22, 30
  Not compelled to accept illegal conditions........22
  Married women and infants as members........22
  Contracts with married women........22
  Purposes of membership........22
  Purposes not material........23
  Is debtor to the association........23 and n, 59, 63
  Entitled to be credited with profit........23
  Association bound to lend to members........24
  Withdrawal of, terminates membership........24
  Issuing of pass book........24
  Payments, how credited on pass-books........24
  Pass books prima facie evidence of membership........24
  Procedure when pass-books are lost........24
  Certificates of stock how issued........24
  Rules concerning when upheld........24
  Estopped to deny incorporation........25
  Illustration of rules........25 n

## Member.

Right to deny incorporation in the state........................25
One receiving membership benefits estopped................25, 29 n
Directors should keep within corporate powers....................25
Stockholders may restrain illegal action of directors .......25 n, 39
Association when estopped to deny membership.................25
Death of stockholder.................... .........................26
Death dissolves membership...................................26
Heirs or devisees as members...................................26
Becomes such by owning stock without signing any agreement...30
Not bound by amendment of by-laws without notice.............28
By-laws requiring members to sign obligation are directory......29
By-laws are part of contract between member and association....30
Violating by-laws cannot complain if waived by association......30
Cannot complain if holding shares contrary to by-laws, but
   not contrary to statute................................... ...............30
Has but one vote.............................................. ...........33
Not relieved from duties by acts ultra vires.....................51
Effect of tender when sued....................................54
Default of other members will not relieve him................... 59
May be shareholder and creditor..............................60
Pro rata interest in reserve fund..............................60
Borrowing entitled to pro rata part of profits.......................60
After enjoying benefits of by-laws cannot question legality of.....62
May inspect books of association...............................63
May invest without borrowing..................................63
Formerly denied in England....................................63
May be sued for dues.........................................63
Should give written notice of withdrawal.......................64
Member withdrawing is creditor of association................65, 66
Amount member may recover on withdrawal....................65
Legal status of withdrawing, defined..........................66
Withdrawing, liability of.......................................66
Withdrawing not bound by new rules..........................66
Withdrawing may sell his interest.............................67
Withdrawing from insolvent association, rights of..............67
Withdrawing must show funds in treasury to enforce demand...66
Defaulting cannot transfer stock..............................70
Forfeiting membership, effect of...............................71
Defaulting, disposition of.....................................71
Borrowing, status of.......................................71, 72, 73 n
Borrowing, selection of.......................................74
Not deprived of ordinary benefits by mortgage in ordinary form.82
Should be accommodated before outsiders on loans.............83
Cannot be compelled by creditor to apply stock payments on
   loan.................................................................86
Withdrawing borrower's manner of repayment.................86

**Member.**
Withdrawing borrower, credit how ascertained...............87
Losses, liability for.................................89, 90
Liability on stock................................90, 127
Fines only collectible from members......................101
Lenders to association entitled to payment over...............111
Defaulting entitled to share in profits..........  ...............123
When may compel settlement.........................124
Cannot participate in assets until creditors are paid............126

**Membership** fee.....................................3
Form of application for.............................158

**Method** of loans..................... 133, 134, 135, 136
Of charging premiums.......................75, 76, 135
Of dissolution...................................119

**Meetings.** See General and Special Meetings.
Of directors.............................  .................37

**Michigan** associations ...........................140

**Minimum** premium..............................78

**Minnesota** associations..........................142

**Minutes** of meetings..........................41, 47

**Misapplication** of funds, liability of directors for.............39

**Misnomer** ....................................11

**Mississippi** associations........................142

**Missouri** associations ..........................142

**Mistake** of law..............................98

**Mode of Amendment** as prescribed must be strictly followed..33
Of charter.....................................19 n

**Money** of association should be loaned........... ...............74

**Mortgage Foreclosure,** See Foreclosure of Mortgage.
Loans ..........................................4
Association has implied power to take.......................55
Association has no power to sell........................116
Assignment effect of...............................116
Registration of....................................91
Acknowledgment of.................................90
Of borrower does not secure liability for debts of association,
    unless so provided.......................88, 89, 128
Not void for uncertainty...  ......................83
May be deposited for collateral security.............111, 112, 113
In ordinary form does not deprive member of benefits..........82
Provisions of.....................................81
Satisfaction of....................................92
Release of by association when there is a second mortgage.......88
Preparation of....................................84

**Mortgage Foreclosure.**
Satisfaction of by president............................98
Note, form of...........................................187
Form of................................189, 206, 213, 219

**Mutual** Home and Savings Association...............136, 137
Form of mortgage of...................................217

**Name** ...............................................11, 12

**Nebraska** associations...............................144

**Necessity** of fines..................................99

**Neglect** to elect officers does not dissolve association.............119

**Negligence** gross, liability of director for.......39

**New Hampshire** associations..........................140

**New Jersey** associations.............................139
Bond ................................................211
Mortgage ............................................213

**New York** associations...............................138

**Non compos** cannot be member.........................22

**Non user** of franchise does not dissolve............119

**North Carolina** associations.........................141

**North Dakota** associations...........................144

**Notary Public,** when disqualified................90, 91

**Note,** provisions of..................................81
Form of mortgage note................................187
Form of stock note...................................194

**Notes,** association cannot traffic in................55

**Notice,**
Of amendment of by-laws should be given..............28
Character of notice..................................28
When shareholder entitled to personal notice of general meeting.37
General meeting must be held pursuant to notice.......37
Required for special meeting.........................37
For special meeting, how served......................37
Of withdrawal should be written......................64
Of withdrawal, how served............................65
Notice of forfeiture not necessary unless required...71
Of junior incumbrancer to association................126
Recording subsequent incumbrance, is not notice......126
Actual, effect of....................................126
To stockholders, when not necessary..................13

**Nul tiel** corporation, plea of.......................53

**Office,** association should have.....................36

**Officers.**
Compensation ........................................................4
To be selected.......................................................4
Stockholders elect..............................................11, 35
Consist ordinarily of president, vice-president, secretary,
    treasurer and attorney...............................35, 36, 42
Election of, by ballot.............................................36
Election to be provided for by by-laws.............................36
Secretary and treasurer should give bond...........................36
May include abstracter and appraisers..............................42
Manner of election as fixed by by-laws to be strictly observed....48
Cannot be removed by stockholders..................................48
Cannot be removed by courts........................................48
Removal of, should be provided for in by-laws......................49
Cannot use position for personal benefit...........................49
Relation of officers to association................................49
Liability of, in distributing funds............................60, 62
Fines against delinquent...........................................99
Rules for, in fixing interest charges.............................106
Neglect to elect, does not dissolve association...................179

**Ohio** associations ..............................................137

**Opinion,** directors not liable for mistake in...............39, 40

**Oregon** associations ............................................144

**Organization** ....................................................9
Promoters of association............................................9
Services of promoter, proof of...................................9 n
Preliminary contract...............................................10
Expenses of........................................................10
Stockholder, how constituted.......................................10
Subscription for stock.............................................10
Stock subscription for.............................................10
Association may enforce stock subscription.........................10
Articles of incorporation......................................11, 12
Preparation of articles of incorporation...........11, 12, 14, 15
Preparation of charter of incorporation............12, 14, 15
Name...........................................................11, 12
Signing of articles of incorporation...............................12
Charter, preparation of.......................11, 12, 13, 14, 15
Registration of articles of incorporation..........................13
Shareholders adopt by-laws.........................................11
Shareholders elect officers........................................11
Certificates of stock..............................................13
Defects in organization cannot be collaterally attacked........16, 17
Form of agreement for incorporation...............................158

**Outsider,** when may borrow.......................................83

**Overdrawing** bank account.......................................114

**Paid up** stock, issue of.................................................60, 61 n

**Partnership**.................................................76 n, 77 n

**Pass Book,** issuing of.................................................24, 36
When must be produced on withdrawal.............................69
Prima facie evidence of membership.............................24
Procedure when lost.................................................24

**Payment** of lenders to association before members..................111
Of dues cannot be required except as stipulated.................81
Of dues at secretary's place of business, when valid.............63
Of dues ceases when association is in hands of receiver..........81
Of dues should be to authorized officer.........................63

**Payments.**
Application of.................................................84
Credited on pass books.................................................24
On re-assigned stock.................................................87
On stock not ipso facto payments on loan.......................85
On stock application, effect of.................................88

**Penalty** for failure to take loan.................................74

**Pennsylvania** associations.................................138
Bond.................................................202
Mortgage.................................................206

**Per centage** of value to be loaned.................................46

**Permanent** association, retiring stock in.................121
Change of to serial.................................................130
Plan of.................................................6

**Perpetual** succession.................................................50, 51

**Plea** of nul tiel corporation.................................53

**Pledging** shares.................................................3

**Pledged** stock cannot be withdrawn.................................69

**Premium** charges.................................................3
Stockholders need not pay for priority of payment of matured
shares.................................................29
Paid as a preference.................................................74
Methods of charging.................................................75, 76
When usurious.................................................76, 102, 103
When not usurious.................................................77, 78 notes
Have general legislative authority.................................77, n, 104
Auction premiums when must be complied with.................77
Fixed unchangeable.................................................78
Horizontal or uniform.................................................78
Minimum premium.................................................78
Chargeable to maturity only.................................79
One premium only chargeable.................................79
Interest not chargeable on.................................80, 105

**Premium.**

Not usurious as formerly................................. ........102

When authorized by statute, recoverable.....................103 n

Effect of disregarding statute.............................104

Enforceable only against members...........................105

Methods of charging...................................134, 135

Unearned...........................................135, 143

**Powers.**

When courts may interfere with exceeded powers.............17

Corporate functions not enlarged by assuming unauthorized
    powers............................................................17

Association has power to amend by-laws.....................31

Supreme power of management vested in stockholders assem-
    bled in general meeting.....................................36

Of special meetings.......................... ..............37

Of directors to remit fines or compromise debts............42, 55

Of courts to remove officers...............................48

Of stockholders to remove officers........................48

Of directors to rescind contract of agent.................49

General powers of association.............................50

    To have a common seal.................................50

    To contract...........................................50

    To hold real estate..............................50, 56

    To sue and be sued....................................50

    To make by-laws.......................................50

Incidental association has such as are necessary............50, 52

Of agents should be defined...............................52

Of special agent..........................................52

Of general agent..........................................52, 53

Delegation of, by secretary or appraisers.................53 n

To loan money.............................................55

To take mortgages.........................................55

When may issue stock to another corporation...............56, 57

To borrow money........107, 108, 109, 110, 111, 112, 113, 114, 115

To sell mortgages.........................................116

**Power** of building associations to borrow money

Act of Parliament 1874...................................110

American authorities.....................................111

English authorities......................................109

Implied power............................................113

Legislative intention....................................108

Necessary to meet demands for loans......................108

Necessary to pay off a series............................107

Necessary to cancel matured stock........................107

Remedy of lenders where statutory limit is exceeded......111

To borrow for authorized purpose.........................114

Of state to withdraw charter for exceeded powers.........16

**Preference,** bidding for............................................74

**Preferential** stock, issue of............................................60

**Preliminary** contract ............................................10

**Preparation** of articles of incorporation................11, 12, 14, 15
  For loan............................................80

**President.**
  Should issue call for special meetings......................37
  Duties of............................................43
  Should appoint auditing committee......................47
  Should make record cancellations......................98

**Profits,** Division of............................................7
  Division of in serial......................................122
  Members entitled to be credited with......................23

**Promoter,** services of............................................9n

**Provisions** of agreement to take shares......................11
  Of mortgage............................................81
  Of note or bond............................................81

**Proxies,** when may be used............................38 and n

**Public Policy.** By-laws must not be contrary to..........29

**Purchaser** of property may compel application of stock payments on loan......................................86, 88

**Purposes** of membership............................................23

**Quorum,** how estimated......................................37, 38

**Ratification** of agent's unauthorized act, effect of..........53

**Real Estate** holding beyond power, effect of..........56
  Holding beyond power does not dissolve association..........56
  Power of association to hold......................50, 56

**Receiver,** Appointment of, for insolvent association..........123
  Dues and interest cease on appointment of..........120
  Payments of dues, etc., cease when association is in hands of....81

**Recording** subsequent incumbrance not notice to association......126

**Refusal** of association to transfer shares, remedy for..........70

**Registration** of incorporation............................................13
  of mortgage............................................91

**Reissue** of stock............................................131

**Relation** of officers to association............................................49

**Remission** of fines......................................42, 55

**Removal** of directors............................................48
  Of officers............................................48
  • Of officers should be provided for in by-laws..........49

**Repayment** by withdrawing borrower............................................86

**Report** of auditors, impeachable when............................................47

**Reserve Fund,** each member has pro rata interest in..............60

**Resignation** of director.......................................48

**Resolution** to borrow, form of.................................115

**Retiring** series...............................................121

    Stock before maturity....................................68

**Retroactive Amendments** of by-laws apply fully unless
vested rights are impaired......................................32

**Revenues** of association........................................4

**Rhode Island** associations....................................141

**Rules.**

    Concerning issue of stock certificate....................24

    Needed by the association.............................33

    May be amended as by-laws............................33

    Unwritten will govern when acted on, if reasonable...........33

    By-laws should be kept distinct from...................33

    For general guidance of directors...................40, 41

    Withdrawing member not bound by new rules...............67

    Form of.............................................185

**Sale** of money by auction......................................74

**Satisfaction** of mortgage.....................................93

    of mortgages by president...........................98

**Seal.**

    Use of, by statutory corporations......................20

    When seal should be attached.........................20

    Any device or form will answer.....................20, 52

    Common, power of association to have...................50

    Custody of..........................................51

    Contracts requiring...................................52

**Secretary.**

    By-laws defining his duties part of sureties' contract......30

    Should give bond....................................36

    Receiving dues at his office...........................36

    Duties of...........................................43

    Liability of.........................................44

    When guilty of embezzlement.........................49

    Estoppel ...........................................49

    May delegate power.................................53 n

    Payment of dues at place of business, when valid..........63

    Should enter notices of withdrawal ...................65

    Form of bond of....................................234

**Security,** character of..........................................3

**Securities,** association should not take unlawful...............50

**Selection** of borrower........................................74

**Serial,** division of profits............................................122

   Maturity of stock............................................123

   Change of, to permanent............................................130

**Series,** maturity of............................................121

   Of stock, association may borrow to pay off............................................112

**Service** of notice of withdrawal............................................65

**Services** of promoter, proof of............................................9 n

**Set off,** borrower entitled to............................................92

**Settlement,** when member may compel............................................124

   When required............................................121

**Shares.** See Stock

   Pledging............................................3

**Shareholders.** See Stockholders.

**Signing** of articles of incorporation............................................12

**Special Agent,** how far may bind association............................................52

**Special** legislative act, incorporation by............................................13

**Special Meetings.**

   Notice required............................................37

   Call for, how made............................................37

   Notice for, how served............................................37

   Power of............................................37

   Acts of majority present, binding............................................37

**Specifications** building, form of............................................227

**State** has power to forfeit charter............................................119

   May annul charter, when............................................51

   Powers of, to withdraw charter for exceeded powers............................................16

**Status** of borrowing member............................................71, 72, 73 n

**Statutes.**

   By-laws must be consistent with............................................29

   Right of withdrawal usually defined by............................................64

   Effect of failure to strictly comply with............................................16

   Strict compliance with, in charter unnecessary............................................16

**Statutory References.**

   Alabama,............................................153

   Arkansas,............................................153

   California,............................................153

   Colorado,............................................153

   Connecticut,............................................153

   Dakota,............................................153

   Delaware............................................153

   Florida,............................................154

   Georgia,............................................154

   Illinois,............................................154

## Statutory References.

Indiana, ............................................................154
Iowa, ..............................................................154
Kansas, ............................................................154
Kentucky, ..........................................................154
Louisiana, .........................................................154
Maine, .............................................................154
Maryland, ..........................................................154
Massachusetts, .....................................................154
Michigan, ..........................................................154
Minnesota, .........................................................155
Mississippi, .......................................................155
Missouri, ..........................................................155
Montana, ...........................................................155
Nebraska, ..........................................................155
New Hampshire, .....................................................155
New Jersey, ........................................................155
New Mexico, ........................................................155
New York, ..........................................................155
North Carolina, ....................................................156
Ohio, ..............................................................156
Oregon, ............................................................156
Pennsylvania, ......................................................156
Rhode Island, ......................................................157
South Carolina, ....................................................157
Tennessee, .........................................................157
Texas, .............................................................157
Virginia, ..........................................................157
Wyoming, ...........................................................157
Utah, ..............................................................157
Washington, ........................................................157
West Virginia, .....................................................157
Wisconsin, .........................................................158

**Stock,** dues are partial payments on ...........................2, 4

Transfer of ........................................................3
Pledging of ........................................................3
Maturing of ........................................................4
Value of ...........................................................5
Loans ..............................................................3
Subscription for ...................................................10
Association may enforce ............................................10
Certificates of ...........................................13, 24, 36
Association cannot hold stock in another corporation ...............25
Become members by subscribing for ..................................22
After maturity of, stockholders need not offer premiums for
    priority of payment ........................29
When may be issued to another corporation .....................56, 57

## Stock.

Preferential, issue of...............................60
Paid up, issue of.............................60, 61 n
What may be recovered on withdrawal.................66
Retiring of before maturity........................68
Right to withdraw limited to present funds.........68
Pledged cannot be withdrawn........................69
Transfer of........................................69
Must be transferred on books.......................70
Certificates should be surrendered on retirement...70
Transfer of, effect on member's liability..........70
Transfer cannot be made by defaulting member.......70
Assignment of, as collateral security..............85
Payments on stock not ipso facto payments on loan..85
Withdrawing borrower may retain and pay off loan...87
Value of, on withdrawal, how ascertained...........87
Re-assigned payments on............................87
Assigned cannot be credited on loan................88
Fines are lien on.................................101
Association may borrow to cancel..................111
Cancelling, effect of.............................121
When to be retired................................121
Maturity of.......................................122
Pledged may be sold as against purchaser..........124
Assessment on.....................................127
Certificate of, form of...........................165
Reissue of........................................131
Form of stock register............................224

## Stockholders.

How constituted................................10, 13
Adopt by-laws......................................11
Elect officers.....................................11
When notice not necessary..........................13
May restrain illegal action of directors.......25, 51
Death of...........................................26
Should have notice of by-laws..................27, 62
Power to enact by-laws resides in..................28
Need not pay premium for priority of payment after maturity
     of shares......................................29
Assembled in general meeting have supreme power....36
Should have copy of report of association..........36
When entitled to personal notice of general meeting..37
General meetings must be held in locality of.......37
Cannot remove directors............................48
Cannot take advantage of acts ultra vires when....51
Bound by judgment against association..............54
Liability of, not terminated by withdrawal.........64

**Stockholders.**
Legal status of, defined.................................................66
Shown by book, entitled to profit................................70
Liability on stock..........................................90, 127
Death of, does not dissolve association........................119
Cannot maintain suit to forfeit charter........................119
Account of, when association is in liquidation.............120 n

**Stock** register form of......................................224

**Subscription** for stock......................................10

**Suit** by withdrawing member, necessary allegations...........66
To foreclose mortgage, constitution and by-laws not proper
    exhibits under Indiana Code................................82
May be on bond or mortgage.....................................82
For dues by association........................................63

**Sureties.**
By-laws defining secretary's duties part of sureties' contract......30

**Sureties,** Responsibilities of, how ascertained............47, 48

**Surety** may compel application of stock payments on loans.........88
Discharge of.................................................48
Liability of................................................48
Effect of failure to read bond...............................48

**Surrender** of certificate of stock...........................70

**Suspension** of business, borrower not relieved from interest
    during....................................................120

**Systems** of loaning...........................133, 134, 135, 186

**Tables**.......................................146, 147, 148, 149

**Taxes,** covenant to pay enforceable............................84

**Tender** effect of, by sued member.............................54

**Tennessee** associations.......................................139

**Texas** associations...........................................144

**Transfer.**
Of stock....................................................8, 69
Of stock, effect on member's liability.........................70
Of stock on books, effect of failure to.......................70
Cannot be made by defaulting member...........................70
Fee enforceable............................................70 n
Shares, refusal of association to, remedy.....................70

**Treasurer.**
Should give bond.............................................86
Duties of...................................................43
Warrant of, not negotiable................................44 n
Liability of................................................45
Is only a bailee............................................45
When guilty of embezzlement.................................49

**Treasurer,**
Estoppel .................................................................49
Form of bond..........................................................235

**Trustees,** directors as...........................................38, 39

**Trust** deed, form of................................................194

**Ultra vires,** Unlimited borrowing is, in English societies..........109
Acts, effect of......................................................50, 51
Liability of directors for..............................................89
When stockholder cannot take advantage of...........................51
When association estopped to deny its acts..........................51
When charter may be annulled for....................................51
Do not relieve members from their duties............................51
Do not of themselves end corporate existence........................51
When subject to collateral attack..................................52

**Unauthorized** transaction void.......................................50

**Unearned** premium...............................................135, 143

**Uniform** premium..:...................................................78

**Unwritten Regulations.**
Will govern when acted upon, if reasonable..........................33

**Use,** name acquired by..........................................11, 12

**Usurious** interest, measure of damages on recovering back..........105
Interest may be recovered back.....................................105
Refunded clears of taint...........................................105
Charged against outsider...........................................105
Not as formerly....................................................102
When premium is not.........................................77, 78 notes

**Usury** definition of.................................................102
Not avoided by complicated transactions.............................102
Combination of interest and expenses at a higher than a legal
    rate is tainted with..........................................102
If the arrangement makes higher than the legal rate it is........103
Avoided on the partnership theory.............................103 n
When cost of money, not usurious.............................103, 104
Interest payable monthly or weekly, not usurious................104
Charging interest on the principal without regard to weekly
    or monthly reductions, is not.................................104
A personal defense.................................................105
When loan not subject to...........................................105
When premiums are usurious.....................................76, 77 n

**Value** of shares .......................................................5
Of shares upon withdrawal, how ascertained..........................87
Of stock not recoverable on withdrawal.............................66
Per centage of, to be loaned.......................................46

**Vested Rights,** amendments of by-laws cannot affect..............91

**Vice President,** duties of............................43
**Voluntary** repayment, amount of....................96, 97
   Repayment, under English Rule, computation for............94
   Repayment, natural and logical rule for................96, 97
   Repayment, rule as to computation for................94
**Vote,** member has but one............................38
**Waiver** of liens, form of....................233, 234
**Washington, D. C.** associations....................137
**Warrant** of treasurer not negotiable............44 n
   Of treasurer, form of............................225
**West Virginia** associations....................142
**Winding up.** See Dissolution
   Rights of withdrawing members on............68, 69
   Stockholders may wind up by unanimous agreement........119, 122
**Wisconsin** associations....................141
**Withdrawing** borrower, manner of repayment............86
   Credits entitled to............................6, 87
   Not compelled to make application of stock............87
   Member of insolvent association, rights of............67
   Liability of............................66, 128
   May sell his interest............................67
   Rights of, against other members............68
   Rights of, on winding up............68, 69
   Not bound by new rules............................67
   Is creditor of association............65, 66
**Withdrawal.**
   Of members............................3, 8, 64
   Terminates membership............................24
   Should be attended with restrictions............64
   Does not terminate all liability............64
   Right usually defined by statute............64
   Written notice of, should be given............64
   Notice of, how served............................65
   Amount payable on............................65, 69
   Amount recoverable on............................66
   Limited to present funds............................68
   Directors should not invest funds to defeat............68
   Pledged stock not subject to............................69
   When pass book must be produced............69
**Wyoming** associations............................143

# BUILDING ASSOCIATIONS.

## CHAPTER I.

## INTRODUCTION.

SECTION 1.  Origin of Building Associations.

SECTION 2.  Definition of Building Associations.

SECTION 3.  General Scheme.

SECTION 4.  Different Types.

SECTION 1. **Origin of Building Associations.** The origin of building associations is involved in much doubt, and no practical purpose will be served in devoting much time to that line of investigation. The Earl of Selkirk is given the credit of founding the building association about the year 1809[1]. The Greenwich Union Building Society was its name, with the object of raising by monthly subscription a fund or capital to be laid out in building houses, and of dividing the same among members, under rules created in a deed of rules and regulations[2]. A mention of " building clubs " occurs in Birmingham, England, in 1772. Some writers have given their origin to Germany, connecting the frugal and accumulative dispositions of this people, probably, with the institution;

---

[1] Davis Building Society.

[2] The author states at length the objects of this association as expressed in the deed.

but there is no authentic support of the claim.' The first building association in America is generally conceded to have been The Brooklyn Building and Mutual Loan Fund Association.' However, the earlier associations found existence in the city of Philadelphia, about 1840; their spread was south and west. Frequently, they were put into operation as unincorporated societies', flourishing in some states and failing in others. Generally they have become the subject of statutory creation and regulation, and being independent corporations, they have become vast depositories of savings and controllers of enormous property. Their influence upon economic affairs is far reaching and the multiplicity of their interests invites the attention of the lawyer, legislator and jurist.

SEC. 2. **Definition of Building Association.** The building association as now existing, is a private corporation, designed for the accumulation by the members of their money by periodical payments into its treasury, to be invested from time to time in loans to the members upon real estate for home purposes, the borrowing members paying interest and a premium as a preference in securing loans over other members, and continuing their fixed periodical installments in addition, all of which payments, together with the non-borrower's payments, including fines for failure to pay such fixed installments, forfeitures for such continued failure of such payments, fees for transferring stock, membership fees required upon the entrance of the member into the society, and such other revenues, go into the common fund until such time as that the installment payments and profits aggregate the face value of all the shares in the association, when the assets, after payment of expenses and losses are prorated among all members, which in legal effect, cancels the borrower's debt, and gives the non-borrower the amount of his stock.

SEC. 3. **General Scheme.** The periodical installment is called dues, and is a partial payment on the certificate of

---

'Endlich Building Associations p. 3.

'Bibb Co. etc. Association v. Richards, 21 Ga. 592.

'Merrill v. McIntire, 13 Gray, 157; Baxter v. McIntire, 13 Gray, 168; Delano v. Wild, 6 Allen, 1; Atwood v. Dumas, 149 Mass. 167.

stock issued to the member'. When the share reaches face value, it is matured. Shares are commonly for $200.00, sometimes for $100.00 or $500.00. Fines are imposed for failure to pay the dues at the fixed time. The stock is sometimes forfeited after a certain time for continued non-payment of dues. When shares of stock are assigned by a member to any person, they have to be transferred on the books, and it is usual to charge a small fee for that trouble.

The membership fee is to cover the expense of issuing the stock. When a member desires to build a home, he takes from the association the amount needed, and assigns shares of the face value of the loan, as collateral security, and agrees to keep up his payments thereon. This is pledging shares. He pays a premium for the loan. The amount of the premium is reached by offering money to the highest bidder, and the proposed borrower bids a few cents on each share, payable with the dues, or a lump amount to be deducted, for the right to have the money. Upon securing that right, he designates his security, and a committee appointed by the association, values it, and if it is sufficient security for the proposed loan, the borrower submits his abstract of title to the attorney of the association, who upon pronouncing it perfect, prepares the necessary papers for the loan. The borrower thereafter pays an additional sum into the association by way of premium and interest. The association, through its proper officers, keeps an account of the receipts and disbursements. Members, except those pledging their shares, may withdraw upon certain notice, and receive the withdrawal value of their shares, which is sometimes fixed by statute, and is the lawful interest. The rest of the profits attaching to those shares, goes into the common fund. Each member may borrow if he can give security. The association usually requires a note or bond secured by mortgage on unincumbered real estate, or a trust deed, or any sum not exceeding the withdrawal value of the shares may be borrowed, and their assignment is taken as a collateral security. A loan secured by pledge of shares, is a stock loan,

'The words "members," "shareholders" and "stockholders" are used synonymously throughout this work.

and when secured by mortgage on real estate, it is a mortgage loan.

When the time arrives that the assets are sufficient to mature the stock, a division must be had, after payment of losses and expenses. The controlling rule of this division is that the assets must be divided equally according to the stock holdings. The non-borrowing member receives the value of his stock, and the borrower's debt is satisfied. The stock is thus matured and cancelled. But a borrower is usually given by statute the privilege of repaying his loan at any time, and thereupon withdrawing. So that he is not compelled to stay in to maturity.

The revenues of the association usually consist of membership fees, dues, premium, interest, fines, and transfer fees. The gross profits consist of membership fees, interest, premium, share of profits left by withdrawing shareholders, fines and transfer fees. Dues are not profits, as they are partial payments on the capital stock. The association will have expenses. They are sometimes provided for by statute; if not, they should be paid out of the general profits from time to time, before any division is made. The directors should only incur such expense as is necessary to the proper conduct of the business. The same care used in private business should be exercised here, for if the directors extravagantly and needlessly make expenses they grossly violate their trust.

This is the general design of a building association, but there are different modifications of this general scheme.

This corporation, just as any other, must have officers, who usually consist of directors, president, vice-president, secretary, treasurer, attorney and appraisers. The business of the association may call for assisting officers to manage a great volume of business. Compensation of the officers depends, as in any other business, upon their work and the amount of business. The borrowers usually pay the attorney for his services in examination of the title and preparation of papers for loans. The scheme is so simple that it almost carries itself, and attached as it is primarily to land security, which after all is the basis of all security, it does not include so many uncertain problems in its management as does a bank, and unless grossly mismanaged, will show the finest results of financial co-operation.

SEC. 4. **Different Types.** In this country we have two distinct and prevailing types; one, serial, and the other permanent. The general plan of the serial association is to issue a certain portion, say one-tenth of its capital stock in one series, providing that it shall be paid in weekly or monthly dues, and that whenever such payments, with accumulated profits, equal the face value of the shares, each share shall be retired and the holder thereof shall receive the amount thereof in cash; provided that if he is an advanced or borrowing member, i. e., one receiving the face value of his shares before maturity, his debt shall be considered paid and cancelled. When one series is full or the demand is satisfied, then a second series is issued, and so on until the entire capital stock is exhausted. The plan of issuing in series is only for convenience of persons desiring membership, who for any reason do not care to pay dues back to the formation of the association. The profits are the total profits, divided by the number of shares in all series having regard to the age of the shares. The serial association does not credit the profits on the shares to any further extent than to keep the assets *in solido* for the benefit of all the shares. The value of the shares is ascertained from the assets by calculating, though not making, a division. The fundamental principle in ascertaining this value is equalizing all shares. The total net profits, excluding dues, losses and expenses, when there is one series, should be divided by the number of shares. The result is the value of the shares. When there is more than one series, the profits to be apportioned to each series must be ascertained, and then the division of the apportioned profits by the number of shares in the series. The calculation simply proceeds upon the theory that a sum representing the net profits of the association is to be divided among certain series of different ages, and the quotients again divided by the number of shares in each series or class. All shares in any one series have the same value and mature at the same time.

Very frequently an applicant for membership will enter a series of some months standing, and pay back to the beginning. In such cases, the rules should provide for an additional cost of shares, equal to the present value, as it is readily to be seen his shares would be entitled to profits from the date of the series, whereas the association had not had the benefit of his money. Fines for default in payment of dues, a small expense charge, interest and premium charges and withdrawal privileges are provided for. These associations resemble the English terminating society, differing in that the former makes only a part instead of an entire issue of its stock. In some of these associations, the premium on advancement on stock is deducted at the time the money is loaned; in others, it is charged with the payment of dues. The permanent association imitates the English permanent society in allowing entrance at any time without back payment of dues. These societies are said by an authority, to be " decidedly the best of all societies, as they contain more of the elements of certainty and equity, if the rules are properly drawn and observed."' The chief distinction between the two kinds is that a person may enter the permanent association at any time, without the back payments. So far as the names are concerned, one is not more permanent than the other. The " serial " by issuing new series continues, as does the "permanent" by issuing new stock. The permanent association has another important difference from the serial, and that is by the system of crediting dividends on the pass books of members, it actually divides up the profits of the association annually or semi-annually as the case may be. The withdrawing member thus can ascertain the amount he is entitled to; the borrowing member, the amount of his debt, and the investor, the value of his shares. As the permanent system is practiced in England, it is said it holds out the greatest inducements to the borrower, for by enabling him to extend his repayments over any fixed number of years the present cost is not so burdensome, and he has in addition the

' Davis Building Society 69.

right of withdrawal of his shares with an ascertained value, and may thus at any time free his property of incumbrance.[*] With us the permanent is not of greater advantage to the borrower than the serial, unless it is in the ascertainment of the value of his stock by the crediting of his profits on his pass book. But in one respect it is of decided disadvantage. And that is in the system of permanent societies in crediting dividends at stated periods, with privilege of withdrawing the full amount of payments and dividends.

Of all the members the borrower is most likely a continuing member. Under the system of dividing up the profits at stated times, any member desiring to withdraw receives not only his payments, but carries away a pro rata part of the profits. This is a decided innovation upon the original scheme which may result in injustice. The association is endeavoring to mature its stock, yet it permits withdrawing stockholders to take away a part of its ability to do so. Then the profits might only be apparent. An association running over a series of years may properly expect some vicissitudes. These may eat into the profits, which having been distributed, the burden must fall upon the members who have been the sustaining force of the association. The seeming profits which had been handed out, were then actually losses. In Ohio, this defect is undertaken to be remedied by requiring associations to carry 5 per cent. of the net earnings to a contingent fund to bear these possible losses. This is a step in the right direction, but in our judgment does not go far enough in justice to staying members. The Ohio law provides that after the payment of expenses and setting aside a sum for contingent fund, the the entire remainder of such earnings shall be transferred as a dividend to the credit of all members. Under this statute, the bureau of building associations has decided that after the payment of expenses and the setting aside of the contingent fund, the entire amount left, even to the fraction of a per cent. must be credited on the members' stock. In dividing

* Davis 70; compare Davis 64-73 for description of English societies.

the profits, it very often happens that a small sum is left over after fixing the dividend, and as it would only amount to a fraction of a per cent., the work in calculating each member's share would be very laborious. It is customary, generally, to carry this amount over as undivided profits. But the Ohio bureau holds such action contrary to the statute. It seems to us that the greater benefits should be given to the continuing member. While the withdrawing member should not be a loser, he should not be a gainer. The association in its relation to him should endeavor to keep him whole as long as it does not infringe the rights of the other members. But if he is unable to comply with his contract and carry out his promises to the end, because a liberal statute has given him the right to terminate it, the equities are pushed too far in his favor, by bestowing upon him, besides his full payments, a pro rata part of the profits. It is foreign to a proper conception of the scheme, and while the Ohio statute provides some protection, it does not compensate the continuing member, and the bureau, it would seem, should have resolved the doubt in favor of the continuing member, rather than against him. This would not only be justice, but save minute divisions. The withdrawing member will be justly dealt with by payment to him of the amount of his installments and adding thereto legal interest. The borrower then whose property is charged with the profit bearing mortgage, will have compensation and protection for his continuing support of the association, as will the staying non-borrowing member, who has shared with him the burdens and responsibilities of the association's career. The association as any other institution, must conserve its strength and should offer inducements to members to continue instead of offering compensation for their withdrawal. If the withdrawing member receives legal interest, he is compensated, and if there is a remaining profit, it should go to the staying member.

# CHAPTER II.

## PRELIMINARY ORGANIZATION.

SECTION 1. Preliminary Agreements.

SECTION 2. Agreements Legally Considered.

SECTION 3. Articles of Incorporation.

SECTION 4. Corporate Name.

SECTION 5. Preparation of Corporate Articles.

SECTION 6. Conformity with Creative Law.

SECTION 7. Procedure After Registration.

SECTION 1. **Preliminary Agreements.** When a number of persons have decided to organize a building association, a first step must be taken, and that is a preliminary organization.

The promoters of the association should be very careful of the expenses incurred in organizing,[1] providing for their

---

[1] The implied liability of a corporation for the services of a promoter may be rebutted by proof that they were gratuitously given, and when the services are those of an attorney in organizing a building association, there being no express contract as to services, it is proper to show in rebuttal of the implied contract, that the attorney had rendered like services gratuitously in getting up other building associations when the same persons were among the promoters, and the proofs should not be limited to what was said and done at the time of service. Subsequent admissions also may be shown, but it is proper to reject a question as to the understanding of the parties. Third Ward, etc., association v. Lotze 11, Bull. 285.

payment, as they are liable individually, for the amount of expenses. To attach liability to each proposed incorporator, they should also carry the preliminary steps to a legal contractual obligation between the organizers, for each to bear his part of the expenses incurred in the preliminary organization. There should also be an agreement that the preliminary arrangement will become binding for incorporation. That arrangement takes the form of an agreement to subscribe for shares in the association to be incorporated. No particular form is required, unless prescribed by statute, and as it is a matter of simple contract, it rests more upon general principles than statutory requirement. These two simple contracts, for all to bear the expense and to take shares in the new association, are the only contracts needed until incorporation is ready. If the association is incorporated and does business, all proper expenses may be charged against it. The agreement to bear expenses is intended to have effect when there is a failure to incorporate.

SEC. 2.  **Agreements Legally Considered.**  From a legal standpoint, the agreements may be said to be supported by two considerations; mutual promises and the stronger one of benefit received by the promissor and detriment to the promisee[1]. Until a charter is obtained, or incorporation otherwise perfected, an agreement to take shares is a mere offer, revocable or not, as the nature of the agreement may determine. When it rests on a valuable consideration, such as a promise for a promise, then as a rule it becomes an irrevocable option, provided, incorporation according to the terms of the offer is perfected within a reasonable time. This would constitute the offerer in substance a stockholder. So if an offer which has no valuable consideration to rest on, be permitted to stand until it is accepted by incorporation according to its terms, this it seems would be an irrevocable subscription of stock[2]. The corporation may enforce the agreement, although it is not a party to it, on the ground that it was made

[1]See Taylor Priv. Corp. sec. 92.      Knox v. Childersburg, etc.,Company,
[2]Morawetz P. C. secs. 47, 128;    86 Ala. 180.

for its benefit.[1] The mere entering into a valid agreement to take shares, does not constitute the persons as partners; there must be some agreement showing an intention to divide and share profits and losses before there is a partnership.[2] The agreement to take shares should be one to take a certain number of shares of designated face value in the association to be thereafter formed, to be paid for in weekly or monthly installments, as the by-laws may provide, with the further provision that if the incorporation never took place, the expenses of the attempt should be equally borne by promoters.[3]

Sec. 3. **Articles of Incorporation.** The promoters of the association having entered into a binding arrangement to take shares in the association, and bear the expense of the organization, the next step is to examine the requirements of the statute on incorporation. A certain number of incorporators and a certain amount of stock subscribed may be required. The statute should be consulted as to any precedent requirements and if there are any, they must be adhered to. These provisions, if any, being observed, the preparation of the articles of association follows. This should be entrusted to a competent attorney.

Sec. 4. **Corporate Name.** Before the articles are drawn, however, a corporate name must be selected. It is necessary for purposes of identification, at least to the existence of a corporation, and is usually given by the charter, but where not expressly given, may be acquired by implication and use.[4] The misnomer of a corporation in contracts or pleadings has an effect similar to the misnomer of an individual. If from the body of a written contract, in which a corporation is misnamed the corporation intended can be ascertained, the misnomer is immaterial.[5]

[1]Haskett v. Flint, 5 Blkf. 69; Farlow v Kemp, 7 Blkf. 544; Eastern, etc., Company v. Vaughan, 14 N.Y. 546; Athol, etc. Company v. Carey, 116 Mass. 471; Buffalo, etc., Company v. Gifford, 87 N. Y. 294.

[5]Shibley v. Angle, 37 N. Y. 626.

[2]No notice is necessary in reference to calls on subscriptions: Morrison v. Dorsey, 48 Md. 461.

[4]Smith v. Plank Road Company, 30 Ala. 650; Minot v. Curtis, 7 Mass. 441.

[4]Hoboken etc. Association v. Martin, 13 N. J. Eq. 427.

A building association cannot by user, acquire an exclusive right to use in its title of incorporation, a general term, descriptive merely of the locality with which its business is connected.[1] The name should have some significance as a matter of policy and should not resemble existing corporate names to prevent confusion.

SEC. 5. **Preparation of Corporate Articles.** The name having been selected, the attorney prepares the articles of association. The incorporating statute usually defines what the articles shall state, so it is a matter of sticking closely to the statute. Wherever the statute is general in its definitions as that "the articles shall state the objects of such association," it becomes a matter of care to define the objects broad enough to meet the requirements of the association, and yet limited enough to be clearly within the spirit of the statute. When the articles are drawn the organizers sign in manner prescribed by statute before some officer capable of taking acknowledgments. The latter is for the purpose of procuring their registration.

The beginning of the corporate existence is signing, acknowledging and filing in the places prescribed by law, the articles of association.[2] The injunction should be strong, that the articles be prepared with great care by an experienced draughtsman. Unskilled work here, will bring on endless trouble and embarassment. The English courts, in several cases, have observed that the articles were so drawn as to perplex the understandings of the ablest men.[3] American courts have patiently endeavored to untangle some serious complications rooted in unintelligible charters.

SEC. 6. **Conformity with Creative Laws.** If the incorporation is by letters patent from the Chief Executive, the articles must conform to the statute vesting the authority in the executive to issue letters; in the case of special legis-

[1]Colonial, etc., Company v. Home, etc., Company, Lim., 33 L. J. Ch. 741.

[2]Carmody v. Powers, 60 Mich. 26.
[3]Davis Building Society 17.

lative act,[1] the charter is the constitution and the by-laws must not subvert the intention of the legislature. If the incorporation is by general statute, the provisions therein must be given substantial adherence. Too often does the charter invade the province of the by-laws, and prescribe rules belonging legitimately to the by-laws. If they prove unwise, amendment or repeal is difficult.

The charter should be general in its character, adhering to the letter and spirit of the creative law, and leave to the by-laws the proper limitations as they may be needed.

SEC. 7. **Procedure After Registration.** When the charter is signed, as required by statute, and the signers duly acknowledge the execution of the instrument, it is then to be filed in the places provided by law for registration. Thereupon the association becomes a body corporate with all the duties and liabilities of a corporation. The individuals who were active in its promotion have changed character, and are now stockholders. They become so by operation of law, and are not entitled to any notice by the association that they are stockholders, subject to its rules and to the payment of dues. The first act of the new corporation after the adoption of by-laws and the election of officers, is to issue certificates of stock to the members. They are shareholders from the date of incorporation, and they should adopt by-laws and elect officers.[2] The certificates are not issued until after the officers are chosen. Their issue does not change their legal status, as the certificate only evidences the holder's interest, as a promissory note is not the debt itself, but evidence of it.

Before discussing the member as he is thus created, the importance of understanding the charter and its legal significance should not be overlooked.

---

[1] An act of the legislature incorporating an association by its constitution and by-laws, without embodying the same in the act, is valid and constitutional: Bibb Co., etc., Association v. Richards, 21 Ga. 592.; and where incorporation was by decree of court, the petition failing to specify the objects, it was competent for the court to do so: Redwine v. Gate City, etc., Association, 54 Ga. 474.

[2] The adoption of by-laws and election of officers are discussed at chapters V. and VI.

# CHAPTER III.

## CHARTER.

SECTION 1. Importance of charter.

SECTION 2. Must generally adhere to statute.

SECTION 3. What constitutes charter and its legal effect.

SECTION 4. Effect of failure to observe statute.

SECTION 5. Construction.

SECTION 6. Amendment.

SECTION 7. Corporate seal.

SECTION. 1. **Importance of Charter.** After the preliminary organization, a charter is necessary, and as was stated in the preceding chapter, it should be drafted carefully and by an experienced person. Its preparation should be referred to the attorney of the association.

This fundamental instrument largely gives and measures the powers of the association. The promoting persons by its execution, have changed character and have been merged into the body corporate. As individuals their identity is gone, but as parts of the corporation, it is preserved, so far as rights and liabilities are concerned. The law has invested them with new duties and new rights, and ignorance of them will not serve as an excuse to stay the consequences of ignoring them. It is important to know something of the charter and the legal status of the association and the member, when a charter is issued and the corporation first has a legal existence.

(14)

Sec. 2. **Must Generally Adhere to Statute.** The state statutes generally define the provisions of the charter. In drawing it, substantial adherence to the statute must be observed. As has been previously stated, it is unwise to say too much in the articles of association. They should not particularize too much, for subsequently it may be found necessary to change some material provisions, and serious difficulty is then encountered. As a suggestion, the provisions of the statute should be given a general observance, and while adhering to the letter of the statute, it should be construed by its patent intent. The articles must keep within the scope of the statute, but where it makes no specification, for instance as to the face value of the shares, it is best to leave that to the by-laws as they may be adopted by the stockholders. Experience may show the advisability of changing the denomination of shares after incorporation, which may be readily done under such a charter. Other matters, such as the internal government of the association, for instance, as to the number of directors, may be treated in the same way; but the corporate objects should be clearly and amply specified so that the association may be able to perform its natural functions without question.

Sec. 3. **What Constitutes Charter and its Legal Effect.** The articles of incorporation of an association formed under the general laws of the state, are its charter and subject to the constitution and general laws of the state, its fundamental and organic law.[1] They fix the rights of the stockholders, and are in the nature of a fundamental contract in form between the corporators, and in practical effect between the association and its stockholders, which neither party is at liberty to violate.[2] By the filing of the articles of association and the passing to the incorporators of a legislative grant of incorporation, there arise contractual relations which are said

[1] The constitution of the state is the higher law of course than the legislative enactments, so that a charter is amenable first to that law. The legislature can not invest an association with rights conflicting with the constitution: State v. McGrath, 95 Mo. 193.

[2] Bergman v. St. Paul, etc., Association, 29 Minn. 275.

to have a triple character, being one between the state and the corporation, between the corporation and the stockholders, and between the stockholders and the state.[1] In determining the rights of these contracting parties, reference must be had to the creative law.[2] It is the primary source of these contractual rights, but the articles of incorporation and constitution and by-laws may be examined for the purpose of determining some of these rights.[3]

SEC. 4. **Effect of Failure to Observe Statute.** The charter should conform to the statute; as to powers, it must conform, for if it wantonly exceeds the legislative authority, the state may exercise its inherent right to withdraw the charter and from that source lies danger. The safe course is to follow the statute, but failure in strict compliance will not always defeat incorporation,[4] as where the certificate of incorporation was acknowledged before a wrong officer, it was held that upon correction, the corporation was de jure from the date of its organization, not only as against persons dealing directly with the association, but as against all others.[5] And the defects in organization can not be attacked in a collateral suit.[6] The courts generally declare that if there has been a bona fide attempt to organize a corporation, persons as members and borrowers will not be allowed to say the association can not enforce its contracts, because it is defectively organized.[7] The refusal of the courts to assist persons in defeating their agreements with associations, extends only to imperfections in organization. If the association is so defectively organized that it can not legally carry on its corporation

[1] Cook Stock, etc., sec. 492; it has long been settled that as between the state and the corporation the charter is a contract: Dartmouth College Case, 4 Wheat. 518.

[2] McCahan v. Columbian etc., Association, 40 Md. 226; Michigan, etc., Association v. McDevitt, 77 Mich. 1.

[3] McCahan v. Columbian etc., Association, 40 Md. 226.

[4] Lord v. Essex Building Association, 37 Md. 320.

[5] Spinning v. Home, etc., Association, 26 Ohio St. 483.

[6] Williamson v. Kokomo, etc., Association, 89 Ind. 389.

[7] Hagerman v. Ohio, etc., Association, 25 Ohio St., 186; Payette v Free Home, etc., Association, 27 Ill App. 307.

business, it should re-incorporate and transfer the property to the new corporation or wind up its affairs and pay its debts and distribute its assets.

The corporation may be so defective as to render the franchise wholly invalid in a proceeding against it by the state, still its corporate existence when acting under color of a franchise, cannot be questioned in a suit where it would arise collaterally.[1] But if the association steps beyond its corporate authority and clearly violates its charter, the remedy may not be alone with the state. The court fully cognizant of its exceeded authority, and having no equities of third persons to preserve, will pronounce its contracts void and leave the association stripped of all rights assumed by the transaction.[2] And the association cannot enlarge its functions by incorporating powers in its charter that are not authorized or contemplated by statute.[3]

SEC. 5. **Construction.** Care should be taken that in framing the charter, the domain of the by-laws is not invaded. The by-laws yield readily to amendment, while the charter is an inflexible compact, changeable only by the power granting it. The inflexible character of the charter and its importance as the instrument of corporate existance, are too often overlooked. It is frequently framed without care, regardless of the duties and rights that spring from it. Considered as a contract, its construction is one of intent of the parties, the state and the incorporators. This intent is discoverable by the legislative utterance on the part of the state and from the instrument itself on the part of the incorporators. So long as the instrument is the subject of construction, the work is a possible one, but when its amendment is considered, the rights of both contracting parties intervene and must be carefully adjusted without legal injury.

[1] Lincoln, etc., Association v. Graham, 7 Neb. 173; Williamson v Kokomo, etc., Association, 89 Ind. 389; Building Association v. Morganthal, 2 Pears. 343; Winget v. Quincy, etc., Association, 128 Ill. 67; Payette, etc., v Free Home, etc., Association, 27 Ill. App. 307.

[2] Anderson v. Cleburne, etc., Association, 16 S. W. Rep 298; Simpson v. Building Association, 38 Ohio St. 349.

[3] Albright v. Building Association, 102 Pa. St. 411.

Sec. 6. **Amendment.** The power to amend, pre-sup-poses legislative authority. All powers rightfully exercised by corporate bodies, being conferred by the government, either in express terms or by clear implication, authority for every corporate act must be found in the grant or requirement of some legislative act.[1] In determining whether or not the charter, the creative instrument, may be amended, it is neces-sary to examine the legislative act under which it is given. No vote or act of a corporation can enlarge its chartered authority, either as to subjects on which it is intended to operate, or the persons or property of the corporators. If created with a fund limited by the act, it cannot enlarge or diminish the fund, and if the capital stock is divided into a fixed number of shares, this number cannot be changed with-out authority from the legislature.[2] The legislature has the inherent right to amend where no vested rights are impaired, with the consent of the majority of the stockholders[3], but no material amendment can be made, except by unanimous consent of the stockholders.[4] The legislature may reserve power to amend. When the legislature reserves power to amend, it may do so in a way reasonable and consistent with the scope and object of incorporation.[5]

Of every corporation formed under the general law, the law itself becomes the charter, defines and enumerates the pow-ers which are to be exercised, the nature and extent of cor-porate franchises and privileges. The declaration of incor-poration, the constitution and by-laws adopted for corporate government, do not form the charter or define or enum-erate the corporate powers. These are the acts of the incor-porators. The charter is the grant from the sovereign power of the state; and by that source only can be amended or enlarged.[6]

[1] State v. Washington, etc., Com-pany, 11 Ohio, 96; but see Wange-rien v. Aspell, 47 Ohio St. 250.
[2] Salem Mill-Dam Corp. v. Ropes 6 Pick. 23.
[3] Delaware R. R. Company v. Tharp, 1 Houst. Del., 149.
[4] Cook Stock, sec. 495.
[5] Shields v. Ohio, 95 U. S. 319.
[6] Grangers, etc., Company v. Kam-per, 73 Ala. 325.

"The power to alter and modify does not give power to make any substantial addition to the work."[1] Within these limits the legislature may exercise reserved power without the consent of the corporation.[2] If the amendments exceed these and alter contract relations, the consent of the stockholders must be had.[3] If the amendment be merely auxiliary, that is merely an assistance to carry out the original plan, the consent of the majority of the stockholders is sufficient.[4] But if the amendment is fundamental, materially changing the original plans unanimous consent is necessary.[5]

If the incorporation is under a general statute, the legislative amendment may be by a general enactment, and if the incorporation is by special enactment the amendment of the charter would be by special statute.

When it is proposed to amend the charter, legislative authority is prerequisite. The legislature can amend with consent of stockholders; if the amendments are material, unanimous consent is necessary; if incidental, a majority consent is sufficient. If the statute authorize amendments they may be made,

[1] Zabriskie v. Hackensack etc. Company, 18 N. J. Eq. 178.
[2] Cross v. Peach Bottom, etc., Company, 90 Pa. St. 392.
[3] Illinois, etc., Company v. Zimmer, 20 Ill. 654.
[4] Illinois, etc., Company v. Zimmer, supra.
[5] Mills v. Central, etc., Company, 81 N. J. Eq. 1; Cook Stock, sec. 500. In a Connecticut case, the court said: "Some amendments or laws affecting corporations are binding with or without their assent. Others bind the corporation and every member thereof, if assented to by a majority of the stockholders. And others are not binding upon non-consenting members, although assented to by the majority. All general laws, and mere matters of police regulation, are embraced in the first class. Additional powers, duties and privileges, which do not change essentially the nature and character of the corporation, or the purpose for which it was created, and have for their object the promotion of the enterprise originally contemplated, fall within the second class. All amendments which work a radical change in the nature and character of a corporation, or the purpose for which it was created, are within the third class." New Haven, etc., Company v. Chapman, 38 Conn. 56. It should be observed that there is a distinction between the obligation of a contract and the remedy given by the legislature to enforce that obligation. Without impairing the obligation of the contract, the remedy may be modified or changed as the legislature may direct; Sturges v. Crowninshield, 4 Wheat. 122.

although the charter is silent on the subject,[1] but under such power, a majority of stockholders cannot make a fundamental change and bind a non-consenting stockholder. Where the amendments are merely auxiliary, a majority may consent and make them binding. The application of the law to the facts of each particular case, renders the subject full of difficulties, and the right to amend the charter should be carefully investigated before any attempt is made, or the whole corporate existence may be involved in confusion.

Sec. 7. **Corporate Seal.** Building Associations can better carry on their business with a regular corporate seal. The ancient rule applied to corporations existing by the common law was that they could only act by their common seal; the rule has no application to corporations created by statute.[2] The rule is however, that the corporate seal need not be attached to a corporate contract, unless a similar contract, when made by an individual, would require a seal.[3] Thus, a building association in a deed, would need to use a seal as required of an individual; however, any device or form will operate as a seal if there was an intent to bind the association and a seal of some kind was used.[4] This rule would not apply in states where the statutes require a corporate seal to be used.

[1] Wangerien v. Aspell, 47 Ohio St. 250. If the charter itself provides a mode of amendment, it must be adhered to: McKeown v. Building Association, 5 Bull. 52.

[2] Curry v. Bank, 8 Port. Ala. 361.
[3] Cook Stock, etc., sec. 721.
[4] Cook Stock, etc., sec. 722 and cases cited.

# CHAPTER IV.

## MEMBERS.

SECTION 1. Effect of incorporation.

SECTION 2. Membership Qualifications.

SECTION 3. Purposes of Membership.

SECTION 4. Purpose not material.

SECTION 5. Right to borrow.

SECTION 6. Right to withdraw.

SECTION 7. Certificate of stock and pass-books.

SECTION 8. Members estopped to deny incorporation.

SECTION 9. Illegal to invest funds in other corporations.

SECTION 10. Death of Stockholder.

SECTION 1. **Effect of Incorporation.** By the issuing of the charter, the association is erected as a corporation. Considered either as an artificial person or as a body of stockholders, in law it is a legal entity in that it remains a whole, although its component parts may change. The stockholders, as the persons to whom the corporation belongs, have, by becoming stockholders, assumed contractual relations with each other, with the corporation and with the state. The building association, being a modified type of private corporations, to perform its peculiar functions embraces a variety of unusual rights and liabilities for the stockholder. Upon his subscription for stock he pays an entrance fee. There are no other prerequisites of membership unless they are the legal disabilities of infancy and coverture, which are sometimes removed by statute. Of course, a non-compos could not be a member. The law does not recognize him except by its guardianship.

**Sec. 2. Membership Qualifications.** A person becomes a member of a building association by subscribing for and holding stock.[1] He acquires status as a stockholder in this way. The incorporating statute usually provides for the manner of the holding, and the by-laws, in accordance therewith, give the rules governing his membership; but he is not compelled to accept any conditions of membership imposed by the by-laws, and not authorized by statute.[2] Any person, capable of entering into a binding contract, may become a member of a building association; although, in some states, this ability is extended by statute to married women and infants, who, at common law, are unable to enter into contracts, they are not thereby given the power to borrow money and execute a valid mortgage therefor, unless the statute expressly enables them to do so. The association, when authorized by statute, may receive them into membership; but further contracts, entered into without express legislative authority, will be taken at its peril. In some states, general married women enabling acts have been passed, whereby they may contract for certain purposes; under these statutes, the association may safely enter into contracts beyond the membership agreements, but, as the statute is in derogation of the common law, it must be strictly construed.[3] Any contract thus made must strictly adhere to the statutory improvements. In making contracts with married women, as in loaning money to them, it should be carefully understood in writing that the money is going for the purposes for which they are enabled to contract.

**Sec. 3. Purposes of Membership.** A person enters a building association for one of two purposes; to deposit his

[1] Robertson v. Homestead Association, 69 Am. Dec. 151, note.

[2] Building Association v. Robinson, 46 L. I. Pa. 5.

[3] But where a married woman purchased stock prior to an enabling act, but continued paying monthly installments after its passage, she cannot set up her disability at the time she entered into the contract; Dilzer v. Building Association, 103 Pa. St. 86.

money or to borrow. His deposits, generally of required periodical amounts, are applied by the association as payments on his stock. The dues are nothing but partial payments on stock. Thus the depositing member by his small payments is enabled to accumulate and put his accumulations at work. The association adds those accumulations to his stock payments—dues—and when the aggregate is equal to the face of the stock it is retired, the membership ceases. In thus re-receiving stock subscriptions and distributing the earnings thereof in part payment of the subscription debt, to itself, the association occupies a position between a private corporation and a partnership. The statute thus conceives it and for convenience has endowed it with a corporate character. Out of this process correlative rights grow. The association is entitled to require the payment of dues as agreed by the member, and if they are not paid, to enforce a penalty.[1] The member, on the other hand, is entitled to have the net profits pro-rated and so credited on his stock.[2] No other corporation is given such powers and no other stockholder has such rights. In ordinary corporations, the stock subscriptions are presently due, and the profits are declared as dividends, and are withdrawable interest on the investment.

Sec. 4. **Purpose not Material.** The purpose of the member's stockholding is not material to the association. He may invest for profit or to meet debts or to acquire a fund for business or to get a loan.[3] His status as a stockholder is not affected by his purpose of entering. For him it is merely a savings institution in which he places his money and holds stock.

Sec. 5. **Right to Borrow.** One of his important rights is to borrow money from the association. Whenever the dues and other revenues create a surplus in the treasury, he has the

---

[1] From the moment a member joins, until he withdraws or his stock matures, he is a debtor to the association for the unpaid balance of his stock; Michigan, etc., Association v. McDevitt, 77 Mich. L.

[2] People v. Lowe, 117 N. Y. 175.
[3] Mutual Savings etc. Association v. Wilcox, 24 Conn. 147.

right to take it upon such reasonable terms as the association may fix. The legislature invests the association with the power to loan money, in fact it imposes upon it the duty of lending it to the members who have a right to compel its loaning. He takes on additional rights and burdens by borrowing money, but he has the right to borrow as he has also the liability of the debt and its cost in the shape of premium and interest.

SEC. 6. **Right to Withdraw.** The member may terminate his membership, stop future payments and liabilities upon notice to the association. He is invested with the right to surrender his stock upon equitable terms with or without the consent of the association. In this he differs from an ordinary stockholder, and is somewhat like a partner, who by retiring, dissolves the partnership. The withdrawing member does not affect the corporation or the other stockholders, but he effectually terminates his membership, as does the retiring partner his partnership. The member has the legal attributes of both partner and shareholder so adapted as the purposes of his existence require, yet he holds legal status as a stockholder and must be so considered.

SEC. 7. **Certificates of Stock and Pass-Books.** When a person has entered an association, a pass book is issued to him upon which his periodical payments are to be credited. The pass book is accompanied by a certificate of stock. The pass books are prima facie evidence of membership.[1] But the holding of a pass book and certificate of stock is not necessary to constitute membership.[2] If lost, the association may replace it upon proper indemnity that it will suffer no loss thereby.[3] Reasonable rules concerning the issuing of certificates will be upheld, so where the by-laws provide that a defaulting member might take a new certificate for a less number of shares, and the payments on the old were to be applied on the new, the court held that all arrears on

---

[1]Germantown, etc., Association, v. Sendmeyer, 50 Pa. St. 67; Dobinson v. Hawks, 12 Jur. 1037.

[2]Chester, etc., Co. v. Dewey, 16 Mass. 94.

[3]Cook Stock, etc., sec. 870.

the old must be paid before the member was entitled to the privilege.[1]

SEC. 8. **Members Estopped to Deny Incorporation.** It is the rule well established, that a party dealing with the association and receiving the benefits of a contract, cannot claim that the association is defectively organized or that the creative law is unconstitutional. This right is in the state;[2] and a person receiving membership benefits from the association may become estopped to deny his membership.[3] The result of this rule is that contracts of the association beyond its power may be sustained as against a benefitted party or a stockholder, yet the directors should not knowingly venture beyond the corporate scope,[4] as their acts might invoke remedies with a different result.[5]

The association by receiving dues is likewise estopped to deny the existence of stock.[6]

---

[1] Fulton v. American, etc., Association, 48 N. W. R. 781; Eaton v. American, etc., Association, 49 N. W. R. 865.

[2] Winget v. Quincy, etc., Association, 128 Ill. 67.

[3] Bates v. People's, etc., Association, 42 Ohio St. 655. So one whose mortgage recites that he is a member, cannot deny membership in an action for foreclosure. Howard, etc., Association v. McIntyre, 3 Allen 571; a borrower cannot deny the right of the association to loan or more than the number of shares limited by law, and his creditors are likewise estopped: Building Association v. Arbeitur Bund, 6 Bull. 823. And where it is required that the whole capital stock be taken in an association where the amount of capital stock is fixed and the number of shares ascertained, yet if a shareholder knowing the full stock has not been taken, attends meetings, votes for the expenditure of money, and the purchase of property, or does other acts from which it may fairly be inferred that he intends to waive such right, he will be estopped to set it up as a defense upon his stock subscription: Morrison v. Dorsey, 48 Md. 461.

[4] The "corporate scope" is the purpose of the association as ascertainable from the articles of association, together with such purposes as are necessarily implied in properly conducting the business.

[5] A minority of the stockholders may maintain a bill in equity to prevent illegal action on the part of the majority after request to the proper officers to interfere, and their failure or refusal so to do. Memphis, etc., Co. v. Woods, 88 Ala. 630.

[6] North America, etc., Association v. Sutton, 35 Pa. St. 463.

SECTION 9. **Illegal to Invest Funds in Other Corporations.** It may be taken as a general proposition that a building association has no power unless authorized by statute to hold stock in another association or corporation.[1] The reason of this is patent, as it was intended by the legislature that the corporate resources should be entirely applied to furthering the objects of the corporation.

SECTION 10. **Death of Stockholder.** In case of death of the stockholder, the by-laws should make some provision for the retirement of the stock or the manner by which it may be carried on.

When it is provided that in the event of the death of a stockholder, his heirs or legal representatives were entitled to continue the relation of stockholder, the death of the member operates a dissolution of his membership, terminating his connection with the association; and upon his heirs or devisees and not upon his personal representatives is conferred the privilege of succeeding to or continuing the membership; and if such privilege is exercised by the heirs or devisees, they become members not in a representative capacity, but in their own right, and they are subject individually to the duties and liabilities of membership.[2]

---

[1] Mutual, etc., Association v. Meriden, etc., Co., 24 Conn. 159.

[2] Montgomery, etc., Association v. Robinson, 69 Ala. 418.

# CHAPTER V.

## BY-LAWS.

SECTION 1. Framing and adoption.

SECTION 2. Definition. Power to enact and amend.

SECTION 3. Notice of amendment.

SECTION 4. Character of by-laws.

SECTION 5. Construction of by-laws.

SECTION 6. Amendment of by-laws.

SECTION 7. Resolutions and amendment.

SECTION 8. Mode of amendments.

SECTION 9. Provisions of by-laws.

SECTION 1. **Framing and Adoption.** The incorporators should select a committee to frame the by-laws and fix a time when its report is to be heard. Notice should be given of the time and place of the meeting. The discussion of the by-laws should be full, and their character well understood, as the by-laws being the law arranged for the internal government of the association, and affecting the stockholder's rights throughout he should know what they mean. The suggestion applies with equal force to the association, as in the case of litigation, the result is most often dependent upon the construction of the by-laws. The by-laws, upon their adoption by the incorporators, should be printed and circulated among the stockholders. Each stockholder should have actual notice of their contents. It may be said as much particularity should be exercised in framing by-laws as the charter.

**Sec. 2. Definition—Power to Enact and Amend.**
A by-law is a rule by which the affairs of the association are
to be conducted. The power of corporations to enact by-laws,
exists independent of statute, but the incorporating statute
usually gives the power. The power to make by-laws resides
in the stockholders; the directors have no inherent right to
make them.[1] Usually, in the promotion and incorporation of
an association, part of the promoters and incorporators act as
the first board of directors. The by-laws should not be
adopted by them as directors, but as stockholders, unless the
charter expressly confers on the directors such power. Very
often it is inconvenient for the stockholders to be called
together to amend the by-laws, and when it is done, it is generally a perfunctory matter, so it is convenient to have the
power of enacting and amending by-laws delegated to the
directors by the stockholders. This may be done in the by-
laws.[2] But the exercise of this right by the directors does not
dispense with the necessity of giving full notice of the amendments to each stockholder.

**Sec. 3. Notice of Amendment.** Notice should be
given, as provided in the by-laws, or, in the absence of any
provision it may be given by mail, or by posting up the
amended by-law in the office of the association, and calling
each member's attention to it. The safest course is by mail, as
the member may not be in the office. A person has the right
to treat the by-laws, given him on his becoming a member, as
all the by-laws of the association, and he is not bound to take
notice of modifications of such by-laws on the record
of the company simply, without further notice to him.[3] And
the burden of showing that notice was given is upon the association, so it should adopt the method that is a sure conveyance of notice to each stockholder. But a member cannot
resist payment of stated dues, fines, etc., on the ground that
by-laws of the association have not been adopted by a vote of

---

[1] Morton, etc. Co. v. Wysong, 51.
Ind. 4.

[2] Heintzelman v. Druids', etc., Association, 36 N. W. Rep. 100.

[3] McKenney v. Diamond State,
etc., Association, 18 Atl. Rep. 905.

the members or directors, where it appears that they have been recorded, acted upon and enforced as the by-laws of the association.[1]

SEC. 4. **Character of By-Laws.** Too much care cannot be exercised in their construction, for the association, as well as the member, is bound. In framing by-laws, assistance will be had in consulting the by-laws of other associations, adopting a clear, concise and explicit expression. Nothing should be left in doubt as to meaning. As a general rule for guidance, the by-laws must be reasonable, equitable, and consistent with the purposes of the association. They must not be contrary to public policy or the established law of the land. Neither must they attempt to oust the jurisdiction of the courts by prohibiting an aggrieved party from seeking legal remedies beyond the jurisdiction of the corporation.[2] There is no objection to the rules providing for settlement of disputes between the association and its members by arbitration, a practice common to English societies, but, if adopted, it should be considered only a means of ascertainment, and not the final determination of the dispute. The authority to pass by-laws is an authority to pass such only as are consistent with the articles of incorporation and the statute.[3] There are limits beyond which the corporation, by its by-laws, cannot go. For instance, the amount of fines must be reasonable. The delinquent cannot be fined twice for the same offense.[4] A building association cannot, by a by-law, compel its stockholders to offer a premium for priority of payment after its shares have become worth par.[5] A by-law providing that each member shall sign

---

[1] Hagerman v. Ohio, etc., Association, 25 Ohio St. 186; Morrison v. Dorsey, 49 Md., 461. After enjoying benefits for years, member cannot say he did not sign by-laws: Parker v. United States, etc., Association, 19 W. Va., 744.

[2] Bauer v. Samson Lodge, 102 Ind., 262.

[3] Bergman v. St. Paul, etc., Association, 29 Minn., 275.

[4] Hagerman v. Ohio, etc., Association, 25 Ohio St. 186; Forest City, etc., Association v. Gallagher, 25 Ohio St., 208.

[5] Rodgers v. Building Association, 7 W. N. C., (Pa) 95; see Building Association v. Jones, 2 L. T. N. S., (Pa.) 17.

a certain instrument containing an obligation to obey the charter and laws, is only directory. If a person becomes the owner of stock, he acquires membership without signing any agreement whatever.[1] These are examples showing a violation of the general principles cited as those guiding framers of by-laws. The by-laws, by operation of law, become a part of the contract between the association and the members. They may be examined, for instance, for the purpose of determining when the mortgage contract terminated.[2] So by-laws defining the duties of a secretary become a part of the contract of the sureties on his bond.[3] This fact exerts an important influence upon the right to amend as a vested right cannot be impaired.

SEC. 5. **Construction of By-laws.** The construction of by-laws must be a fair one, and a construction which would operate with harshness and oppression upon the party in default, will not be indulged by the Courts.[4]

If a by-law consists of several distinct and independent parts, although one or more of them may be void, the rest are equally valid, as though the void clause had been omitted.[5] If the association waive the rule of its by-laws, the member violating it has no right to complain, nor has any other person standing in the relation of surety for him, any cause of complaint. So a member holding a greater number of shares than is allowed by its by-laws, but not in excess of the number limited by statute, cannot defend against a claim the association has on account of such shares.[6] And if the association, having an express power to loan money upon real estate, upon terms prescribed in the by-laws, a loan not in conformity with and in contravention of the by-laws is not void as *ultra vires*.[7]

SEC. 6. **Amendment of By-Laws.** The amendment of by-laws is an important matter, and should be carefully

[1] Building Association v. Robinson, 46 L. I., (Pa.) 5.

[2] McCahan v. Columbian, etc., Association, 40 Md. 226.

[3] Humboldt, etc., Society v. Wonnerhold, 81 Cal. 528.

[4] Monumental, etc., Society v. Lewis, 38 Md. 445.

[5] Shelton v. Mayor etc., 30 Ala. 540.

[6] Hagerman v. Ohio, etc., Association, 25 Ohio St. 186.

[7] Kelly v. Mobile, etc., Association, 64 Ala. 501.

done. Power to make by-laws implies power to repeal them.[1] By-laws may be amended so as to effect future benefits but not vested claims.[2] Plaintiff in a case became a member of defendant building association at a time when a by-law thereof provided that all non-borrowing stockholders wishing to withdraw, shall be privileged so to do, upon giving notice to the directors of his or her intention, and shall be entitled to receive the amount of installments actually paid in without interest. Held that plaintiff's right of withdrawal was a vested right, of which defendant could not deprive him without his consent by a subsequent repeal of the by-laws.[3]

When a member has contracted upon the faith of a by-law, and has acquired rights under it, the association has no power to change the by-law so as to affect him. The by-law became a part of his contract, and the association can no more rescind that part of his contract without his consent, than it can any other part; and amendments or rules made after the contract, cannot by any construction have an ex post facto effect, when his rights would be thereby impaired.[4] Suppose the by-laws provided that upon the payment of a certain amount, the mortgagor should be entitled to a reduction of his mortgage interest and premium. The association has no legal right to subsequently repeal or amend that by-law, so as to deprive the mortgagor of his benefit thereunder. He had executed his mortgage with that right in contemplation; it had become vested in him, and the association cannot, without his consent, wrest it from him. This is a fair illustration of the rule.[5]

[1] King v. Ashwell, 12 East, 22.

[2] Stohr v. San Francisco, etc., Society, 82 Cal. 557; Weise v San Francisco, etc., Society, Ib. 646.

[3] Holyoke etc. Association v. Lewis, 27 Pac. R. 872.

[4] Christie v. Northern Counties, etc., Society, L. R , 43 Ch. Div. 62.

[5] Other illustrations: Where majority of members in a depreciated association passed a rule that a certain amount should be deducted, it has held ultra vires, and members who had given notice of withdrawal after the resolution, were entitled to be paid the whole amount at their credit. Auld v. Glasgow etc. Society, 12 App. Cas. 197. So where a by-law provided that "all non-borrowing members wishing to withdraw shall be privileged so to do upon giving notice to the directors of his or her intention, and shall be entitled to receive the amount of installments actually paid in without interest. Held, that the member's right of withdrawal was a vested right of which defendant could not deprive him without his consent by a subsequent repeal of the by-law: Holyoke, etc., Association v. Lewis, 27 Pac. R. 872.

But amendments having a retroactive effect, apply fully, unless a right vested under prior laws is impaired. A constitution originally provided that a member whose shares were unpledged for loans, might give notice of withdrawal, at any time, and that from and after such notice, all dues on such shares should cease. In June, 1876, all holders of unpledged shares gave notice of withdrawal, and thereupon the section of the constitution requiring the payment of dues on shares, was amended so as to provide that no dues be thereafter required from the unpledged shares. Another amendment was also then adopted, changing the manner in which withdrawal shares were to be paid off, instructing the directors to close the business of the association. Held, by the court, that these amendments in no manner changed the contracts evidenced[1] by the note and mortgage or released either party from any obligation thereon.[1] While amendments not impairing vested rights may be made to have a retroactive effect, yet they must be brought to the knowledge of each member to bind him.

SEC. 7.   Resolutions and Amendments.   The rule that a by-law cannot be passed so as to impair a vested right, applies to resolutions of a board of directors.[2]   A resolution of a building association providing that the value of all stock borrowed on to a certain amount, should be allowed to such holders as wished to redeem, can not be rescinded to the prejudice of a member who has made application to withdraw and had refrained from paying his monthly dues in the belief that his application had been accepted.[3]   A resolution permitting borrowers to withdraw on certain terms, the stock to be cancelled, when acted on by a member, is conclusive on the

---

[1] Hekelnkaemper v. German, etc., Association, 22 Kan. 549.

[2] Neither rules nor resolutions can have an ex post facto effect, when rights are impaired: Christie v.

Northern Counties, etc., Society, L. R. 43 Ch. D. 62.

[3] Eyre v. Building Association, 17 L. I. (Pa.) 148.

association; it amounts to an accord and satisfaction.' The rules must be in conformity with the by-laws and charter. In the management of the association, unwritten regulations sometimes govern, simply because they are reasonable and have been acted on by the members, but, if they are inequitable, the courts will not enforce them.'

SEC. 8. **Mode of Amendments.** The mode of amendment prescribed in the statute, charter, or by-laws, themselves, must be strictly followed, or the amendment is nugatory.' The by-laws usually provide how and when they may be amended; in such case, the procedure, as defined, must be followed.

The by-laws should not be incorporated in any part of the charter, and the rules of the association should be kept distinct from the by-laws. This is especially necessary, as amendment of the by-laws may be attended with delay. The association needs a simple code of rules, governing the manner of making loans, and their payment, and such other matters as relate to its routine business. The directors may amend these rules upon the principles that by-laws are amended.

SEC. 9. **Provisions of By-Laws.** In its by-laws, the association should specify the character of its shares and the manner of their issue; its officers, the mode of election, term of office, and the manner of filling· vacancies; the duties of the officers; the place and time of annual meetings of shareholders, and regular meetings of stockholders; the manner of calling special meetings of stockholders and directors; the number necessary to constitute a quorum; the appointment of an auditing committee, and such other committees as may be necessary; the seal to be used by the association; the fine

¹ Miller v. Second Jefferson, etc., Association, 50 Pa. St. 32.
² Winterer v. Building Association, 44 L. I. (Pa.) 122. In this case it was held that a custom to charge interest on money bid, when the loan is subsequently refused, is not a binding custom.
³ McKeown v. Building Association, 5 Bull. 52.

3

and other charges'; transfer fees; dividends and manner of declaring and paying; the place and time of paying dues; the manner of making loans and the security; the granting of withdrawals, with the notice required, and manner of payment; the replacing of lost or stolen pass-books; the disposition of the stock of a deceased member, and making of amendments. These are generally the subjects covered by the by-laws.

' The fine, charges and forfeitures against delinquent members must be created by unambiguous language, or they will not be upheld: Occidental, etc., Association v. Sullivan, 62 Cal. 394. When the association can protect itself sufficiently against the acts of defaulting members without applying increased penalties or forfeitures of stock, their omission from the by-laws in an equitable one.

# CHAPTER VI.

## GOVERNMENT AND OFFICERS.

SECTION 1. Officers and election.

SECTION 2. Pass-books and dues.

SECTION 3. General meetings.

SECTION 4. Special meetings.

SECTION 5. Quorum. Voting and proxies.

SECTION 6. Objects of general meeting.

SECTION 7. Character, duty and liability of directors.

SECTION 8. General guidance for directors.

SECTION 9. Minutes of meetings.

SECTION 10. Powers of directors.

SECTION 11. Term of election of directors.

SECTION 12. Duties of president.

SECTION 13. Duties of vice-president.

SECTION 14. Duties of secretary

SECTION 15. Duties of treasurer.

SECTION 16. Duties of attorney.

SECTION 17. Appraising committee.

SECTION 18. Per centage of value to be loaned.

SECTION 19. Executive committee.

SECTION 20. Auditing committee.

SECTION 21. Officers' bonds.

SECTION 22. Sureties on official bonds.

SECTION 23. Resignation and removal of directors.

SECTION 24. Officers' relations and responsibilities to the association.

SECTION 1. **Officers and Election.** The association after incorporation and adoption of by-laws, should, in shareholders' meeting, elect officers to serve until the next general meeting. The officers to be elected are, ordinarily, president, vice-president, secretary, treasurer and attorney. If the business requires, assistant officers may be elected. The mode of election is by ballot. The manner of election and time of holding should be prescribed in the by-laws. After the election of the officers, two of them at least should give bond, the secretary and treasurer, with sureties satisfactory to the directors. This is pre-requisite to their entering upon the discharge of their duties.

SEC. 2. **Pass Books and Dues.** The association then issues its pass books and certificates of stock, and is ready for receiving dues. The by-laws should fix the time in the week or month when dues are to be paid, having reference to the time when shareholders can best pay them. In factory towns, Monday evening may be the best time, and in railroad centers a monthly payment would be convenient. By adjusting these pay times, the association will accommodate its members and strengthen its membership. If the person selected as secretary has a convenient office, the association might receive dues at all times, with the express stipulation that they must be paid before the expiration of the week or month, as the case may be. Whenever the business will justify, the association should have its own office, a place where the shareholder feels he may come at any time and have inquiries answered and make such examination of the workings of the society as he desires.

SEC. 3. **General Meetings.** The supreme power in the management of the affairs of the association is vested by law in the stockholders assembled in general meeting. This power must be exercised with regard to the statute, but it cannot be defeated by rules adopted by the corporate directors. The general meetings should be held annually and properly occur shortly after the end of the fiscal year, allowing time enough for the officers, after the close of the year, to balance their books and submit their annual reports. If the association makes semi-annual reports, the general meeting can be held after the last half of the year. The stockholders do not generally attend these meetings as they should, and the directors should place in the hands of each shareholder a copy of the report of the affairs of the association. The date of the general meeting should be fixed by the by-laws, when the business to be done by the stockholders may be transacted. Then all members are affected with notice of the general meeting and are bound by the acts of the meeting,[1] but the by-law must fix, also, the hour of the meeting.[2] If the by-law make no such provision, the shareholder is entitled to personal service.[3] Unless the meeting is held at the proper place, as indicated by the by-laws, the measures taken will be of no validity.[4] The meeting must be held in the locality of the shareholders.[5]

SEC. 4. **Special Meetings.** If the meeting is a special one, or there are special and unusual matters to be considered at the general meeting, notice specifying the time (giving the hour), place and nature of the business of the meeting, should be given to each stockholder and the by-laws should provide for such notice and the manner of its issuing, as the notice is absolutely essential to the validity of the meeting. The by-laws should provide that the president and secretary shall issue a call for special meetings, upon the request of a certain number of stockholders. The notice must then be issued, as provided by the by-laws, and served on each stockholder a reasonable time before the meeting. The notice may be served in any manner that will reach the shareholders, as by mail, which is the usual method. A special meeting can only do the business for which it was called, and, upon adjournment, the shareholders may do those things which they were authorized to do at the original meeting,[6] but no new business unless notice is given.[7] The same rules apply to the meetings of directors.

SEC. 5. **Quorum—Voting and Proxies.** Where there is no provision in the statute or by-laws to the contrary, the acts of the majority present, at a properly called meeting, are binding, if there is a quorum present. And in estimating a majority of the quorum present, a majority of those voting will be counted, so that members cannot by abstaining from

[1] State v Bonnell, 35 Ohio St. 10.
[2] San Buenaventura, etc , Company v. Vassault, 50 Cal 534.
[3] Stebbins v. Merritt, 10 Cush. 27.
[4] Reg v. Pratt,118 E. C. L. 6 B. & S. Q. B.) 672.
[5] Reg. v. Registrar of Friendly Society, 7 L. R., Q. B. 741.
[6] Cook Stock, etc., Sec. 601.
[7] Reg v. Grimshaw 10 Q. B. 747.

voting, defeat the power of the meeting. If they refuse to vote, the majority of those voting will determine the question involved and be binding on the association. If members are present but refuse to vote or take any part, yet they will be counted for the purpose of having a quorum.[1] The vote must be cast in person unless proxies are authorized by the by-laws. It requires special authority in the by-laws for the use of proxies, unless the statute authorizes them.[2] It is a tacitly accepted custom in absence of any regulation on the subject, that a member has but one vote, independently of the number of shares he holds, a custom which seems to be founded on the strictly co-operative character of the scheme.[3] In those states where the borrower's stock interest is extinguished, he then loses his right to vote.[4]

Sec. 6. **Objects of General Meeting.** The usual objects of a general meeting are to elect officers, to receive statement of the association's condition, to pass by-laws and to determine upon the general policy of the association.

Sec. 7. **Character, Duty and Liability of Directors.** The Board of Directors has the supervision and management of the affairs of the association, and as a body, acts as its agent.[5] It is elected by the stockholders, and, in a sense, the members are trustees for the stockholders.[6] The rules

[1]Rushville Gas Company v. City of Rushville, 121 Ind. 206.

[2]Craig v. First Presbyterian Church, 88 Pa. St. 42: Davis Building Society, 101. A duly incorporated church, owning shares which it is entitled to vote at an election of officers, may do so by proxy duly authorized by the Board of Trustees: State v Rohlffs, 19 Atl. R. 1099.

[3]Endlich Building Associations, sec. 113.

[4]Mechanics, etc., Association v. Conover, 1 McCart. 219. In Virginia he loses his vote: Winchester, etc., Association v. Gilbert, 23 Grat. 787. While in Michigan, the statute divests him of the right, although

he remains a member and debtor. Mich. etc. Association v. McDevitt, 77 Mich 1.

[5]Allen v. Curtis, 26 Conn. 456.

[6]Thompson's Liabilities of Officers and Agents 351; Hodges v. New England Screw Company, 53 Am. Dec. 637, note. Officers of a building association, although trustees of the property of the association do not occupy that relation toward one to whom they sell their individual stock, and therefore if they make representations to him as to its value, which do not turn out as expected and represented, they are not liable in the absence of an allegation of deceit: Cook v. Henderson, 8 Rec. (Ohio) 429.

should prescribe their duties. Generally the directors elect the officers of the association and pass upon loans and transact whatever business is of interest to the association. While the board is, in a sense, trustee and agent, it can only bind the association in the scope of the corporate business, and this is true of officers. The directors are only held to the exercise of reasonable care and diligence in the management of the corporate affairs, as it is conferred on them.[1] If they act beyond the corporate power[2] or fraudulently,[3] or misapply the funds,[4] or are guilty of gross negligence and inattention to duty,[5] they may be personally liable either to stockholders or creditors of the corporation, when injury results.[6] Thus, managers of an association are not personally liable for losses resulting from an honest mistake in estimating the value of the stockholder's lands on which they loaned money, nor for a defect in the ackowledgement of a mortgage which rendered it worthless. But, they are liable for losses from loans made on personal security of the stockholders, in violation of a by-law limiting the amount of such loan.[7] Any member may compel the directors to keep within the corporate powers.[8] Certainly, a director is not liable for a breach, or act beyond the corporate power, or improvident act, committed by his co-directors, when he was not present when it was decided upon,

[1]Sullivan v. Lewiston Institution for Savings, 56 Me. 507. It has been recently held that where their services are gratuitous, they do not owe creditors of the corporation such care as a reasonably prudent man exercises in his own business, but are liable only for such gross negligence as amounts to fraud: Swentzel Penn. Bank, 23 At 1 Rep 405. This decision relaxes the rule heretofore applied.

[2]Moses v Ococe Bank, 1 Lea, 398. A rule of a building association provided that a director should not be answerable for, and might reimburse himself for, any loss which might happen in the execution of

the powers given to him by the rules of the society. Held that this rule did not apply to acts, *ultra vires* and beyond the powers which the society itself could confer: Cullerne v. London, etc., Society, L. R. 25 Q B. Div. 485.

[3]Koehler v. Black River Falls, etc., Company, 2 Black, 7, 715.

[4]Bank, etc., v. St. John, 25 Ala. 566, 611; Citizens, etc., Association v. Lyon, 29 N. J. Eq. 110.

[5]Robinson v. Smith, 24 Am Dec.212.

[6]Hodges v. New England Screw Company, 53 Am. Dec. 637, note.

[7]Citizens, etc., Association v. Coriell, 34 N. J. Eq. 383.

[8]Davis Building Society, 120.

took no part in it and had no knowledge of it, unless he might have prevented it by ordinary attention to his duties.[1] He cannot, by absenting himself from his duties, avoid the responsibilities of them. If he has been guilty of a legal fraud on the association, whether intended or not, he cannot share in the assets with other members.[2] The directors cannot bind the association by mere expression of opinion concerning its work; as, when, in a laudatory statement they set out the advantages of the association, one claiming to be misled thereby, who had a copy of the by-laws, in which were fully stated the rights and obligations of members, cannot rescind his contract on the ground of fraud;[3] nor do expressions of opinions as to the maturity of shares amount to a fraud entitling the party relying thereon to relief in equity.[4]

Sec. 8. **General Guidance for Directors.** The plain rule for the guidance of the board of directors is, that it must act at a regular or legally called meeting, within the powers conferred on it, and each director must exercise honesty and ordinary care in attending to the corporate business. No liability will then attach to him. The chief difficulty that a director encounters is to determine what powers are conferred upon him, as a director. Each member of the board, in order that he may properly interpret the by-laws touching his duties, should study the scheme of building associations and

[1] Sperings Appeal, 71 Pa. St. 11. Directors of a building association passed a resolution authorizing advances to members on the security of their shares. An advance was accordingly made to a member, and the society incurred a loss thereby. Held that a director who concurred in the resolution, but was not a party to the making of the advance, could not be held liable to the society for the loss, on the ground that the advance was *ultra vires* and was not attributable to the illegal resolution which authorized it, as the cause of the loss was the wrong-ful act of those directors only who made the advance: Cullerne v. London, etc., Society, L. R. 25 Q. B. Div. 485. As to who may enforce the liability against a delinquent director, see Hodges v. New England Screw Company, 53 Am. Dec. 637, note.

[2] Kisterbock's Appeal, 51 Pa. St. 483.

[3] Winget v. Quincy, etc. Association, 128 Ill. 67; See also Quincy, etc. Association v. Winget, 29 Ill. App. 173.

[4] Lake v. Security, etc., Association, 72 Ala. 207.

particularly, that of his association. He will, then, better understand his duties. Generally speaking, the directors have the management of the affairs of the association through its officers. That management is to be conducted by such rules as will accomplish the purposes of the association. They are entitled to exercise such powers as are given them by statute and by-laws and such other incidental powers as are necessary to accomplish its lawful purposes. A legal meeting implies that a quorum is present. If the number constituting a quorum is fixed by the by-laws, and it should be, that determines it. If there is no provision, a majority, usually, constitutes a quorum, and when a quorum is present, a majority of the quorum voting binds the association.

Sec. 9. **Minutes of Meetings.** Minutes of the directors' meetings should be kept by the secretary, signed by him, and attested by the president. It is essential, that the official acts of the directors be thus recorded, as in case of any litigation, the minutes may become important evidence. The value of permanent recording of corporate acts can not be over-estimated.

Sec. 10. **Powers of Directors.** The directors having the power to make such contracts as are authorized by the statute and by-laws, they should in such contracts make it clearly appear that they act as the agent of the association. So a note signed by individuals, as directors or officers, is the individual note of the makers.[1] The contract should be signed by the corporate name by the proper officers. Then, it is the contract of the association. The right of the directors to delegate to agents the transaction of the ordinary and routine business of the corporation, is unquestioned, and is absolutely necessary. But, in matters involving discretion, the decisions are in some conflict, but the better weight of authority is that the powers of the board may be delegated to an executive committee of the board, and the acts and contracts of such

---

[1] Hayes v. Brubaker, 65 Ind. 27. But where a contract not under seal was signed "S. Mather, President," it being alleged that it was executed by defendant corporation, it was held enforceable against it: Hand v. Society, etc., 18 N. Y., Supl. 157.

committee are binding on the association.[1] It very often
expedites business of the association for committees to attend
to certain branches of it, and it is within the power of the
board to create such committees.

Directors, personally interested in a resolution, are not competent to vote thereon,[2] nor can they speculate in the funds
for their own benefit,[3] nor purchase property for resale to the
association at a higher figure,[4] nor enter into any secret agreements for their personal profit.[5] The director's individual
transactions with the corporation are viewed with suspicion
and to be upheld by the courts must be clear of any advantage
taken by reason of his official connection.[6]

The directors must grant loans conformable to the by-laws
and rules, and where they do not specify, the conditions are
much within their discretion. If the attorney pronounces the
title defective, the association, declining the loan for that
reason, cannot be compelled to grant it.[7] They have power,
within reasonable discretion to remit and condone fines, and to
compromise with a borrowing member, who is unable to pay.[8]

Sec. 11. **Term of Election of Directors.** After
the election of directors, at the general meeting, the board or-
ganizes by electing officers. They are president, vice-president, secretary, treasurer and attorney. Some societies will
have other officers, as, abstracter and appraisers. They are,
however, more properly employes of the board. The directors
may be elected annually, or for a longer term. The advantage of an annual election is that unsatisfactory members of

[1] Cook Stock, etc., sec. 715.
[2] Smith v. Los Angeles, etc., Association, 78 Cal. 289.
[3] Redmond v. Dickerson, 1 Stock.
507.
[4] Blake v. Buffalo Creek R. R.
Company, 56 N. Y. 485; European,
etc., R. R. Company v. Poor, 59 Me.
277.
[5] Farmers', etc., Bank v. Downey,
53 Cal. 466; Pangborn v. Citizens,
etc., Association, 35 N. J. Eq. 341.

[6] Twin Lick Oil Company v.
Marbury, 91 U. S. 587.
[7] Conklin v. Peoples, etc., Association, 41 N. J. Eq. 20. If the action
of the board in contracting with an
officer outside of his duties is ratified by the stockholders and no one
else is affected, it will become valid:
Building Association v. Goldbeck,
13 W. N. C. 24.
[8] People v. Lowe, 117 N. Y. 175.

the board, or any officer, may be dropped without any trouble. Building association officers, if they attend to their duties, are usually kept in charge, year after year. The stockholders are averse to changes so long as the affairs of the association are properly managed. Sometimes, one part of the directors is elected for one year, another for two years, and a third for three years. The advantage of this is, that outgoing directors always leave directors in charge who are familiar with the business. Any vacancy in the directory should be filled by the directors, the appointee to hold until the next general meeting.

SEC. 12. **Duties of President.** The duties of the president are to preside at all meetings of the stockholders, and of the board of directors; to call special meetings, unless the by-laws otherwise provide; to sign all certificates of stock, and all drafts drawn on the treasurer for whatever purpose; to execute all satisfactions of mortgages when paid; to make all conveyances of property owned by the association, when sold by order of the board of directors; and to sign all contracts. He should be custodian of the bonds of the officers of the association. He should, also, appoint an auditing committee to serve at such times and in manner prescribed by the by-laws, and also appoint such other special or standing committees as the board may designate from time to time. He is also custodian of the corporate seal, if one is used.

SEC. 13. **Duties of Vice-President.** The vice-president should perform all the duties and have all the powers of the president, during the absence or disability of the latter.

SEC. 14. **Duties of Secretary.** The secretary is often the real manager of the association; and the supervision of the board of directors is too often nominal. It follows, that his office is the important one in the association, and should be occupied by a fit person. The general duties of the secretary are to attend to the correspondence, keep the minutes and the accounts of the association, sign all certificates of stock and other instruments provided in the by-laws, submit reports of the affairs of the association, sign all drafts drawn on the treasurer for the payment of money belonging to the association, and act as the custodian of all notes, bonds, mortgages, deeds, and other legal papers belonging to the association. Sometimes, as a matter of convenience, he will pay money on loans, especially, on loans where periodical payments are made. This is merely for the convenience of the member or the treasurer, and should not be declared a part of his duties by the by-laws. In thus acting without the scope of his duties, he cannot bind the association, without authority of the directors. When a loan has been granted, upon the appraisement, and upon the opinion of the attorney that the title is sufficient, and all papers have been executed by the borrower, the secretary issues a warrant,[1] signed by the president, upon the treasurer, directing him to pay out the money on the loan. Care must be exercised, that all liens on the property mortgaged are discharged and satisfied of record, before any money is paid to the borrower; or if the loan is a building one, the proper application of the money will have to be attended to. This work naturally falls within the province of the secretary. .

The directors should examine the books, at frequent times, however much confidence they may have in the officer. The secretary should give a bond, for the faithful performance of his duties, payable to the association, and approved by the directors. The secretary of a building association is only required to use ordinary care—that is, such as a prudent man would exercise in his own business—as to money, or property coming into his hands, as such officer, and if he uses such care, he will not be liable for the loss of any such money, or property.[2]

SEC. 15.  **Duties of Treasurer.**  The treasurer should have charge of the funds of the association, and be responsible for their proper disbursement. He should disburse the funds upon warrants issued to him, duly signed by the President, and attested by the secretary, or, as authorized to be issued by the by-laws. When he is directed by the by-laws to pay out money upon warrants so issued, he is, thereby, protected. If

---

[1] This warrant is not a negotiable security but subject in any holder's hands to all the equities of the association: Ashland, etc., Co. v. Centra-

lia, etc., Association, 9 **Luz. Leg. Reg.** (Pa.) 41.

[2] Mowbray v. Antrim, 123 **Ind.** 24.

the warrant was improperly issued, the liability attaches to the issuing officer. He should deposit the money of the association not ready for disbursement, in a bank selected by the directors as the depository, and, if a loss follows, as, by failure of the bank, no liability will then attach to him. In accepting payments from members, or remittances from the secretary on account of such payments, he should require cash, and not any other form of payment; for, if there is a loss, he has exceeded his authority to that extent, and the loss falls upon him.[1] He should submit a report, at stated times, of the finances of the association and he should, also, give bond for the faithful discharge of his duties and accounting of the funds in his hands. The treasurer is only bailee of money he receives on account of the society, and does not become a debtor of the society, and, consequently, if he is robbed of its money, he is discharged from liability to repay the amount of the robbery.

SEC. 16. **Duties of Attorney.** The attorney is the examiner of the abstracts of title of property offered as security, and other papers relating thereto. It is his duty to prepare all mortgages, bonds, affidavits and other instruments necessary in making loans, and, in substance, attend to all legal business of the association. He must do his work *bona fide* to the best of his skill and with an ordinary degree of diligence, or he will be answerable in damages; for example, if he rely on an extract from a will, in examining the abstract, instead of examining the whole will, he is guilty of gross negligence and is liable.[2] The fees of the attorney are usually paid by the borrowing member, and are not as large as are, usually, charged for like services in a professional way, but there is a certainty of pay and the quantity of work is often considerable, so that the fees are compensatory. The legal

[1]People's, etc., Association v. Wroth, 43 N. J. L. 70. And the fact that the executive officers were present and consented to payment other than by cash, will not relieve the treasurer's sureties. The rule for making the assessment would be the damage sustained by the dues and fines not being received: Ib; Mutual, etc., Association v. Hammell, Ib. 78.

[2]Walker v. British, etc., Association 21 L J., Q. B. 257.

[3]Wilson v. Tucker, 3 Stark. 154; see Davis Building Society, 126.

contracts, such as bonds and mortgages, are usually printed, and there being only blanks to fill in, much work is saved.

Sec. 17. **Appraising Committee.** The President should appoint an appraising committee. Very much of the association's safety depends upon the wise and careful judgment of the appraisers. They should be selected with special reference to their caution and knowledge of values. If appraisements are loosely or ignorantly made, the keystone of the association is weakened, and the entire superstructure is endangered. The appraisers are, usually, paid a small fee by the proposed borrower

Sec. 18. **Percentage of Value to be Loaned.** A building association can loan more on real estate than an ordinary lender, because the principal is in effect being repaid weekly or monthly. The percentage of value to be loaned is not settled. Circumstances may safely vary any rule, as property in one locality is of a more stable character, or the proposed borrower is a person of more thrift and financial ability. An association should not loan in excess of 75 per cent. of the value, in any case. If there is a default, and foreclosure, the marginal 25 per cent. may be soon taken up in costs and loss of premium. Sixty-six and two-thirds per cent. is a safe rule, when the character of the property is established ; or where it is of some fluctuating value, 50 per cent is a prudent per cent. The by-laws need not provide for any rule on this subject. It is better for the matter to be left to the discretion of the board of directors. The appraisers, by swelling the valuation, could easily bring a loan within the rule if they were corruptly disposed, so that their report should be received in an advisory way, and the decision of the matter left to the board of directors, upon all the facts of the case.

[1]This is deemed unwise by Mr. Davis (Building Society p. 128) as there might be a collusion between the appraisers and borrowers. In the writer's opinion there is not so much danger from that source as there is from the personal relations of the parties. It would be wise to have a sealed report from the appraisers for confidential use. The borrower would not then know what valuation was placed on his property and he could not know the result of his influence for high appraisements.

Sec. 19. **Executive Committee.** Sometimes the directors delegate to an executive or financial committee the work of passing on the securities offered. This committee should organize with a chairman, and the secretary of the association should act as *ex-officio* secretary of the committee, and keep minutes of the committee's meetings, and prepare the report of their work for the approval of the board of directors. This committee is useful when the board holds its meetings at some intervals, and loans are needing attention at more frequent times. There should be, in addition, a special inspection of building loans, as the work progresses.

Sec. 20. **Auditing Committee.** The next important committee to be appointed by the president, is the auditing one It should act at least once a year. The persons selected for this position should be expert accountants, without any relationship to the officers whose books are to be placed under examination. While the report of the auditors is *prima facie* evidence of the condition of the books of the officers, yet their accounts may, after a report has been made, be impeached for fraud.[1]

Sec. 21. **Officers' Bonds.** The directors should require, of the secretary and treasurer, bonds with sufficient sureties, conditioned that those officers will faithfully perform the duties required of them. The duty of approving these bonds is upon the board of directors, and it should exercise care in accepting sureties. The board should exercise care in this matter to avoid personal liability, in the event sureties prove irresponsible. It does not follow that the board, in law, guarantees the responsibility of the bondsman, it must simply be prudent. This is the obligation the law imposes, generally, on the members, and, when they have performed their duties in that manner, they have discharged the obligation.

Sec. 22. **Sureties on Official Bonds.** The manner of ascertaining the financial responsibility of the sureties offered, is either by an examination of the public records, or by a statement of the sureties. The former method will not always

[1] Holgate v. Shutt, L. R., 27 Ch. D. 111; S. C., L. R., 28 Ch. D. 111.

prodnce an accurate statement, as there may be unrecorded
and valid conveyances or liens affecting their property.   If the
latter method is adopted, it is best pursued by requiring an
affidavit, by each surety, as to what he is worth.

A surety is not discharged by the negligence of other
officers of the association, nor, because the by-laws are not
complied with.[1]   If the officer's holding is general and unlimited by the statute or by-laws, the fact that he was appointed
by directors who held but one year, will not limit the liability
of the sureties to that year, but it will continue throughout
the term of the officer's actual holding.[2]   And, if the bond is
for a particular and "any succeeding terms," the bondsmen
are liable for a subsequent defalcation,[3] but, if the term is fixed,
the sureties are not liable beyond that term.[4]   The surety will
be bound, although he signs, in the absence, and, without the
knowledge, of the principal.[5]   If the surety has had an opportunity to read the bond, but did not, and signed it, he is guilty
of such gross negligence, as will prevent him from having relief
against the bond.[6]   The bonds of the officers should provide
that they are to faithfully perform their duties during the particular term, and until successors are elected and qualified.

Sec. 23.  **Resignation and Removal of Direc-
tors.**  If the manner of electing officers is prescribed by by-
law, it must be strictly observed,[7] unless it be waived by the
stockholders, at a legal meeting.

A director may resign and no formal acceptance or entry
thereof is necessary to effect his resignation.[8]   The stockholders have no power to remove directors, before the expiration of their term of office, unless the charter expressly gives
that power.[9]   Courts have no power to remove corporate
officers.[10]   The directors may rescind the contract of an agent

[1] Brandt Suretyship, etc., sec. 425.
[2] Humboldt, etc., Society v. Wennerhold, 81 Cal. 528.
[3] Metropolitan, etc., Association v.
Esche, 75 Cal. 513.
[4] People's, etc., Association v.
Wroth, 43 N. J. L. 70.

[5] Hughes v. Littlefield, 18 Me. 400.
[6] Glenn v. Statler, 42 Iowa, 107.
[7] Roberts v. Price, 16 L. J. C. P.
169.
[8] Blake v. Wheeler, 18 Hun. 496.
[9] Cook Stock, etc., sec. 620.
[10] Neall v. Hill, 16 Cal. 145.

holding at the pleasure of the directors,[1] and he may be removed for incapacity or malfeasance, when he is under contract; but unless these things exist, they cannot remove him during his contract, or term, without paying the amount of his salary.[2]

As the decisions are somewhat in conflict, as to the power of directors to remove officers, the by-laws should, to avoid controversy, provide for removals from office, for cause, specifying the mode of procedure.

SEC. 24. **Officers' Relations and Responsibilities to the Association.** An officer of a building association holds a confidential relation to it, and will not be permitted to take advantage of any knowledge acquired by him by virtue of his position, for his personal benefit; therefore, where he knew it was insolvent, he was not allowed to discharge his indebtedness to it with stock held by him.[3]

He must treat it as a trust, preserving its property and advancing its interests whenever he can. The funds that come into his hands must be held, like life insurance funds, with sacred fidelity. The courts will not tolerate negligence or omission.

So, if the secretary or treasurer receives money, as by check, belonging to the association, and appropriates it to his own use, though, probably, with the intention of returning the money at some future time, he is guilty of embezzlement,[4] and he will not be heard to say, the association has no legal existence.[5]

---

[1]Hunter v. Sun, etc., Company, 26 La. Ann. 13.
[2]Morawetz Priv. Corp., sec. 544.
[3]Quein v. Smith, 108 Pa. St. 325.
[4]Shinn v. State, 32 Grat. 899.
[5]Ib.

4

# CHAPTER VII.

## POWERS.

SECTION 1. General powers.

SECTION 2. Implied powers.

SECTION 3. Powers of Agents.

SECTION 4. Power to sue.

SECTION 5. Power to compromise with shareholders.

SECTION 6. Power to loan money

SECTION 7. Power to hold real estate.

SECTION 8. Power to issue stock to another corporation.

SEC. 1. **General Powers.** Generally speaking, a building association has the usual attributes of a corporation, such as, perpetual succession, to have a common seal, to contract, to hold real estate consistent with its objects, to sue and be sued, to make by laws; and, in addition to have such other privileges as may be conferred by the incorporating statute, together with such incidental powers as are necessary to effect the corporate objects. The corporation must, therefore, pursue its legitimate purposes, for, if it passes beyond the scope of those purposes, its acts amounts to a mere nullity. A transaction not authorized by the statute, or the rules, and not incidental to the conduct of the society's business is void.[1] It should not engage in banking,[2] or invest its money in transactions, or securities, unauthorized by the statute, and not contemplated by the scheme of its organization. In some instances, the law will

[1] Small v. Smith, L. R., 10 App. Cas. 119.

[2] Schober v. Accommodation, etc., Association, 35 Pa. St. 223; Building Association v. Semiller, 35 Pa. St. 225n; State v. Building Association, 35 Ohio St. 258.

not permit advantage to be taken of those *ultra vires* acts, because, such permission will promote, rather than prevent, injustice. If the association exceeds its authority, and the stockholder has consented to such act, or, has reaped a benefit therefrom, the law will not permit him to say the association could not enforce any obligation against him arising out of the transaction,[1] and the rule applies with equal force to the association, so that its mouth is closed to deny its right to make a contract when an innocent party would suffer and when it has received a benefit from the contract. These instances represent cases, where the law will not enforce the consequences of the acts exceeding the corporate powers of the association, but, if an association departs from the authority conferred by statute, and assumes new or enlarged powers, the state, as the other party to the contract of corporate existence, would have the right to annul, through its proper officers, that contract represented by the charter; and any stockholder not a beneficiary of the illegal acts, may invoke this power of the state or apply to a court of equity to restrain their further commission. And the mere act, *ultra vires*, will not, of itself, end the corporate existence, nor relieve the members from their duties, so long as the association continues in existence.[2]

The directors to intelligently exercise the powers of the association, must have an understanding of its scheme, as expressed in the statute and by-laws, and they should keep within the pale of its corporate objects in order to avoid complicated and uncertain results attending a contrary course.

The association continues, uninterruptedly, its existence, notwithstanding there may be changes in officers and members, and, thus, it has, in contradistinction to persons, unchanged existence, although the component parts may change. It is, thus, given the attribute of perpetual succession by the law. The power to have and use a seal is a corporate function. Its custody, if one is required by statute, is impliedly with the president, and the affixing is, usually, by him, but the by laws

[1] Poock v. Lafayette, etc., Association, 71 Ind. 357.

[2] Hughes v. Layton, 10 Jur. N. S. 513.

may provide for other custody and usage, or the general powers of another officer may give him power to affix the seal. Ordinary contracts do not require a seal; only those require a corporate seal which would require a seal if they were the instruments of an individual. Any device will serve as seal if intended as such.[1]

The association has the power to contract, as a part of its corporate existence. It is invested by statute with unusul and extraordinary privileges and rights, and, with reference to those powers, any contract executed by it, to be brought within their operation, should strictly conform to the very terms of the law;[2] and such powers, if unauthorized by statute, but contained in the charter, if invoked by the association, will be considered inoperative, even when the attack is a collateral one.[3]

SEC. 2. **Implied Powers.** Besides these usual powers, expressly enumerated in the statute, there are, implied powers as may be necessary to carry out the object of the corporate existence. The defining of these incidental powers is sometimes troublesome, and, especially is this true, in regard to building associations considered as a peculiar type of corporations; therefore, the incorporating statute and by laws should be explicit and comprehensive enough to meet their necessary requirements as savings and building corporations.

SEC. 3. **Powers of Agents.** The association exercises its power to contract through its officers and agents, including the directors, and when they act within the apparent scope of authority conferred on them, the association is bound by their contracts. It becomes important, then, that all limitations on the authority of an agent be defined, as well as the authority itself, so that persons dealing with the association, through him, have knowledge thereof.

If the agent is only a special one, the person dealing with him is bound to take notice of his limited powers, and, if he manifestly exceeds them, the association is not bound; while, if the

[1]Imprint in red lines held to have such effect: Woodman v. York, etc., R. R. Company, 50 Me. 549.

[2]Birmingham v. Maryland, etc., Association, 45 Md. 541.
[3]Albright v. Building Association, 102 Pa. St. 411.

powers are general, one without knowledge of any limitation can hold the association. It is important for the association to define clearly, in the by laws, the powers of its officers, and, in case of special agents, to draw the lines of authority strictly to the objects of their appointment.[1] However, if the association accept and hold the benefits of an agent's unauthorized act, it will be considered as having ratified the same, and will be bound.[2]

The association is liable to third parties for whatever the agent does or says, whatever contracts, representations, or admissions he makes, whatever negligence he is guilty of, and whatever fraud or wrong he commits; provided, the agent acts within the scope of his apparent authority, and, provided, a liability would attach to the principal, if he was in the place of the agent.[3]

The contracts made by the agent, if executed in the name of the association, and on its behalf, and, it appearing so on the face of the instrument, if authorized, will bind the association. A misnomer of the association in a contract is immaterial if the association was intended, and that it was, may be shown, if it cannot be ascertained from the face of the contract.[4]

SEC. 4. **Power to Sue.** The association may, without any allegation as to incorporation, other than a mere statement of its name, sue a stockholder or other person or corporation,[5] unless the plea of *nul tiel* corporation is filed.[6] If the

---

[1] The rule is that ordinarily an agent cannot delegate the power entrusted to him, but there are exceptions as he may do so when it is the lawful custom or usage, or the act is purely ministerial, or where the object of the agency cannot lawfully be attained otherwise, or where the principal is aware that his agent will appoint a deputy. See Ewell's Evans Agency, p. 42. An appraiser could not delegate his duty, as it is in nature judicial, while the secretary may, as it is merely ministerial.

[2] Jones v. National, etc., Association, 94 Pa. St. 215; Chicago, etc., Society, v. Crowell, 65 Ill. 453.

[3] Ewell's Evans Agency, p. 440.

[4] Franklin Avenue, etc., Institution v. Board, etc., 75 Mo. 408.

[5] Odd Fellows, etc., Association v. Hogan, 28 Ark. 261; Stein v. Indianapolis, etc., Association, 18 Ind. 237. See also Chillicothe, etc., Association, 60 Mo. 218, where it was held that averment that an association was "duly incorporated under and by virtue of the act of the General Assembly of the State of Missouri," was sufficient.

[6] Odd Fellows, etc., Association v. Hogan, Supra.

action is upon a mortgage, and the continuance of default, for a specified time, is a condition precedent to a decree of fore-closure, such continuance should be averred.[1] The defendant member may tender in cash the amount due the association and it is bound to accept it, and, if it refuses, further interest, premium, and costs cannot be collected. If the tender is, after suit is brought, it is bound to accept it, or be liable for costs, and it will be unable to, thereafter, collect interest and premium.[2] The refusal by the association of a tender of the amount due does not relieve the member from paying his dues, although it suspends the association's right to collect interest and premium until it is accepted, or, if it rejects the tender, and secures a decree paying the costs, of course, the right to collect further premium and interest is ended. The dues being payments on the stock and not on the loan, while con-tinuous defaults in their payment, as the stock is pledged, will render the loan due, yet the member is required, even upon refusal of the tender, to continue his stock payments, for that is a separate liability upon which the association could if it chose, predicate a separate action. The bringing of the suit outside of the question of tender, does not relieve the member of the necessity of continuing his stipulated payments in the way of dues, premium, and interest, or suspend his liability to fines for delinquency in his regular payments.[3] The associa-tion represents the shareholders in defending action involving

[1] Schaefer v. Amicable, etc., Com-pany, 47 Md. 126. In computing the period fixed by the statute or by-laws as the limit allowed before the whole debt becomes due, partial pay-ment of dues, it has been held in Pennsylvania, are not to be allowed. For instance, when the period of six months was fixed as the time of de-fault, before the association could proceed on its mortgage, it was held that payment of part of January dues was made, this did not make the judgment rendered in July pre-mature: Barndt v. Gruel, 4 Leg. Gaz. 388. Generally, the legislative intention is that the default should be for a continuous period, and if during that period there were any payments, they would be applied on the first of the defaults, thus cut-ting down the period of defaults to that extent.

[2] Columbian, etc., Association v. Crumb, 43 Md. 192.

[3] German, etc, Association v. Metz-ger, 9 W. N. C. (Pa.) 204; Union, etc., Association v. Masonic Hall, etc., Association, 2 Stew. 389.

their rights, and a judgment against it, in the absence of fraud, binds them.[1]

SEC. 5. **Power to Compromise with Shareholder.** An association has incidental power to compromise with shareholders and retire stock unless prohibited by law. The power must be fairly and reasonably exercised.[2] It may compromise with him, whether the debt arose from loan or on subscription for stock, and, when the parties to the transaction have acted in good faith, the transaction will not be rescinded, because the released member was paid a greater sum than he would have received upon a pro rata distribution of the assets of the association.[3] The association, if solvent, may appropriate and apply the proceeds of a mortgage owing to itself in payment of a debt that it owes to a withdrawing stockholder. The power to compromise debts includes the power to remit fines.

SEC. 6. **Power to Loan Money.** The power of the association to loan money, to hold real estate, and the rates of interest to be charged, and security to be taken, are usually defined by the creative statute, but, in the absence of the statute defining the security, they would have the implied power to loan money on the same security as individuals, notwithstanding, the usual mode is to require the borrower to assign his own stock as collateral to his mortgage.[4] And, where they are authorized to loan money but not expressly authorized to take a mortgage or any other security, the association has power by implication to take a mortgage to secure repayment to it of the funds loaned in regular course of business.[5] But, if authorized to invest surplus funds in notes, this would not give the association the power to buy notes to sell for gain, as that would be clearly beyond its scope.[6] The association would, however, have the right to sell the notes to change its investment. The power to buy implies, to that extent, the power to sell.

[1]Heggie v. Building, etc., Association, 107 N. C. 581.

[2]Wangerien v. Aspehl, 47 Ohio St. 250.

[3]Ib; State v. Building Association, 35 Ohio St. 258.

[4]Union, etc., Association v. Masonic Hall Association, 2 Stew. 389.

[5]Massey v. Citizens, etc., Association, 22 Kan. 624.

[6]Manufacturers', etc., Company v. Conover, 5 Phila. 18.

SEC. 7. **Power to Hold Real Estate.** The power to hold real estate is, generally, defined by statute, and the association cannot go beyond the limits there fixed without incurring the risk of doing an invalid thing. An association, without statutory authority for holding land, might be compelled to take it for payment of a debt, and, in such case, the transaction would not be annulled, as it is necessary to the management of its business,[1] but the duty of the association would be to dispose of it, as soon as practicable. If land is purchased by the association beyond its authority, the effect is not to dissolve the association,[2] but the court will declare the contract void, unless it has gone into the hands of a person protected, by law, as an innocent purchaser.[3] If the transactions still remains between the original parties, they are left by the law as if there had been no contract, but if the rights of an innocent purchaser have intervened, he will be protected, and if a loss falls upon the association, a personal liability therefor may attach to its officers and agents.[4]

The scheme of a building association does not contemplate that it become a land company, engaged in buying, selling, or speculating, in land, as a part of its business. If it is invested with those powers by statute, then, of course, it can lawfully avail itself of them, but, unless expressly granted, they cannot be exercised;[5] however excepting from this general proposition involuntary conveyances, such as, titles invested by court decree, or compromise of debt, which, necessarily, follow in the legitimate line of its business.

SEC. 8. **Power to Issue Stock to Another Corporation.** Whether or not a building association has the right to issue stock to another corporation and advance money thereon, is not settled by the courts. In England it has been

[1] Morawetz Priv. Corp. sec. 327.

[2] Hughes v. Layton, 33 L. J. M. C. 89.

[3] Vos v. Cedar Grove, etc., Association, 9 Bull. 194.

[4] In Pennsylvania it is held that the curative act of 1878 will not validate such a contract as a personal obligation, but a purchase money lien will be restricted to the land itself: Faulkner's Appeal, 11 W. N. C. 48.

[5] Miller's Estate, 2 Pearson, 348; Rhoads v. Hoernerstown, etc., Association, 82 Pa. St. 180.

held, that one society has no power to invest its funds with
another society,[1] and it was, also, held that the society had no
power to advance money to a joint stock company.[2] A corporation cannot hold shares in another company as an investment, unless this be the usual method of carrying on its
proper business.[3] The statutes in some of the states provide
generally, that no corporation shall purchase and hold stock in
another corporation. The reason of this is, that the legislature does not intend, that the capital of a company shall be di-
verted from its declared purposes by investment in stock of
other corporations. In building associations, the reason of the
rule fails, and, therefore, the rule will not apply unless the
statute, specifically, prohibits the association from receiving
other corporations into membership. The issuing of stock is
a device in a building association by which a loan is made.
The stock is one of the instruments of the loan. Only by
holding it, unless there is special statutory authority, can the
loan be granted. Stock is therefore taken for that purpose.
If the other corporation has power to borrow, it has the right
to do those things needed to perfect the loan. If it borrow
from a building association, one of those things is to hold
stock. None of its capital is thereby withdrawn, its payments on the stock are payments practically on the loan and
its cost. For the purpose of borrowing, it would seem upon
sound reasoning, that a corporation may, lawfully, take shares.
If shares are taken for investment, an entirely different question is presented, and the reason of the statute would apply,
and its operation would be invoked. The association would
then have no power to issue the stock.

[1] In re Durham Co., etc., Society,
25 L. T. Rep. N. S 8).
[2] Hardy v. Metropolitan, etc., Company, L. R., 7 Ch. App. 427.

[3] Morawetz Priv. Corp. sec. 431.

# CHAPTER VIII.

## RIGHTS OF MEMBERS.

SECTION 1. Legal status of members.

SECTION 2. Preferential stock.

SECTION 3. Paid up stock.

SECTION 4. Members and officers must observe rules.

SECTION 5. Members' rights to inspect books.

SECTION 6. Member as an investor.

SECTION 7. Payments.

SECTION 8. Right of withdrawal.

SECTION 9. Manner of withdrawal.

SECTION 10. Legal status of withdrawing member.

SECTION 11. Liability of withdrawing members.

SECTION 12. Rights of withdrawing members of insolvent association.

SECTION 13. Right to withdraw limited to present funds.

SECTION 14. Stock pledged cannot be withdrawn.

SECTION 15. Amount withdrawable.

SECTION 16. Construction of by laws concerning withdrawals.

SECTION 17. Transfer of shares.

SECTION 18. Forfeitures.

SECTION 19. The legal status of member as a borrower.

SECTION 20. Duty of association to loan its money.

SECTION 21. Selection of borrower.

SECTION 22. Methods of premium charges.

SECTION 23. Auction premiums.

SECTION 24. Premium fixed, unchangeable.

SECTION 25. Premium chargeable to maturity only.

SECTION 26. Formal application for loan.

SECTION 27. Appraisement.

SECTION 28. Abstract of title.

SECTION 29. Interest not collectable on interest and premium.

SECTION 30. Payment of instalments.

SECTION 31. Provisions of note or bond.

SECTION 32. Provisions of mortgage.

SECTION 33. Complaint upon bond or mortgage.

SECTION 34. Loans to outsiders.

SECTION 35. Loans to married women.

SECTION 36. Mortgage covenants.

SECTION 37. Application of payments.

SECTION 38. Assignment of shares as collateral security.

SECTION 39. Payments on stock not to ipso facto payments on loan.

SECTION 40. Payments on re-assigned stock.

SECTION 41. Assigned shares cannot be credited.

SECTION 42. Liability of borrower under his mortgage for losses.

SECTION 43. Acknowledgement of mortgage.

SECTION 44. Leases by the association.

SECTION 45. Satisfaction of mortgages.

SECTION 46. Borrower entitled to set off.

SECTION 47. Amount payable upon foreclosure.

SECTION 48. The English rule.

SECTION 49. Rule laid down upon voluntary repayment.

SECTION 50. Uncertainty of the foregoing rules.

SECTION 51. The natural and logical rule.

SECTION 52. By laws should provide for record cancellations.

SECTION 1. **Legal Status of Member.** In considering the legal status of a member, we have regarded him as occupying the general position of stockholder in a corporation, with modified rights and liabilities to suit the peculiar nature of the institution. As a stockholder he is either an investor or a borrower. Every member of the association, from the moment he joins, becomes a debtor to the association, and every member remains a debtor until the full amount of the shares for which he subscribed, and became the holder of, is paid, unless his membership is terminated in a legal manner.[1] And default by any other member will not relieve him from his liability.[2] Being fixed as a debtor, he remains such until his stock is matured, unless he chooses to

[1] Michigan, etc., Association v. McDevitt, 77 Mich. 1.

[2] Hoboken, etc., Association v. Martin, 2 Beas., N. J. 427.

terminate his membership. And a person can be both a shareholder and creditor of the association; as shareholder he is liable for his proportion of losses, but as creditor, he is entitled to recover the amount due him, independently of all losses.[1]

SEC. 2. **Preferential Stock.** The building association idea implies absolute co-operation. In the absence of statutory authority, there should be no preferential members. Common strength is increased strength, and by the plan of depositing in one treasury the savings of many people for the common benefit of all, any one depositor receives benefits not attainable by his own unaided efforts. It is a part of the scheme that all members shall share equally in the profits, according to their stockholdings; unless the statute provides otherwise, the net profits should attach pro rata to all the shares. In event of dissolution, the assets must be distributed equally among the members, subject, of course, to the payment of debts, and if there is a reserve fund, each member is entitled to a pro-rata share upon distribution, whether he is a borrowing member or not.[2] If the directors distribute profits in any other way than contemplated by law, they become personally liable to an injured member.

SEC. 3. **Paid-up Stock.** In England, and in some of the States, building associations are permitted under restrictions, to issue paid-up stock; *i. e.*, stock where the full face value is paid up at the time of issue, or has matured by the periodical payments and the profits, and upon this stock fixed interest dividends are paid.[3] The issue of this stock depends upon the creative statute. If it is authorized, and no interest is fixed by statute, it should receive only a limited share of

[1] Henninghausen v. Fisher, 50 Md. 583.

[2] People v. Lowe, 117 N. Y. 175; Seibel v. Building Association, 43 Ohio St. 371. A by-law giving to withdrawing stock 5 per cent interest, applies to borrowing as well as non-borrowing stockholders: Winterer v. Building Association, 44 L. I., Pa., 122. When the constitution provided for payment to a non borrower specified rates of interest on withdrawals, without including the borrower; held the borrower was entitled to the same rate of interest: People's, etc., Association v. Furey, 20 Atl. R. 890.

[3] Davis Building Society, 18.

the profits, and it should be kept in a safe ratio with the assets. The only motive in the issue of this stock should be to acquire money to meet the demands of proposing borrowers. In some associations, where the borrowers are numerous, directors may be compelled to go into bank, and get a temporary loan to satisfy demands that exhaust the ordinary receipts. They may have to do this in order to remove dissatisfaction among the members. In associations accumulating idle money, paid up stock would be superfluous and it should not be issued. An income to the association is secured by this stock from another class of shareholders, and the rules should be so drawn that if at any time the demand from borrowers be light, the association may compel a withdrawal by paying off the stock in the order of its issue. The rule is a safeguard to the association and entirely just. Paid up stock should not be allowed as the predominating stock. It is a source of strength to the association if limited by the demands upon the association, but its unlimited issue might prove a weakness. Stock of this character forms an exception to the rule of equal distribution and should not be entitled to share in the profits beyond the fixed dividends.[1]

¹There is an honest diversity of opinion among building association managers as to the propriety of an association issuing paid up stock. The objection urged by its opponents is, that it allows capitalists to invest their money at oppressive interest rates, to be paid by the poor home-seekers. This objection would be forcible when an association placed such stock on the same footing so far as profits are concerned, as other stock, and paid its pro rata part in cash. But its issue is certainly helpful to an association when temporarily in need of money at a cost not exceeding the legal rate of interest, under the restrictions given in the text. English societies, from whom we have borrowed some equitable features, testify to its value as the present act of Parliament authorizing its issue is the result of their efforts.

In the early history of building associations, the borrowing demands were not heavy. The members willingly waited their turns to receive money, and, in fact, the receipts often exceeded the loans. But in present day associations the constant pressure of borrowing members compels elasticity of the original scheme. When the association is unable to supply the demands from its ordinary receipts, it must either satisfy them by borrowing, or securing, investing money or lose an opportunity to secure a borrower who may not apply when the money ac-

**SEO. 4.   Members and Officers Must Observe Rules.** When a person becomes a member, he thereby obligates himself to conform to the laws of the society.   He should be given a copy of all by-laws and rules in force, and that is notice to him of their contents.   Thereafter he cannot excuse himself of his ignorance of the regulations.   And after acting as a member and enjoying the benefits of the association under its bylaws, the law will not permit him to question the legality of its by-laws.[1]   The members being subject to the regulations have a right to expect and compel the officers of the association to observe the regulations.   If the officers fail or refuse to carry out the rules, they are blameable and a personal liabillty may attach to them.   So if the officers act contrary to the rules and expend the money of the society in an unauthorized manner, they may be compelled to replace the money.[2]

**SEC. 5   Members' Rights to Inspect Books.** Members are entitled to inspect the books of the association for proper purposes, at proper times, and they are entitled to such inspection though their only object is to ascertain whether their affairs have been properly conducted by the directors or managers.   The right exists, although its exercise may be inconvenient to the officers[3].

**SEC. 6.   Member as Investor.** Although the original plan of a building association contemplated that each member should ultimately become a borrower and in some states it is still made obligatory for relief therefrom to be purchased, by a penalty,[4] yet a member is to be regarded as an investor.   He, thereby, assumes duties and acquires rights that are not

---

cumulates.   If this relief is prohibited, premiums naturally go exorbitantly high, and the borrower is the sufferer, and it is unlawful to stifle competition in bidding, by limiting the premium.   See sec. 23 *post.*   So by letting in this money under safe restrictions, the congested condition of the association is relieved without injury to any member and with great benefit to many.

[1] Building Association v. Arbeiter Bund, 6 Bull, 823 ; Building Association v. Minnick. 1 Kulp, 513

[2] Grimes v. Harrison, 28 L. J. Ch. 823.

[3] Huylar v. Cragin, etc., Company, 40 N. J. Eq. 392.

[4] In Maryland this is required by some associations.

removed, though modified and increased by the fact that he becomes a borrower.

When a person becomes a member, he is a debtor to the association until his stock matures,[1] and suit may be maintained against him for monthly dues.[2] Some doubt was expressed in England as to whether it was lawful for an association to receive money from members who did not wish to take loans, but merely wished to allow their monthly payments to accumulate at compound interest until the dissolution of the association, but it has since been decided to be lawful.[4] The practice is general throughout the United States, to provide for the investing class, persons who never contemplate borrowing, but who deposit their surplus in the association for safety and profit. The rights of an investor are different in different associations. In the serial and permanent associations their rights are unlike, and in associations of the same type they may vary. In some states, paid up and deposit shares are issued; while, in other states, but one kind of installment stock is issued. It would be futile to enter into an investigation of the different rules for investing members under these varied conditions. Their rights acquired in such societies are determinable from the laws and rules of each particular association as authorized by the incorporating statute.

SEC. 7. **Payments.** Payments of money by the members should be made to an officer authorized to receive them;[5] otherwise if there is loss the association is not bound to credit the payment in favor of the member. If the by-laws make it the duty of the secretary to receive money, payment at his place of business is valid.[6]

[1] Michigan, etc., Association v. McDevitt, 77 Mich. 1.

[2] Association v. Kribs, 7 Leg. & Ins Rep. (Pa.) 21.

[3] Davis Building Society, 264.

[4] Doe d Morrison v. Glover, 15 Q. B. 103.

[5] Kilpatrick v. Association, 119 Pa. St. 30. And the neglect of an officer of the association to apply to a member for his subscriptions at the proper time and in accordance with the rules, will not excuse default in the payment by the member: Taylor v. Collins, 46 L. T. Rep. N. S. 169.

[6] Schutte v. California, etc., Association, 23 Atl. Rep. 336.

Sec. 8. **Right of Withdrawal.** One of the most important rights conferred upon a stockholder is the right of withdrawal. This right is incorporated in all statutes. A distinguishing difference between the stockholder of a building association and the stockholder in an ordinary private corporation is the right of the former upon giving notice to terminate future liability on his stock. He can arbitrarily divest himself of his membership, cut loose from the association, and end his duties and liabilities. In an ordinary corporation, a subscriber for stock cannot obtain a cancellation of his subscription except by the unanimous consent of the other subscribers, and then he could not do it if there were creditors whose rights would be jeopardized. Even a majority of the stockholders cannot withdraw and refuse to proceed further in the corporate enterprise; and these rules are said to be just and based upon a sound public policy.[1] The liberality of the legislative policy can be readily seen, in making such a radical change in the law of corporations by investing the building association stockholder with the personal right of withdrawal. It being considered in other corporations highly essential to retain the stockholder, it would seem that the legislature never intended to permit a full, unconditional withdrawal and consequent termination of all liabilities. Such important modification of established rules must necessarily, even in a building association be attended with some wise restrictions.

Sec. 9. **Manner of Withdrawal.** The by-laws should prescribe the manner of withdrawal, and in this they generally but re-enact the statute, as it usually defines the right. The withdrawing member should be required to give a written notice[2] of his intention to withdraw. That notice should be

---

[1] Cook Stock, etc., sec. 169.

[2] The written notice may be waived by the association and an oral notice accepted: McKenney v. Diamond State, etc, Association, 18 Atl. R. 905. A co-operative bank is chargeable in a trustee process as the trustee of a member at the withdrawal value of his shares, although he has given it no notice of his desire to withdraw such shares: Atwood v. Dumas, 149 Mass. 167.

served upon the secretary some time before the money is expected, and should be entered by him on a book kept for that purpose. The amount to be paid upon withdrawal is a difficult question, unless the statute determines it, since the enterprise has no certain profits until it is wound up, as there may be losses, idle money, unforeseen expenses or lower premiums or interest, while the association may be completely successful and yield a larger return than calculated. It is inequitable to allow him to take out all the profits accruing upon his shares, as the continuing members take all the burden of the loans upon which the retiring stockholder has received his full share of profits. The association should, therefore, retain a part of the profits. The withdrawal value should be adjusted by the directors upon the time of the membership. If the member retires early in the life of the association, his share should be small, with proper increase as the time of the withdrawal more nearly approaches maturity of stock. In ascertaining the withdrawal value, another element is to be considered, and that is the earning capacity of the association. An arbitrary rule might be unjust in some societies, as approaching too close to the per cent. of earnings. A general rule might, therefore, be unjust when applied. If one could be formulated it would be to repay the dues paid in, less expenses and losses, with the legal rate of interest for the average time. This rule might militate against the association in early withdrawals, but it would be compensated when the withdrawals were late and left a large surplus profit.

SEC. 10. **Legal Status of Withdrawing Member.** When a member gives notice of withdrawal he stops paying dues. He has determined that he will no longer carry his payments, and the association is bound by that determination. His character as debtor is at once reversed, and he becomes a creditor to the amount of his legal claim and is entitled to recover as such.[1] But he is not entitled to recover the value

---

[1] Building Association v. Silverman, 85 Pa. St 394; Building Association's Estate, 12 W. N. C. 207; Haigh v. United States, etc., Association, 19 W. Va. 792. See Wittman v. Building Association, 7 W. N. C. 80.

5

of the stock,[1] nor its par value even though it has matured,[2] but only the withdrawal value as fixed by the by-laws or rules. A complaint to recover thereon must show a compliance with the by-laws in withdrawing, and that payment was refused. And he cannot enforce his demand without showing funds in the treasury, or that the directors consented to such application.[3] The authorities are somewhat confusing in their views of him as he stands in this position. Some hold him as a member; others divest him of membership and qualify him as a plain creditor. In truth he has the attributes of both. As against the other members he is a creditor of the association; but he is not an ordinary creditor, since he cannot come in competition with outside creditors. Their claims must be satisfied before his; but as against the continuing members he is entitled to be paid the amount due him before they can divide the assets.

SEC. 11. **Liability of Withdrawing Member.** In the sense given in the last section, the withdrawing member is a creditor,[4] but so far as the by-laws and rules are concerned, he is in a sense a member until payment[5] and be is bound by them. So that he is held under the by-laws for all liability incurred prior to the notice, coming to the knowledge of the society after the notice had been given. But liabilities incurred after the notice is received by the association cannot be imposed upon him. While he continues a member and subject to the by-laws for some purposes, yet he is not

[1] Laurel Run, etc., Association v. Sperring, 3 Kulp, 67.

[2] Building Association v. Sperring, 106 Pa St. 334.

[3] Texas, etc., Association v. Kerr, 13 S. W. Rep. 1020.

[4] See also *In re* Blackburn, etc., Society, L. R. 24 Ch. D. 421; Sibun v. Pearce, L. R , 41 Ch. D. 354; Wright v. Deley 4 II. & C. 209. In Henninghausen, et al.,v. Tischer, 50 Md. 583, it was held that a person can be both shareholder and a creditor of the corporation; as shareholder he

is liable for his proportion of losses, but as creditor he is entitled to recover the amount due him independently of all losses, as the balances assigned by withdrawing members must be presumed to have been ascertained, after allowing all deductions to which the withdrawing member, assignors, were then subject or liable.

[5] Walker v. General Mutual, etc., Society, L. R , 36 Ch. Div. 777, 786; Siburn v. Pearce, L. R., 44 Ch.D. 354

subject to dues and fines after notice to withdraw. The society retains his membership until he is paid, for readjusting of any liability that may legally attach to the stock before the actual retirement. After he has been paid off, on his withdrawal, and there is a final settlement between him and the society, in the absence of mutual mistake or fraud, he cannot be compelled to make good a deficiency occurring before the withdrawal and discovered before the winding up of the association[1]. In order to remove any doubt as to the liability of withdrawing members for losses, the by-laws should explicitly and clearly define it. Where a by-law provided that a withdrawing member was "entitled to receive the amount actually paid in by him, less all fines, interest, insurance, due from him with average interest at the rate of 6 per cent per annum," the court refused to allow losses because they did not come under any of the heads mentioned in the by-laws.[2] While he would be equitably chargeable with all losses incurred prior to the notice, the amount withdrawable is a proper subject for the by-laws and the liability for such losses should be carefully provided for. The withdrawing member is not bound by new rules made after he has given notice to withdraw.[3] He may sell and assign his shares, or rather his claim, and the purchaser takes them subject to all liabilities, just as a purchaser before withdrawal becomes liable to the duties of a shareholder.[4]

Sec. 12. **Rights of Withdrawing Members of Insolvent Association.** While a withdrawing member is in a sense described a creditor of the association and can obtain judgment, yet when the association was insolvent at the time of his withdrawal, he cannot compel payment of the money due from the association to the exclusion of claims of general creditors, or those of his fellow stockholders,[5] for if the

---

[1] *In re* West Riding, etc., Society, L. R., 45 Ch. Div. 463.

[2] McKenney v. Diamond State, etc., Association, 18 Atl. Rep. 905.

[3] Armitage v. Walker, 2 Jur. N. S. 13.

[4] Handley v. Farmer, 29 Beav. 362.

[5] Hanney v. Building Association, 16 W. N. C. 450.

society is known to be insolvent although proceedings may not have been taken to wind it up, the withdrawing rules cannot be invoked.[1]  But the association cannot withhold a part of his withdrawal on the ground of apprehension of ultimate insolvency of the association, because of the liability of the member to contribute,[2] yet he cannot withdraw without considering losses,[3] though they are probable,[4] nor necessary expenses.[5]  The association ordinarily has no right to retire stock before the terminating period and force out the stock holder against his will, so long as he performs his duties.[6]

SEC. 13.  **Right to Withdraw Limited to Present Funds.**  The right of members to presently withdraw deposits, is practically limited to funds on hand.[7]  And the withdrawing member must show that there are funds for that purpose before he can enforce his demand, but it is an abuse of discretion for the directors to so invest the entire funds in real estate so as to leave none applicable to the payment of withdrawing members, and thus defeat their rights.[8]  When notice of withdrawal is given the association, it should arrange the disposition of its receipts so as to meet its payments when due.  While the right to withdraw is only grantable out of funds designated for that purpose, it is not intended that rightful lack of funds shall defeat the right as against the members.  So, if the association is solvent and a member gives notice of withdrawal, and the notice had matured- before the association is being wound up, he is entitled to be paid out of the assets, after outside creditors, in priority to those members who had not given notice, notwithstanding the fact that

[1] *In re* Sunderland, etc., Society, 24 Q. B Div 394.
[2] Jungkuntz v. Building Association, 6 Bull. 428.
[3] Friel v. Association, 1 Leg. Rec. Rep. (Pa.) 217.
[4] Knoblanck v. Building Association, 25 P. L. J. 89; Paffert v. Building Association, 25 P. L. J. 40 The probable loss may be ascertained by an appraisement.
[5] McGrath v. Hamilton, etc., Association, 44 Pa. St. 383.
[6] Bergman v. St. Paul, etc., Association, 29 Minn. 275.
[7] State v Redwood Falls, etc. Association, 45 Minn. 154.
[8] National, etc., Association v. Hubley, 34 Leg. Int. 6.

after he had given the notice, there were no funds for payment.[1] The intention of the rule is to prevent the application of the funds to withdrawals to such an extent that its operations will be crippled; and when it winds up, the reason of the rule does not apply, which readily defeats the application of the rule itself.

SEC. 14. **Stock Pledged Cannot be Withdrawn.** When a loan is made to the member his stock is pledged as collateral security. The right to withdraw is thereby curtailed to the extent that he pay off his loan before he can withdraw.[2]

SEC. 15. **Amount Withdrawable.** The withdrawal by the member includes only his credits on his stock. So, under an ordinary by-law for withdrawals, he is not entitled to have premium, interest, fines, transfer fees or charges of that character refunded to him.[3]

SEC. 16. **Construction of By-Laws Concerning Withdrawal.** The by-laws providing for withdrawal, are favorably construed for the member, but any privileges therein given, if not taken advantage of by the member as therein specified, are forfeited.[4] And if the by-laws provide that no money is to be paid on a withdrawal unless the pass book is produced, its production is a condition precedent to payment.[5]

SEC. 17. **Transfer of Shares.** The by-laws should provide for transferring of stock by a shareholder. The certificate of stock should have a blank assignment indorsed on it, to be acknowledged before the secretary, or a power of attorney to the transferee to make the transfer, and the by-laws usually provide that upon payment of a transfer fee, the secretary shall

[1]Walton v. Edge. L. R. 10 App. Cas. 33; In re Middlesbrough, etc., Society, 53 L. T N. S. 203; In re Blackburn, etc., Society, L. R, 24 Ch. Div. 421; In re Mutual Society, 24 Ch D. 425.
[2]Building Association v. Sperring, 106 Pa. St. 334; State v. Red Falls, etc., Association, 45 Minn. 154.
[3]Security, etc., Association v. Lake, 69 Ala. 456.
[4]Fuller v. Salem, etc., Association, 10 Gray 94; Booz's Appeal, 109 Pa. St. 592.
[5]Atkinson v. Bradford, etc., Society, L. R., 25 Q. B. Div. 377.

enter the transfer upon the books of the association.[1] The title will pass by an assignment of stock, without transfer on the books of the association, but until the transfer is so entered the transferrer as against the association, and creditors of the association, is liable on the stock.[2] The association, with knowledge of the assignment, may choose to accept the transferree as a member, but the legal liability to do so, does not attach until there has been a transfer on the books. The officers of an association are not liable where they divided the assets among those whom the books show to be stockholders, to one whose name does not appear on such books, but who held certificates assigned to him with power of attorney to transfer.[3] However, the directors should not, as a matter of precaution retire any stock without the certificates being surrendered to the association, but in declaring dividends, they would be justified in giving them to the stockholders shown by the books. A transfer of stock properly effected, will not relieve from accrued liability, but only from future liability. A by-law that no stockholder shall be permitted to transfer his stock while he is in default, is valid.[4] A building association's rule that each member on transferring his shares to another shall pay to the association a transfer fee on each share, has no application where one who has subscribed to a number of shares in his own and others' names, and seeking to exercise his right of withdrawal on all, produces proper vouchers from such others for payment.[5] When the association refuses to transfer shares, the general weight of authority is that mandamus will not lie to compel its transfer, and that the proper action is for damages.[6]

[1] The transfer fee is enforceable: McGannon v Central, etc., Association, 19 W. Va. 726.

[2] Cook Stock, etc., 260.

[3] Bank of Commerce's Appeal, 73 Pa. St. 59 In a case where the registered holder of shares held in trust for plaintiff who held the certificates and such trustee was allowed to withdraw the shares without producing the certificates, it was held the society was not liable to transfer the shares to plaintiff: Nolloth v. Simplified, etc. Society, 53 L. T. N.S. 859.

[4] Cunningham v. Alabama, etc., Company, 4 Ala. 652.

[5] Building Association v. Henderson, 3 Bull. 386.

[6] Galbraith v. Bldg. Ass'n, 43 N. J. Law, 389; Cook, Stock, etc., sec. 289.

**Sec. 18. Forfeitures.** Almost all associations provide that in case of a certain number of defaults in his payments, the member shall forfeit his membership. The right of an association to declare a forfeiture of stock for non-payment of dues, etc., must be clearly authorized by the charter or general incorporation laws;[1] it cannot be created by by-law.[2] A power of this character must be constructed strictly, and the validity of the forfeiture depends upon a strict compliance with the law.[3] Forfeitures are not favored in law, and the right must be expressly conferred and exercised in accordance with the granted power. But if the forfeiture is authorized, the courts will not relieve a member for a willful neglect of his duties,[4] and he cannot recover back the money paid on his stock after it has been forfeited for non-payment of dues, and assessments, where such forfeiture is authorized by the charter of the association.[5] No notice, unless there is one prescribed by the charter or by-laws, is necessary before declaring the forfeiture.[6]

When the association holding the bond of a member forfeits his membership and proceeds upon the bond, it can only recover the amount actually advanced with interest, deducting payments.[7] The association having declared the borrower no longer a member, can only enforce against him as though he were a stranger.

The most equitable plan in case of default, after the imposition of fines becomes ineffective, is to provide, after a certain time upon failure to pay all back charges, for a compulsory withdrawal, deducting such charges.

**Sec. 19. The Legal Status of Member as a Borrower.** When the association has accumulated funds suffi-

[1] Cook Stock, sec. 123; Perrin v. Granger, 30 Vt. 595; Henderson, etc. Association v. Johnson, 10 S. W. Rep 787.
[2] Master Stevedores' Assn v Walsh, 2 Daly, 14; Rosenback v Salt Springs, etc., Bank, 53 Barb 506; In re Long Island, etc., Company, 19 Wend. 37.
[3] Germantown, etc., Company v. Fitler, 60 Pa. St. 124.
[4] Freeman v. Ottawa, etc., Association, 114 Ill. 182.
[5] Holmes v. Smythe, 100 Ill. 413; Freeman v. Ottawa, etc., Association, 114 Ill. 182.
[6] Ibid.
[7] Bechtold v. Brehm, 26 Pa St. 269; Denny v. West Philadelphia, etc., Association, 39 Ib. 154; Premium Fund Association's Appeal, Ib. 156.

cient to loan, a member under its rules may become a borrower. Upon receiving a loan, the member has increased obligations. In order that the rights and duties of the borrower may be understood, his legal status should be defined. The borrower is sometimes called an advanced, prepaid or redeemed shareholder. It matters little by what name he is known so long as it is kept in mind that his act of borrowing money does not in law divest him of membership. By borrowing, he takes advantage of a right as a member which is vouchsafed to him by the statute. The right to borrow is inseparately connected with his membership; it flows naturally from that endowment. To say that he loses his membership upon becoming a borrower is to assert that the assumption of a right effectually destroys its source. And it is equally untenable to say that his status as a member is modified by borrowing. When a member bids for an advance on his shares, he asks for a loan. Stripping the transaction of all devices as "advance on" or "redemption of" shares, it is the act of the association lending to its member a sum of money to secure the repayment of which the member gives a mortgage and assigns his stock as collateral security. What change is effected in the member's condition? He is to pay dues; that he is already bound to do; he is to pay premium and interest which represent the cost of the loan. So the borrower has not modified his contract, as a member, but he has added to it the cost of a right he has chosen to exercise, and has secured the repayment of the money gotten by the exercise of that right. He has not surrendered his interest in the society's assets; neither has he parted title with his stock; he has pledged it with the full right reserved to redeem it at any time. The borrower's interest in the assets of the society are unmodified but it is burdened with the pledge. His substantive rights, as a member, remain unchanged, except, he has agreed not to exercise his right of withdrawal as long as the loan is unpaid. His stock matures as the stock of the non-borrowers, and he shares in losses and expenses. Regarding the borrower as such, in legal effect, simplifies his position and enables us to clearly understand it. So when his stock has matured, the debt or the loan is still due the association in the full amount, but if he chooses, or the association elects, the stock may be used to cancel the debt. Until that application has been made, his debt is entirely unpaid and he remains the owner of the stock with the lien upon it. But he can compel the association in equity,[1] if not by the rules, to resort to that lien and exhaust his stock, representing his interest in the distributive assets of the association, before reaching the security given by him, as, if it satisfied the debt, the association must then release the mortgage.[2] This is the legal status of the member who secures the face value of his shares from the association in advance of their maturity.[3]

[1]Red Bank, etc., Association, v. Patterson, 27 N. J. Eq. 223.

[2]Tyrrell, etc.,Association v. Haley, 139 Pa. St. 637.

[3]The writer is aware that this view is not in accord with all the courts. In Virginia it is held that borrowing extinguishes the membership, and, consequently, the borrower is not entitled to participate in the final division of the funds: White v. Mechanics, etc., Association, 22 Grat. 233; Winchester, etc., Association v. Gilbert, 23 Grat. 787. But he is yet held by the court to his covenants as a party to the articles of association, and to make his regular monthly payment of dues and fines, obligations secured by his mortgage. As has been said: "Observe the inconsistency; he has lost his membership but is bound as a member to the duties of membership, and has even put himself under bonds to be a good member." Endlich Building Associations, p. 182. The better rule sustained by the courts is to regard the advance as a loan: Pfeister v. Wheeling, etc., Association, 19 W. Va. 676; Mills v Salisbury, etc., Association, 75 N. C. 292; Lincoln, etc., Association v. Benjamin, 7 Neb. 181; Martin v. Nashville, etc., Association, 2 Cold. 418; Gordon v. Winchester, etc., Association, 12 Bush 110; Security, etc. Association v. Lake, 69 Ala 456. In a Maryland case it is held that advanced or prepaid members are obliged to pay interest on the sum advanced besides their weekly dues—they have not ceased to be members by the prepayments, but continue to hold an interest in the management and success of the association, as upon that depends their earliest relief, not only from the payment of the weekly dues, but their final release from their mortgage. The unpaid members are not absolved from the punctual payment of weekly dues. They are entitled to any residium of profits, the exclusive interest in which has been devolved upon them by virtue of the contract, with the prepaid members, through the act of the company furnishing the equivalent consideration. Both are interested and under mutual obligation to contribute to the accumulation of the common fund by the payment of their weekly dues, until the time provided for its final distribution and settlement: Lister v. Log Cabin, etc., Association, 38 Md. 120.

The member as a borrower is still a member with all his rights, except as pledged. He may vote,[1] hold office, transfer his shares subject to the lien, and in fact do everything another shareholder may do.

SEC. 20. **Duty of Association to Loan its Money.** When the association accumulates the amount of a share it then becomes its duty to loan it, and not only is it a duty to the state that created it for the purpose of lending to its members, but it is a duty to the members, as through the earning power of its accumulations does the association expect to realize the profit which is to assist in maturing its stock.

SEC. 21. **Selection of Borrower.** The next step is to select a borrower among its members.[2] The most equitable way to make this selection, as determined by experience, is by providing for bidding among the members for preference of the loan. The method, is usually, to offer a sum upon the auction plan, and the highest bidder pays whatever amount he feels justified in paying for the privilege of getting the money. This he pays in addition to interest. Evenings are most convenient to the shareholders for the sales of money, who are generally employed during the day. The president of the association is the officer who acts as auctioneer, but any officer present may do so. Upon a bid being received which is the highest, the secretary takes a memorandum of it with the name of the bidder; additional sums, if any are offered, in the same manner. The by laws should provide for a penalty in a small amount for failure to take a loan after bidding it in. These sales should be conducted upon fair principles; by-bidding, especially from a director, should not

---

[1] In Michigan, by statute the right to vote is withheld, although he remains otherwise a member: Michigan, etc. Association v. McDevitt, 77 Mich. 1.

[2] In some states associations are permitted to make loans outside of their membership, but from the nature of the scheme, all borrowing members should be satisfied before loans are made to other persons.

be tolerated. If the member feels such unfairness is being practiced upon him, he can injure the society before its members and outsiders.

SEC. 22. **Methods of Premium Charges.** The preference so paid is called generally the premium, and the manner of its payment varies in different associations.

The manner of charging premiums has been measurably changed since the earlier societies. The old plan of deducting the full amount of premium at the time of making the loan was the prevailing method at one time, and is still practiced in some localities. For instance if a borrower paid 25 per cent. on a $2,000 loan, he received $1,500 in cash and paid full interest on the $2,000.[1] In some states this method was invalidated as usurious, while in others it was upheld. These associations, to prevent inequality in the cost of money, adopted the minimum premium plan, requiring all bidders to pay at least a certain premium. When the borrower desired to repay his loan the face value was not required, i. e. from the $2,000 he was allowed a rebate of premium having reference to the unexpired time. The system has generally been found so complex in the keeping of its accounts and so uncertain in its earnings that it has been modified in many states, and entirely superseded in others.[2] One modification of this plan was to give the borrower the face of the loan, less his bid, and to charge interest on the net loan only. It involved the same intricacies as the other plan, and has not been generally adopted. The most popular system throughout the United States is that by which the borrower pays with his installments his interest and premium. If the borrower desires to repay his loan, he only pays premium up to the time of repaying his loan. This system is simple to the

[1] It has been recently held that in an association operating under this plan, a stockholder who had bid 25 per cent premium for a loan of $100 was entitled to receive $80, since the per centage of the premium is to be computed on the actual sum received by him: Mutual, etc., Association v. Tascott, 28 N. E. Rep. (Ill.) 801; Affirming Tascott v Mutual, etc., Association, 37 Ill. App 274.

[2] The statute of Indiana in force contemplates this style of an association, but they are not received with as much favor as the newer plans.

borrower, which is a strong point, and it lays a less heavy burden on him, lessening the amount of the premium and making its payment easy. In New York, the premium is charged as a bonus, is so understood by the borrower, and is then deducted from the loan. He gives security for the face of the loan and pays interest on that. The premium is settled; there are no rebates, and with this understanding the borrower governs his bidding, and there is a consequent tendency to lower the bids. The merit of the plan is in impressing upon the borrower that the premium is a bonus for the preference in the use of money. That is the true function of premiums. Primarily, the association uses the method of charging premiums to make an equitable selection of a borrower; and secondarily, to make a profit; but premiums should be bid by borrowers on the theory that they are paying that much for the right to have the money over fellow stockholders. There are many different schemes for charging premiums indigenous to different localities, but those outlined are the general ones.[1] To an uninformed mind, this additional cost of money, in the charge of premiums, seems an exorbitant cost, but in view of the profit attaching to the borrower's stock with which he can pay the debt, the apparent cost is materially reduced and it is not oppressive. In charging premiums the association should be guided by the statute. If the premium charge is not authorized by the statute, and it increases the cost of the loan beyond the rates of interest fixed by statute, it is usurious and void,[2] but if the statute authorizes the charge, then usury laws do not apply.[3]

[1] An investigator in this line will consult Dexter's Co-operative Savings and Loan Association, pp. 70 et seq.

[2] Citizens', etc. Company v. Uhler, 48 Md. 455.

[3] Home, etc., Association v. Boning, 7 Bull. 174; Montgomery, etc. Association v. Robinson, 69 Ala. 413; Security. etc. Association v. Lake, 69 Ala. 456.

Note. In some courts the transaction of an advancement is treated as of a partnership character: Silver v. Barnes, 6 Bing N C. 180; Burbridge v. Cotton, 8 Eng. L. & Eq. R. 57; Seagrave v. Pope, 15 Eng. L. & Eq. 477; Robertson v. American, etc. Association, 10 Md. 397; Shannon v. Howard, etc. Association, 36 Md. 383; Lister v. Log Cabin, etc. Association, 38 Md. 115;

**Sec. 23. Auction Premiums.** The manner of charging the premium by auction of money is the one usually contemplated by the statute, and is more in harmony with the general scheme. The power of determining its cost is thus placed with the borrowers themselves, and the managers cannot impose upon them an arbitrary rate. If the statute shows that this method was the one intended by the legislature, the courts require compliance with it. So, under statutes providing that money on hand shall be sold to the member who will pay the highest premium for the preference in taking the loan, the bidding must be competitive and the directors cannot

Williar v. Baltimore, etc. Association, 45 Md. 546; Massey v. Citizens, etc. Association, 22 Kans 624; Delano v. Wild 6 Allen, 1; Clarksville, etc. Associati n v. Stephens, 26 N. J. Eq 351; Shannon v. Dunn, 43 N. H. 194; Bibb County, etc. Association v. Richards, 21 Ga. 592; Parker v. Fulton, etc., Association, 46 Ga. 166; Patterson v. Albany, etc., Association. 63 Ga. 373. In these cases it was held the question of usury is to be left to the jury, and if it is found that the organization is not intended to evade the usury laws, but has for its purpose the accumulation of monthly savings to procure homes, there is no usury in the charge. In other courts the advancement is regarded as a mere loan: Mills v. Salisbury, etc. Association. 75 N. C. 292; Overby v. Fayetteville, etc. Association, 81 N. C. 54; Vann v. Fayetteville etc , Association, 75 N. C. 494; Latham v. Washington. etc. Association, 77 N. C 145; Hanner v. Greensboro, etc., 78 N. C. 188; Hoskins v. Mechanics, etc., Association. 84 N. C. 338; Smith v. Mechanics. etc., Association. 73 N. C. 372; Columbia, etc., Association v. Bollinger, 12 Rich. Eq. 124; Lincoln, etc., Association v. Graham, 7 Neb. 173; Lincoln, etc., Association v. Benjamin, 7 Neb. 181; Martin v. Nashville, etc., Association, 2 Cold. 418; Herbert v. Kenton, etc., Association, 11 Bush. 296; Gordon v. Winchester, etc., Association, 12 Bush, 110; Bechtold v. Brehm, 26 Pa., St. 269; Reiser v. William Tell, etc. Association, 39 Pa. St. 137; Burlington, etc., Association v. Heider, 55 Iowa, 424; Building Association v. Timmins, 3 Phila. 209. In these cases the premium charge is held usurious, being unauthorized by statute. In unincorporated associations, or in associations without statutory permission to make a premium charge, it would become a question whether the transaction was to be regarded as a partnership in character so as to take it out of the usury law, or that it was a mere loan falling within the pale of that law.

The partnership theory sustained by courts with a liberal and friendly disposition, enabled associations without legislative sanction, to enforce premiums. Premiums have now a more general legislative authority, and the transaction is more regarded as a loan In building association parlance, it is treated as

refuse a bid if the security is properly tendered;[1] hence they have no right to fix a minimum rate of premium,[2] but the loan made by the association having a by-law to that effect, but not made in pursuance of such by-law, and unaffected thereby, is binding on the borrower.[3] It often happens in actual practice where there is a steady demand for money, that horizontal or uniform premiums based upon a just profit to the association, are of advantage to the association, and of more fairness to the members, as all are paying the same cost. In that case, a member's bid at the uniform rate without deceit or compulsion by the association, would be binding, even if the statute contemplated bidding, but if he refused to make a bid so high, the directors have no discretion with surplus funds on hand, but to loan him if his bid is the highest offered, and his security sufficient.

Sec. 24. **Premiums Fixed, Unchangeable.** But the premium once fixed cannot be afterwards changed. The proportion of premiums which shall be paid each week cannot be increased by subsequent action as to existing mortgages,

such, and in law it is logically a loan, since there is a fixed interest and premium charge, with security for full repayment. These conditions are absolute, and their performance is required until the stock security increases in value sufficient to satisfy the debt, when the association obligates itself to take it in full satisfaction. It is merely a mode of payment, and if it fails the debt remains unpaid and enforceable. The proposition laid down in the text seems to be safe for observance. The conflict in the cases upon the subject of premium as usurious has led to the opposite theories of the transaction represented in the two lines of cases cited, but since premiums latterly are authorized in nearly all of the states, the views of the courts in those cases cannot apply to associations operating under such statutes. The directors of the association should be guided by the statute in charging premiums, as the power is safely statutory, notwithstanding the partnership theory supported by some courts, and this is the tendency of the recent cases

In Illinois, premium is regarded as liquidated damages and not usurious: Holmes v. Smythe, 100 Ill. 413; Freeman v. Ottowa, etc., Association, 114 Ill., 182.

It was recently held by the Arkansas Supreme Court that as it was uncertain how much would be paid as interest until winding up, premiums are not usurious: Reeve v. Ladies', etc., Association, June, 25, 1892.

[1] State v. Greenville, etc. Association, 29 Ohio St. 93.

[2] Stiles Appeal, 95 Pa. St. 122.

[3] Orangeville, etc., Association v. Young, 9 W. N. C. 251.

unless the constitution and by-laws of the association clearly
and unmistakably confer such authority. And where the
constitution provides that the installments of premium shall
be 50 cents per week for four years, and after that time the
directors shall determine the amount to be paid weekly, this
language does not clearly give such authority and will be construed prospectively and to authorize a larger weekly installment only as to loans made after the change.[1]

Sec. 25. **Premium Chargeable to Maturity
only.** A premium bid for the right of precedence in taking
a loan, cannot be collected after the maturity of the loan. So
held in a case where the loan was for a specified time, and the
premium a percentage on the amount payable periodically.[2]
And this is true though the time of payment be extended by
renewal or forbearance.[3]

But one premium can be charged upon a loan, so that where
after a sheriff's sale on a mortgage, the stockholder received a
second loan, at a higher premium, he is entitled to be repaid
his first premium.[4]

Sec. 26. **Formal Application for Loan.** The
amount of premium to be paid by the proposed borrower being
determined, it is advisable for formal application for the loan
to be made to the association. The application should give
the interest and premium the applicant is to pay; the number of shares to be pledged, a description of the real estate
offered as security, including a description of the improvements thereon or those proposed to be placed thereon, the
market value of the property, its rental value, description of
liens, the purpose of borrowing,[5] the age, residence and occupation of applicant. These are chief points to get the security
before the directors and the value of reducing this prelimi-

---

[1]Burke v. Home, etc., Association,
7 Bull. 114; Home, etc., Association v. Boning, 7 Bull. 174.

[2]Savings, etc., Association v. Stevens, 5 Bull. 113.

[3]Ib.

[4]Flounders v. Hawley, 78 Pa. St.
45.

[5]The association is not required to
ascertain the use of the proposed
loan: Hagerman v. Ohio etc. Association, 25 Ohio St. 186, but it is advisable and even necessary in some
states where the borrowers are married women.

nary contract to writing, cannot be overestimated, as in controversies between the association and the borrower, it may be the vital point of the whole transaction.

SEC. 27. **Appraisement.** The application should be submitted to competent appraisers, appointed by the directors, and the property personally viewed by them. They should give their written opinion as to its value. The application thereupon becomes a subject of investigation by the board. The report of the appraisers is merely advisory. The directors then decide upon the facts thus presented, whether or not to grant the loan.

SEC. 28. **Abstract of Title.** Upon the acceptance of the loan, an abstract of the title to the property offered as security should be placed in the hands of the attorney of the association by the proposed borrower. If the title is reported sufficient by the attorney, then the papers, usually consisting of a note or bond, secured by mortgage or a deed of trust, and such affidavits as may be necessary, should be prepared by the attorney or a skilled draughtsman, and executed by the borrower. The association is then ready to pay the money, seeing that all existing liens are paid and satisfied of record. If the loan is a building one, the association must use precaution to see that all mechanics' liens against the property are satisfied and that there are no enforceable claims superior to its mortgage arising out of the improvements. The surest precaution is to take an indemnifying bond, with sufficient surety, at the time the loan is made.

SEC. 29. **Interest not Collectible on Interest and Premium.** Building associations cannot collect interest on premiums or interest and thus compound it; so under a statute authorizing a deduction of premiums at the time of the loan, interest cannot be charged upon the par value of the shares but upon the money actually advanced.[1]

---

[1] Forrest City, etc., Association v. Gallagher, 25 Ohio St. 205; Risk v. Delphos, etc., Association, 31 Ohio St. 517; Pfeister v. Wheeling, etc., Association, 19 W. Va. 676; Parker v. United States, etc, Association, 19 W. Va. 769; Edelin v. Pascoe, 22 Grat. 826.

SEC. 30. **Payment of Instalments.** Instalments must be paid as stipulated until the accumulated fund suffices to pay the sum agreed, which cancels the debt.' If, however, the association is dissolved by a vote of the shareholders before maturity the instalments cease.' And where the borrower is required to pay monthly instalments and interest thereon, he cannot be required to pay in a different manner as *in solido.* If the association is unable to perform its contract, as when it goes into the hands of a receiver, a borrower is not liable to pay further dues, etc.'

SEC. 31. **Provisions of Note or Bond.** Building associations, with power to loan money, have the right to take security therefor, as provided by statute, and this generally is first mortgage on real estate.' The bond or the note is the principal debt and it usually provides for an indefinite number of small periodical payments in the shape of dues on the stock, together with the premium and interest charges on the loan and for the payment of fines and assessments, if any, on the stock assigned. The mortgage is given to secure the performance of this bond as authorized by statute' and the by-laws.' Consequently, the mortgage must conform to them.'

SEC. 32. **Provisions of Mortgage.** If the statute prescribes the conditions and covenants to go into the mortgage, it must strictly be adhered to, but if the statute merely gives the general scheme of the association without making any requirements, any form which will accomplish the purposes of the statute will be sufficient. But when the statute makes no provisions for covenants and conditions in the mortgage, and the association uses a note or bond, as is commonly

'Cason v. Seldner, 77 Va. 293.
'Cason v. Seldner, supra.
'Low Street, etc., Association v. Zucker, 49 Md 448.
'Union, etc., Association v. Masonic Association, 2 Stew. 389; Massey v. Citizens', etc., Association, 22 Kans· 624.
'Franklin, etc., Association v. Mather, 4 Abb. Pr. 274.

'Shannon v. Howard, etc., Association. 36 Md. 383.
'Building Association v. Schuller, 3 W. N. C, Pa 431; Smith v. Mechanic's, etc., Association, 73 N. C. 372; Baltimore, etc , Society v. Taylor, 41 Md. 409; Birmingham v. Maryland, etc., Association, 45 Md. 641.

6

done in the different states, those instruments really express the contract between the association and its borrowers. The provisions necessary to accomplish the results, contemplated by the statute, are incorporated in them, and the mortgage securing their performance merely incorporates and identifies them as the provisions of the bond which it secures. In such cases, in drafting a bond, the statute should be consulted, that the objects of the association may be carried out, and in drafting the mortgage, the bond and its provisions should be incorporated and identified, adding such other provisions as may be necessary to effectuate the purposes of the mortgage as security, and as the statutes of the state may generally require concerning mortgages of real property. The association cannot deprive the member from the ordinary privileges of the association by making the mortgage in the ordinary form.[1]

SEC. 33. **Complaint upon Bond or Mortgage.** The association may sue upon either the bond or mortgage or upon both,[2] and the complaint should show the necessary defaults to render the debt due. The amount due the association should be alleged in the suit, as no greater sum can be recovered.[3] When the association has shown in evidence that there are shares outstanding, the burden is on the defendant to show the shares had matured and that he is entitled to have his mortgage discharged.[4] If he seeks to take advantage of any failure by him to comply with the charter, as by signing a paper, the burden is upon him to show that he did not sign it.

---

[1] Building Association v. Robinson, 46 L. I , Pa. 5.

[2] Building Association v. Hetzel, 103 Pa. St 507. In a suit on a note given to an association, wherein the payment of the note depends on the payment of assessments, the manner of making the assessments need not be particularly described in a complaint on the note: Borchus v. Huntington, etc., Association, 97 Ind. 180.

[3] Mutual, etc., Association v. Tas-cott, 28 N. E. Rep. 801. Under the Indiana code, in a suit to foreclose a mortgage, the constitution and by-laws of the association are not proper exhibits to the complaint: Newman v. Ligonier, etc., Association, 97 Ind. 295.

[4] Concordia,etc.Association,v.Read, 93 N. Y. 474; Tyrell, etc , Association .v. Haley, 20 Atl. R-1063.

[5] Nicely's Estate, 3 Kulp, 47; Building Association v. Lyons, 2 Kulp 409.

Sec. 34. **Loans to Outsiders.** The association may take the mortgage of a third person to secure a loan to a member, and it need not notify such third person of the failure of the member to pay the obligation,[1] and the surety is liable to the same extent as his principal,[2] and this is true where a member becomes surety for another member.[3] Unless it is authorized by statute, the association cannot loan money to outsiders,[4] but a loan so made cannot be defeated by the borrower on that ground.[5] Even if outside loans are authorized, members should be first accommodated.

Sec. 35. **Loans to Married Women.** The mortgage of a married woman cannot be enforced beyond the powers conferred upon her by an enabling statute,[6] since at common law she has no right to make such contracts, but where her husband joined in the bond and has full benefit of the loan, he is not within the rule.[7] Extreme care should be exercised in drawing papers where married women are under legal disability or where it is partially removed. The matter should come under the immediate supervision of the association's attorney, who by custom is the custodian of the legal blanks used by the association.

Sec. 36. **Mortgage Covenants.** The mortgage running during the association's existence without fixed termination is not void for uncertainty,[8] nor is the bond, although

[1]Pfeister v. Wheeling, etc., Association, 19 W. Va. 676.

[2]Saving Fund v. Longshore,8 Luz. L. Reg. 199.

[3]Johnson v. Elizabeth, etc., Association, 104 Pa. St. 394.

[4]State v. Oberlin, etc., Association, 35 Ohio St. 258; Wolbach v Lehigh, etc., Association, 81 Pa. St. 211. See Mechanic's, etc , Association v. Wilcox, 24 Conn. 147; Mechanics, etc., Association v. Meriden, etc., Company. Ib. 159; St. Joseph, etc., Association v. Thompson, 19 Kans. 321.

[5]Poock v. Lafayette, etc., Association, 71 Ind. 357.

[6]Building Association v. Rice, 8 W. N. C. 12; Building Association v. Mixell, 84 Pa. St. 313; Association v. Steele, 11 W. N. C. 204.

[7]Tanner's Appeal, 95 Pa. St. 118; Wiggins Appeal, 100 Pa. St. 155; Building Association v. McDermott 2 Kulp. 203.

[8]Robertson v. American,etc.,Association, 10 Md. 397. If the by-laws fix a time for the maturity of the mortgage debt and the borrower pays dues to that time the mortgage obligation is then extinguished: Lime City, etc., Association v. Wagner, 122 Ind. 78.

the articles provide for the termination of the association when its funds attain a certain sum.[1] Covenants on the part of the mortgagor to pay taxes,[2] fines,[3] insurance[4] are enforceable, but unless incorporated in the mortgage, it is not security for them.[5] These are usual provisions in mortgages of this character.[6] And a stipulation that the borrower is to re-pay the principal sum with interest and penalties, if there is default, is not a provision for a penalty that equity will relieve from, and may be enforced.[7] The mortgage should conform to the provisions of the charter or by-laws, and where it was taken for too much money in violation of such provisions, a conveyance of land under it will be enjoined[8]

Sec. 37.  **Application of Payments.**  Payments by a defaulting borrower not appropriated to any portion of his several sources of indebtedness, were directed by a court of equity to be applied (a) in payment of monthly fines, (b) dues,

[1]Merrill v. McIntire, 79 Mass. 157.
[2]Huntington, etc., Association v. Melsheimer, 14 W. N. C. 344.
[3]Hagerman v. Ohio, etc., Association, 25 Ohio St. 186.
[4]Chicago, etc., Society v. Crowell, 65 Ill. 454. It was held in this case that an action will lie against the association for breach of an agreement to insure. The measure of damages would be the dividend the insurance company would be able to pay in case the insurance had been perfected before loss and not the sum agreed upon. The association would be estopped to deny it had the right to make such contract. The secretary, having made similar contracts without personal interest, and the company received the personal benefits of them, the court held it would be inferred that he acted with knowledge of directors and was authorized to so act.

[5]Hamilton, etc., Association, v. Reynolds, 5 Duer, 671; Hazel, etc., Association v. Groesbeck, 41 L. I. 16; but where fines were not provided for in the mortgage, but were paid by the borrower, it was held he could claim no credit on the mortgage debt: Clarkville, etc., Association v. Stephens, 26 N. J. Eq 351.
[6]But if the parties incorporate unusual but lawful provisions, the courts will uphold the contract, as where a mortgage provided for payment of the principal in one year and interest monthly and one dollar per month for monthly contribution, it was held that the mortgage remains as security for the monthly dues: Everham v. Oriental, etc., Association, 47 Pa. St. 352.
[7]Concordia, etc., Association v. Read, 93 N. Y. 474.
[8]Smith v. Mechanics', etc., Association, 73 N. C. 372.

(c) interest.¹ But upon the principle that a creditor may apply payments upon such items of the debt as he may elect, it would seem that the association in justice to itself and without injury to the borrower, might apply his payments when not directed by himself to the discharge of (a) fines, (b) interest and premium, and (c) the balance on his stock. This application would seem forcibly right when it is considered that he is debtor to the association in two ways, first on his stock, and second on his loan, and the association should have the right to treat a payment as discharging the cost of the loan debt, since it cannot enforce interest on that cost if delinquent, whereas, it may protect itself on the stock debt by fines. The application we have given is the just one.

In case of non-borrowers, the same application is to be made, omitting, of course, the interest and premium.

SEC. 38. **Assignment of Shares as Collateral Security.** Usually in borrowing money, the shares of the borrower are assigned to the association as collateral security. This assignment does not relieve him from his covenant to make monthly payments on his stock or on account of fines.² Upon such assignment, the association is invested with their ownership for all purposes of dominion of the debt secured.³ After a sale to the association in liquidation of the shares, a member cannot again sell the shares,⁴ as he has thereby lost membership.

SEC. 39. **Payments on Stock Not Ipso Facto Payments on Loan.** The borrower's liability on his stock and his liability on his loan being different, payments on his stock are not ipso facto payments on the mortgage debt or loan. The distinction is not clearly kept in the practical management of the association, but the law holds the distinction, and requires appropriation by the association or application by the

¹Clarksville, etc., Association v. Stephens, 26 N. J. Eq 351. But, see, Building Association v. Taylor, 13 W. N C. 13.

²White v. Mechanic's, etc., Association, 22 Grat. 233.

³Schlessinger's Estate, 1 Law Times N. S 15.

⁴Michigan, etc., Association, v. McDevitt, 77 Mich. 1.

member, to effectuate that purpose. A member may, then, at any time apply his stock payments as a credit on his debt by paying in cash the balance, if any. A creditor of the member cannot compel such application to reduce the mortgage,[1] but the law regards a person holding a second mortgage on the property mortgaged to the association,[2] or a purchaser of the property,[3] as holding more favored positions, and to be equitably entitled to have the application made by the association, so as to reduce the lien on the property.

When a borrower desires to withdraw, he gives the association such notice as may be provided in the by-laws. He may then elect to have the withdrawal value of his shares applied on his loan, by paying the balance, and his shares of stock will be cancelled, which will terminate his membership. Or if he has defaulted in his payments, he may elect to have the value of his stock applied on his debt and the society is entitled to recover the balance.[4] The borrower is, therefore, not entitled

[1] Conrow v. Spring Garden, etc., Association, 21 Leg. Int., 109; Building Association, v. Raber, 11 Phila. 546; Kehler v. Miller, 4 Leg. Gaz. 125; Spring Garden Association v. Tradesmen's, etc., Association, 46 Pa. St. 493; Sunbury, etc., Association v. Martin, 1 Luz. L. Reg. 147; Delaware, etc., Association v. Keller, 2 W. N. C. 29; Selden v. Building Association, Ib. 481; Building Association v. George, 3 Ib. 239; North America, etc., Association v. Sutton, 35 Pa. St. 463; Barker v. Bigelow, 15 Gray, 13); Mechanics, etc., Association v. Conover, 1 McCart (N.J.), 219; Hoboken, etc., Association v. Martin, 2 Beas. (N. J.), 427; Hekelnkaemper v. German, etc., Association, 22 Kans. 549; Houlette's Estate, 2 Chest. 511; Link v. Building Association, 89 Pa. St. 15; and see Building Association v. Roan, 9 W. N. C. 15; Flynn v. Saving Fund, 37 L. I. (Pa.) 333; Diemer v. Egolf,

Chest. 55; Greenfield's Estate, Ib. 356; Whilden v. Broomall, 1 Del. (Pa.) 142; Harris's Appeal, 18 W. N. C. 14; In re Treffeison, 3 Kulp, 308; Oliver's Estate, 1 Del. (Pa.) 358.

[2] Hoboken, etc., Association, v. Martin, 2 Beas. (N. J.) 427.

[3] Herbert v. Mechanics, etc., Association, 17 N. J. Eq. 497; People's, etc., Bank v. Collins, 27 Conn. 142; Phillipsburg, etc., Association v. Hawk, 27 N. J. Eq. 355. See Authorities, p. 88 n. 4.

[4] When the by-laws provided that if the mortgagor desired to redeem from his mortgage he should apply to the directors, " who should decide the amount to be paid," it was held the borrower should pay the sum advanced, adding unpaid interest, deducting the amount of dues already paid, without interest, and making no deduction for entrance fee: Barker v. Bigelow, 15 Gray,

to any credit for payment of dues, unless the association
chooses to make such application; or, unless he elects for the
association to make such application.[1] And the credit is the
withdrawal value of the shares[2] to be ascertained by the charter and by-laws without regard to the improper withdrawal of
shares by other stockholders.[3] The "value," it is held, is to be
ascertained by the number of stock payments (dues) excluding
interest or profit and less expenses.[4] But he is not entitled to
the value of shares in another series.[5]

The borrower is not compelled to make this application of
his stock; he may pay off the loan and retain his stock.[6]
When the borrowing stockholder elects to apply his stock in
payment of his loan, the proper course is to deduct from the
ascertained value of the stock all arrearages thereon, and to
credit the balance on the loan.[7]

SEC. 40. **Payments on Reassigned Stock.** Where
stock is reassigned on a second loan, payments thereon are to
be applied to such loan in the absence of any specific appropriation.[8] If the association with knowledge of a second

130; but see People, etc., Association v. Furey, 20 Atl. R. 890, where
it was held, on foreclosure, as between the society and member, the
former is not bound to apply the
stock payments on the debt as the
member is not injured, as he will
receive the benefits of those installments on the increased value of the
shares.

[1] Assignments of shares to a third
person will prevent such application.

[2] Saving Fund v. Cake, 2 Leg. Rec.
Rep. 172; Watkins v. Building Association, 97 Pa. St. 514; Building Association v. Morgan, 2 Kulp, 19.

[3] Building Association v. Gallagher, 3 Law Times, N. S. 101.

[4] Building Association v. Groesbeck, 41 L. I. 16; Mechanics, etc.,
Association v. Conover, 1 McCurt.

219; Watkins v. Workingmen's, etc.,
Association, 10 W. N. C. 414. Under
a by-law providing upon the death
of a member, his legal representative might upon notice receive the
net value of his shares, it was held
the proper mode of determining that
value was to ascertain the market
value of the shares: Babcock v.
Middlesex, etc., Company, 28 Conn.
302.

[5] Saving Fund v. Cake, *supra.*

[6] Springville, etc., Association v.
Raber, 33 Leg. Int. Pa. 329.

[7] Building Association v. Rood, 2
Kulp., (Pa.) 246.

[8] Philadelphia, etc., Association v.
Moore, 47 Pa. St. 233.

mortgage, releases its mortgage, its debt, so far as the subsequent mortgage is concerned, is satisfied to the extent of the value of the stock;[1] if the borrower elects to have such application made, only the balance, if any, over such application, can be reached by creditors,[2] for it is an absolute payment.

SEC. 41. **Assigned Shares Cannot be Credited.** The right to have such application, if not directed by the member, cannot be had by his creditors,[3] but a purchaser at sheriff's sale is entitled to have the value of the shares credited,[4] and a surety of the member is entitled to have such stock applied.[5] But a borrower who has assigned his shares to a third person as collateral security, is not entitled to a credit for the value thereof.[6]

Sec. 42. **Liability of Borrower under his Mortgage for Losses.** The mortgaged property of a borrowing member cannot be charged under his mortgage, to make up general losses for the benefit of the non-borrower. Unless the mortgage so provides, that is a personal liability. When a covenant is to pay weekly dues and fines until such time as the association might have sufficient funds to pay all the holders of unredeemed shares, the par value thereof, clear of all losses and liabilities, it was held that the mortgagors could be required to contribute to losses and liabilities only by the prolonged payment of weekly dues in the continued operation of the association.[7] So where the conditions of the borrower's mortgage have been wholly fulfilled by him in good faith, whilst the building association was in actual operation as a

---

[1] Washington, etc. Association, v. Beaghen, 27 N. J. Eq. 93.

[2] Early's Appeal, 7 W. N. C. 184; and see Building Association v. Bayley, 1 Kulp, 215.

[3] Kreamer v. Saving Fund, 6 W. N. C. 267; Building Association v. Hungerbuehler, 93 Pa. St. 258; Building Association v. Mangan, 2 Kulp, 210. See authorities p. 86 n. 1.

[4] Kupfert v. Guttenberg, etc., Association, 30 Pa. St. 465; Hughes's Appeal, 30 Pa. St. 471; Overruling

Building Association v. Eshelbach, 7 Phila. 189; Kelly v. Accommodation, etc., Association, 2 Phila. 237; Saving Fund v. Murray, 14 Leg. Int. 133; Columbia, etc., Association v. Dobbins, 15 Ib. 45; Building Association v. Rowe, Ib.

[5] Massey v. Citizen's, etc., Association, 22 Kan. 624.

[6] Schober v. Accommodation, etc., Association, 35 Pa. St. 223.

[7] Low St. etc., Association v. Zucker, 48 Md. 448.

going corporation, and before its being placed in the hands of a receiver, the borrower is entitled to a cancellation of his mortgage, although his personal liability to share in the losses continues.[1] This rule would apply to associations having a fixed period of termination or crediting dividends at stated times. In a serial association, that does not make a tangible division of its profits until it matures its stock, as long as there were losses, they would, in effect, postpone the maturity of the stock, and, thus, necessarily the cancellation of the mortgage. But where the by-laws provided that on payment of an amount equal to the sum advanced, with interest and other charges, the mortgage should be released, and the mortgagor should should "at once cease to be a member," he was not liable to contribute as his memebrship was terminated.[2]

When there is a loss, it is deducted from the profits, and the effect is to postpone the maturity of the shares, and therefore the payment of the debt. But, suppose the loss exceeds the profit fund, and there is immediate necessity to extinguish the claim against the society, the next resort is to the assets. Building associations, legally speaking, seldom have available assets of any consideration, since mortgage debts are not regarded as such, as they are only a source of revenue which constitutes what little available assets they may have.[3] An assessment on the stock then becomes necessary, and questions may arise as to whether or not the mortgage secures such assessment. If the mortgage contemplates securing such assessment then it is an essential part of the indebtedness. If it is not provided for by that instrument, it is hard to see why the borrower should be discriminated against, by requiring the mortgage given by him to secure a loan, should also hold his property for an assessment, when the investor escapes with only a personal liability. The logical rule would seem to be, in the absence of a mortgage contract, the borrower and

---

[1] Everman v. Schmitt. 24 Bull. 56; Sparrow v. Farmer, 26 Beav. 511; Farmer v. Smith, 4 H. & N. 196; Handley v. Farmer, 19 Beav. 362; [2] In re Doncaster, etc., Society, L. R., 3 Eq. 158.

[3] Lister v. Log Cabin, etc., Association, 38 Md. 115

[4] McGrath v. Hamilton, etc., Association, 44 Pa. St. 383.

investor are precisely in the same situation and are personally liable for losses up to the par value of the stock held by them. Each has subscribed for stock in the corporation upon which each is indebted. The investor is paying his with the intention of securing a lump sum as the result of his savings; the borrower is maturing his stock for the further expectation of cancelling a debt. Both have contracted with the association to make an indefinite number of payments until the stock is fully paid up. So, by their contracts, they are debtors until that time is reached and the measure of their liability is the amount of their stock subscription.[1] The fact that one is a borrower, cannot change this liability. This liability would be enforceable in favor of creditors upon insolvency, as in ordinary corporations; but the liability may be usually terminated under the statute by notice of withdrawal, providing the stockholder is not in arrears to the association, does not owe it or there are no losses.

Sec. 43. **Acknowledgment of Mortgage.** The borrowing member must, of course, give some evidence of his indebtedness to the society and this generally takes the form of a bond or note comprehending his contract. This follows the certification of the title by the attorney of the society. To secure payment of the bond or note, the mortgage is given, but the contracts are separate.

Upon signing the mortgage, it should be acknowledged by the mortgagors before a competent officer, usually a notary public. An acknowledgment is an authentication of an instrument that enables it to be used for purposes of evidence in a manner different from what it could have been previously. The duties of an officer taking an acknowledgment seem to be at the same time judicial and ministerial. Judicial in that the officer has to determine upon the identity of the parties etc., and ministerial in that he has to give a certificate of the facts found. Regarding his duties as judicial, no officer may take an acknowledgment of a deed in which he is interested,

[1] State, etc., Association v. Kellogg, 63 Mo. 540.

for no one may be a judge in his own case; besides it would be an attempt to create evidence in one's favor, an attempt, too, which must in the majority of cases, be altogether unavailing.    It has even been held, a notary public who is a stockholder in a bank, cannot protest a note.[1]

The general rule seems to be when a notary is a party in interest, he is disqualified to take the acknowledgement.[2] However, an inferior court in Ohio has held the secretary of an association who was a stockholder, may take the acknowledgement of parties to a mortgage.[3]  The taking of the acknowledgment by an officer of the association is, to say the least, improper, and in view of the conflicting authorities, it is wiser to have work of that character performed by persons not having connection with the association, as stockholders or officers.    Upon the execution of the mortgage, it should be registered in the proper office to give notice of the association's claim as to all persons dealing with the mortgaged property.

Sec. 44.   **Leases by the Association.**   The officers of the association in loaning money sometimes realize that the margin is close for security and deeds are taken and leases given for a rental equal to the dues, premium and interest, so as to vest the title in the association, and avoid, in case of default, expensive foreclosure and delay in perfecting title and recovering the money invested.   It should be borne in mind, that every conveyance of land without regard to its form, which is, in fact, a security for an antecedent debt, or for a contemporaneous loan in the contemplation of a court of equity, is a loan.[4]   In considering such a transaction, the important inquiry with a court is, was the form of contract adopted intended to secure the payment of money loaned or advanced? And that inquiry is to be determined by considering the contract, the relations of the parties, and all the attending circum-

[1]Bank v. Porter, 2 Watts, 141; Withers v. Baird, 32 Am. Dec. 754, note.

[2]Wilkowski v. Halle, 95 Am. Dec. 374, note.

[3]Horton v. Building Association, 6 Bull 141.

[4]Bryant v. Cowart, 21 Ala. 92; Hughes v. Edwards, 9 Wheat. 489.

stances.  Where the circumstances show that the parties
contemplated and intended no more than security to the association for the money loaned or advanced, and that being the
intention, they stand in relation of mortgagor and mortgagee.[1]
So, where a building association having power to loan money
to its stockholders, and also to purchase and lease property to
them, advanced money to one of its stock-holders, or at his
instance, in the purchase of a house and lot, taking the title to
itself. and leasing it to him at a stipulated annual rent, payable
monthly, and the association covenanted to keep the premises
insured to the amount of money advanced, and in case of a loss,
to apply the proceeds of insurance to re-building or repairing,
for the benefit of the stockholder, who covenanted to pay taxes
and repairs; and the stock-holder was to be entitled to a conveyance in fee, during the continuance of the lease, on making
payment of the money advanced, the contract was held to be
a mortgage.[2]

Sec. 45.  **Satisfaction of Mortgage.**  Upon the payment of the mortgage, either by money or maturity of the
stock, the association should enter satisfaction of the mortgage
upon the proper records.[3]

Sec. 46.  **Borrower Entitled to Set-Off.**  A borrower
may not only settle his debt by his stock, or actual money, but
he is entitled, as an ordinary debtor, to pay it all, or any part, by
set-off.  A shareholder who had made a mortgage to the association can set off, or have applied, as against the amount due
from him to the association, under the mortgage, claims held by
him, these claims consisting of balances due from the association to members, who had withdrawn from the association and
assigned them to the mortgagor; and there being nothing in
the constitution or by-laws of the association which made it
inequitable to allow the set-off or application, having regard

[1]Mobile, etc., Association v. Robertson, 65 Ala. 389.

[2]Ib.

[3]And the borrower when sued
upon his mortgage, may show that
a proper application of the profits
would mature the stock and leave
his mortgage satisfied: Tyrrell. etc.,
Association v. Haley, 139 Pa. St.
476. He may set up the maturity of
the stock as an equitable defense to
the suit on his mortgage:  Ib.

to the rights of others;[1] but he cannot set off stock assigned
to him after maturity of his loan.[2] And he cannot prove as
a set off, loss suffered by him by reason of suspension of business by the association.[3]

SEC. 47.  **Amount Payable Upon Foreclosure.**
Whenever a mortgage is foreclosed, the amount payable
by the mortgagor is a question upon which there has been
a wide divergence of opinion. The peculiar character of
the mortgage, calling as it does for an indefinite number of
small payments, for an uncertain time, is likely to cause per-
plexity in establishing a just computation of the amount recoverable in a foreclosure suit, when partial payments have
been made on the borrower's stock.

The manner of estimating the amount recoverable against a
defaulting borrower, may be statutory, or provided for in the
by-laws; in either case, the manner designated must be followed.[4] In the absence of any method being provided by the association, some courts have adopted a rule requiring the probable or possible duration of the society, to be approximated by
proof, and the aggregate of all the subscriptions stipulated for
in the mortgage, to be calculated as they would accrue during
that period; to this sum must be added the arrearages and
fines standing against the mortgagor, and the whole amount
thus found is what the association is entitled to recover; rebating, however, a just sum for interest on the future payments, so that the association will not recover interest on
the loan after it has been repaid to it.[5]

[1]Hennighausen v. Tisher, 50 Md.
583.

[2]Building Association v. Rood, 2
Kulp. 246.

[3]Johnston v. Building Association,
104 Pa. St 394.

[4]Heckelnkaemper v. German, etc.,
Association, 22 Kan. 549.

[5]Robertson v. American, etc., Association, 10 M I 397; McCahan v.
Columbian, etc., Association, 40 Md.
226; Allemania, etc., Association v.

Mueller, 8 Bull. 97; Hagerman v.
Ohio, etc., Association, 25 Ohio
State, 189; Windisch v Korman, 5
Bull. 864; Cincinnati, etc., Association v. Flach,1Cin. S. C. R. 468; Hoboken, etc., Association v. Martin,
2 Beas (N J) 427; Central, etc ,Asso-
ciation v. O'Connor, 5 Bull 853; Fox
v. Cottage, etc.. Association 81 Va.
677; and see Building Association v.
Leyden, 1 Bull. 126; Building Association v. Eggen, 5 Bull. 752. In the

Sec. 48. **The English Rule.** The rule adopted in England, is, that unless the rules provide otherwise the member can only redeem upon the terms of paying all the subscriptions hereafter to become due, taking into account the longest possible estimated duration of the society; such subscriptions to be taken to be a debt presently due from him;[*] adding fines, arrearages, and assessments, if there be any, and taking into account the dues paid by him.[2] It will be noticed that the rule of the American courts is substantially the one supported by the English courts, basing the calculation upon the "possible duration" of the society, modifying it, however, by rebating interest on the future payments.

Sec. 49. **Rules Laid Down Upon Voluntary Repayment.** The statute usually provides for, and it is generally considered, a right of a borrower to repay his loan. The society has loaned its funds to him, with the expectation that he will keep them until the maturity of the stock, but the statute, by its liberal interposition, gives him the right to repay his debt, just as he may terminate his membership, yet seldom has the legislature defined the method of computing the amount to be repaid by him. That has been left to the associations, and in the absence of a definition by them, the courts adopting the rule of "possible duration," have said that where such member is not a defaulter, charged with violating the association's rules, but is exercising a right-vested in him, he is entitled to more consideration than if he had been sued, and to his dues, considered as credits on his debt, a certain proportion of the profits, by way of interest, should be added.[3] And they make the calculation upon voluntary re-

---

last case it was held that a defeasance clause in the mortgage, providing in the event of foreclosure the amount due shall be ascertained by taking the whole amount of the loan, and deducting credits paid in, is void, as depriving the member of the benefits he is entitled to as a member.

[1] Davis Building Society, p. 293.

[2] Mosley v. Baker, 12 Jur. 551; Seagrave v. Pope, 22 L. J., Ch. 258; Fleming v. Self, 24 L. T. Rep. 101; Archer v. Harrison, 3 Jur. N. S. 194; Smith v. Pilkington, 4 Jur. N. S. 58; Farmer v. Smith, 4 H. & N. 196. These are the leading English cases on the subject.

[3] See authorities, *supra* and p. 95, *post.*

payment upon the same theory, adding, however, the same interest on the stock payments, as the non-borrower receives upon withdrawal. These rules underlie the American cases, where the statute or by-laws do not clearly define the manner of calculating the amount of repayment, but they may be, and should be, superseded by by-law provisions for a method.[1]

**Sec. 50. Uncertainty of the Foregoing Rules.** The English rule of estimating the amount due upon voluntary repayment, and upon default by "probable duration," is followed in those jurisdictions which regard the transaction as an advancement on the shares and redemption of those shares. But it seems by retaining the proposition that the transaction is merely a loan, and it certainly defines itself very clearly as such, that the rule of the English courts, or as modified by the American courts, cannot fitly be invoked. In computing the amount to be paid upon voluntary repayment, and upon default, an important distinction, suggested by the different situations of the members, should be observed; but in either case it is of but little effect on the computation, how long the society will possibly run. The fact is fixed and certain, that the member obtained a certain sum; another fact is equally as demonstrable, that he has paid a certain amount on his stock. If he is in default the society may foreclose, and, at his instance, it is bound to apply the value of the pledged stock, measured by the dues paid, on its debt. If he is not in

[1] Hoboken, etc., Association v. Martin, 2 Beas. 427; Somerset Co. etc., Association v. Vandevere, 3 Stock, 382; Citizens', etc., Association v. Webster, 25 Barb. 263; City, etc., Company v. Fatty, 1 Abb. App. Dec. 347; Shannon v. Howard, etc., Association, 36 Md. 383; Lister v. Log Cabin, etc., Association, 38 Md. 115; Robertson v. American, etc., Association, 10 Md. 397; McCahan v. Columbian, etc., Association, 40 Md. 226; Hagerman v. Ohio, etc., Association, 25 Ohio St. 186; Risk v. Delphos, etc., Association, 31 Ohio. St. 517; Richards v. Bibb Co., etc., Association, 24 Ga. 198; Ocmulgee, etc, Association v. Thomson, 52 Ga. 427; Winchester, etc. Association v. Gilbert, 23 Grat. 787; Waverly, etc., Association v. Buck, 64 Md. 338; but see Overby v. Fayetteville, etc., Association, 81 N. C. 56; Hoskins v. Mechanics', etc., Association, 84 N. C. 838; Hekelnkaemper, v. German, etc., Association, 22 Kans. 549; Glynn v. Home, etc., Association, 22 Kans. 746; Watkins v. Workingmen's, etc., Association, 97 Pa. St. 514.

default, the value of his stock, on the basis of its withdrawal value, should be credited on the debt. The debt and credits are certain in figures and enforceable in law. Then, it seems to us, that a rule so complex in its practical application, and including a great element of uncertainty in estimating probable duration, is likely to miscarry justice, and especially is this true where interest is charged to the estimated end. The duration depends upon several conditions, none of which can with any certainty be foretold. For instance, if there is an accumulation of idle money, a financial stringency or loss, the maturity of the shares is postponed. The prosperity may be unbroken, and earlier maturity reached. No proof *in praesenti* can surely establish an intangible matter absolutely *in futuro*, and no one can say how much will be required by dues, to mature shares, unless the margin of profits is excluded. If that margin is excluded, and interest is rebated for the probable duration, under the American modifications of the English rule, it is simply repaying the loan, and the transaction would be simplified by so terming it.

The rule as applied to the repaying or defaulting borrower lacks certainty, and therefore may be productive of injustice.

SEC. 51. **The Natural and Logical Rule.** The advancement of money on the shares is simplified, in considering its legal aspect, by regarding it as a loan. The rules governing repayment follow naturally and logically.

The incorporating statute usually permits the borrower to withdraw, upon repayment of the debt, prescribing the basis of withdrawal, but if it is silent, the by-laws should provide for a withdrawal value to be credited on the debt.[1] If the statute is silent on the subject, the by-laws should provide for the computation of the amount to be paid by the defaulting or repaying borrower. The association, granting that the right of repayment to the borrower is just, must, however, protect itself. If, upon the exercise of a withdrawal right, the member is returned his dues, with in-

[1] Borden State, etc., Association v. Hayes, 61 Md. 597.

terest, there is no reason for any discrimination against the repaying borrower, and he should be given interest on repayment; but if the society is likely to suffer loss by an inability to reloan the money paid back, it should protect itself by by-law, requiring the payment of such additional interest as will cover the time the money remains unloaned. If the borrower is in default, having violated the rules, he has forfeited his right to any interest profit,[1] but he has not thereby forfeited his stock[2], and he can apply that as a credit if he chooses. The transaction thus readily resolves itself into a loan, and the association is entitled to recover the balance with any fines and proper charges.[3] The association, then, can make an equitable settlement with the defaulting borrower, by recovering the amount of his loan, with all arrearages and fines, crediting, however, the stock payments; and if the member voluntarily repays his loan, the association may credit on his debt the withdrawal value of his shares, if the member so elects, and desires to withdraw his membership. If the statute provides for voluntary repayment at the option of the borrower, the association could not impose any conditions upon the repayment, as the charging of interest for the time, sufficient to reloan the money, except on the ground that the regulation is exercised as a reasonable one. If repayment is granted by the association, without statutory compulsion, additional interest may be added without question, to protect it from any loss.

If interest or premium is deducted from the loan, there should be a rebate from the whole amount so deducted, as the unexpired time bears to the past time.

This rule avoids intricate calculation, and places the members upon a certain and just footing.

[1] Watkins v. Workingmens', etc., Association, 97 Pa. St. 514; Matterson v. Elderfield, 4 L. R. Ch. 207; but, see, Building Association v. Eggen, 5 Bull. 752.

[2] Unless there is a forfeiture allowed by statute and it must then be so declared by the Association: Watkins v. Workingmens', etc., As-

sociation, *supra*. So it may bo waived by implication: North America, etc., Association v. Sutton, 35 Pa. St. 463.

[3] Hanner v. Greensboro, etc., Association, 78 N. C. 188.

7

Of course, if the statute provides for a method of computation, that course must be pursued. These suggestions are only available in case no other method is pointed out.

It has been assumed that a borrower is entitled to share in the profits of the association as well as the investor. It is only in those jurisdictions where the transaction is regarded as a redemption of the shares, that it is held that he is not entitled to share in the earnings, while the better weight of authority is to regard it as a loan, and both kinds of members stand so far on the same footing.*

SEC. 52. **By-Laws Should Provide for Record Cancellation.** The by-laws should prescribe the manner of making record cancellations, and vest that authority in an officer, usually the president. Unless the assent of the association is acquired in some such way, it is not bound by the cancellation.* If the satisfaction is fraudulently procured, as where the secretary falsely reported the maturity of the shares, and upon such information the board of directors directed satisfaction to be entered, a court of equity will strike off the entry.* If the borrower voluntarily pays in, to get a release of the mortgage, more money than is required by the by-laws, if he knew all the facts, but was mistaken in his legal rights, he cannot recover it back.*

[1]Overby v. Fayetteville, etc., Association, 81 N. C 56; Winchester, etc., Association v. Gilbert. 23 Grat. 787; Cason v. Seldner, 77 Va. 293.

[2]Winterer v. Building Association, 44 L. I. 122; People v. Lowe, 117 N. Y. 175; Seibel v. Building Association, 43 Ohio St. 371.

[3]Baxter v. McIntire, 13 Gray, 168.
[4]Callahan's Appeal, 124 Pa. St. 138.
[5]Haigh v. United States, etc., Association, 19 W. Va. 792.

# CHAPTER IX.

## FINES.

SECTION 1. Necessity of Fines.

SECTION 2. Must be Reasonable.

SECTION 3. Stop after Foreclosure.

SECTION 4. No Interest on Fines.

SECTION 5. Are Lien on Stock.

SECTION 1. **Necessity of Fines.** Fines are necessarily a part of the plan of an association. The carrying forward of its purposes, conceived of strict mutuality, requires of each member punctuality. Upon that, largely depends the success of the association. If a member neglects his payments, he does an injury to the other members, who are faithfully observing their obligations; it therefore becomes necessary to compensate those injuries by compelling the delinquent to pay a small additional sum each week for the profit of the association. This is, in principle, liquidated damages, and takes the form of fines. Or, if an officer fails to do his duty, a penalty by the way of fines might be assessed against him, if provided for in the by-laws. So while the statute generally authorizes their charge, yet it has been held that fines slightly in excess of the real damages, are recoverable as stipulated damages.[1]

---

[1] Shannon v. Howard, etc., Association, 36 Md. 383; Ocmulgee, etc., Association v. Thomson, 52 Ga. 427. The fine in this case was 10 per cent. on the dollar; and see Lynn v. Association, 117 Pa. St., 1 where it was held that such a fine was unreasonable, and the by-law providing therefor was void.

99

In some other courts it is held that where statutory authority is wanting, they cannot be enforced.[1]

SEC. 2. **Must be Reasonable.** Fines should be assessed in the exercise of statutory power, and must be reasonable.[2] They may, however, be assessed upon the theory of stipulated damages, in the absence of a statute. If they are oppressive and extortionate, the association is hurt as well as the delinquent member. If based on the real damage, or slightly in excess of it, to the association, justice is well measured to all concerned.[3] They can be imposed only by way of punishment, for some delinquency in the performance of a duty, which the member may owe to the corporation by reason of his membership. It is unreasonable to assess more than one fine for the same delinquency; that is, dues payable on June 16, cannot on June 23, be fined for again.[4] Under a power to fine for non payment of dues, fines cannot be charged on delinquent interest;[5] the authority to assess fines for unpaid interest must appear from the by-laws, where the statute does not limit their imposition to dues, and they then may be enforced.[6]

A by-law, which imposes a fine of ten cents monthly, on each dollar due, has been held to be unreasonable, extortionate and oppressive, and therefore void,[7] but a fine of ten cents on each $200, where power is given to impose fines of limited amount, is valid.[8] A fine of five per cent of the total amount

---

[1]Lincoln, etc., Association v. Graham, 7 Neb. 173; Link v. Germantown, etc , Association, 89 Pa. St. 15.

[2]Lynn v. Freemansburg, etc., Association, 117 Pa. St. 1.

[3]Hagerman v. Ohio, etc., Association, 25 Ohio St. 186; Forrest City, etc , Association, v. Gallagher, 25 Ohio St. 208; Building Association v. Schuller, 3 W. N. C. 431; Pfeister v. Wheeling, etc., Association, 19 W. Va. 676.

[4]Hagerman v. Ohio, etc., Association, supra; Forrest City, etc., Association v. Gallagher, supra; McGannon v. Central, etc., Association,

19 W. Va. 726; Monumental, etc., Society v. Lewin, 88 Md 445; see, also, Gouchenour v. Sullivan, etc., Association, 119 Ind. 441.

[5]Parker v. United States, etc., Association, 19 Va. 744; Shannon v. Howard, etc., Association, 36 Md. 383; Clarksville, etc., Association v. Stephens, 26 N. J. Eq. 351.

[6]Parker v. Butcher, L. R., 3 Eq., 762.

[7]Lynn v. Freemansburgh, etc. Association, supra.

[8]Clarksville, etc., Association v. Stephens, supra.

in arrear, was held not unreasonable, and that it included five per cent on the amount of previous fines and other payments, as well as the principal and interest, in arrears, does not make it unreasonable.[1] Fines can only be collected from members.[2] The mortgage may embrace lawful fines, and they may be charged against the land,[3] if they are not included in the mortgage, it will not be considered as security for their payment.[4]

SEC. 3. **Stop After Foreclosure.** When fines are secured by the mortgage, of a borrowing member, after assignment as collateral security for the mortgage money, they do not cease on filing of a bill to foreclose the mortgage, to which the stock is collateral,[5] but after decree of foreclosure, the association cannot assess fines.[6]

SEC. 4. **No Interest on Fines.** The fines should be regulated by the by-laws, which should be explicit and certain on the subject. Interest cannot be charged on fines,[7] but after decree for foreclosure, they become a part of the principal and bear interest.[8]

SEC. 5. **Are Lien on Stock.** The association holds a lien on the stock of a member, for the payment of the fines legally assessed, and he cannot withdraw or apply his stock in cancellation of his debt, until that lien is satisfied, or cannot sell his stock free from the lien.

[1]*In re* Middlesbrough, etc., Society, 54 L. J. Ch. 592.

[2]Hagerman v. Ohio, etc., Association 25 Ohio St. 186; Forrest City, etc., Association, v. Gallagher, 25 Ohio St. 208.

[3]Hagerman v. Ohio, etc., Association, *supra*.

[4]Building Association v. Groesbeck, 4 L. I. (Pa.) 16.

[5]Union, etc., Association, v. Masonic Hall Association, 2 Stew. 389.

[6]Houlette's Estate, 2 Chest. 511.

[7]Ingoldby v. Riley, 28 L.T. N.S. 55.

[8]Provident, etc., Society v. Greenhill, L. R., 9 Ch. D. 122.

# CHAPTER X.

## USURY.

SECTION 1. Definition.

SECTION 2. Premium not Usurious as formerly.

SECTION 3. Premiums Authorized by Statute.

SECTION 4. When Interest is not Usurious.

SECTION 5. Illegal Interest not Recoverable by Association.

SECTION 6. May be Recovered Back by the Borrower.

SECTION 7. A Personal Defense.

SECTION 8. Rule for Officers.

SECTION 1. **Definition.** The mortgage, bond or note of the association to be valid must be free from the taint of usury. Usury is defined as the taking of more for the use of money than the law allows, or the extortion of a sum beyond what is legal.[1]

SEC. 2. **Premium Not Usurious as Formerly.** The question of usury is not involved in the transactions of associations so much now as formerly. In the earlier associations, the legislature was unwilling to grant the privilege of adding a premium charge, thus increasing the cost of money beyond the legal rate. The usury question, in the reported cases, in nearly each instance, arose in the endeavor of the association to make a charge for preference to the right in having a loan. It was held that usury cannot be avoided by complicated transactions.[2] So a combination of interest and expenses at a

[1]Tyler Usury, p. 35; see Association v. Bollinger, 12 Rich. Eq. 124.

[2]Martin v. Nashville, etc., Association, 2 Cold. 418.

102

higher than a legal rate is tainted with usury;[1] if the borrower pays more than the legal rate by arrangement, no matter what its form is, it is usury,[2] but it is not every transaction increasing

[1]Waverly, etc., Association v. Buck, 64 Md. 338. Expenses of loan do not effect the transaction as usurious: Hoboken, etc., Association v. Martin, 2 Peas. 427.

[2]Williar v. Baltimore etc., Association, 45 Md. 546; Bates v. Peoples, etc., Association, 42 Ohio St. 655; Association v. Bollinger, *supra;* Lincoln, etc., Association v Graham, 7 Neb., 173; Mills v. Salisbury, etc., Association, 75 N. C. 292; Melville v. American, etc., Association, 33 Barb. 103; Thompson v. Gillison, 28 S. C. 534. But, see Delano v. Wild, 6 Allen 1; Bowker v. Mill River, etc., Association, 7 Allen, 100; however, it was held in a North Carolina case that a borrowing member paying usury, would not be aided, being considered in *pari delicto:* Latham v. Washington, etc., Association, 77 N. C. 145; but this doctrine is generally denied. In order to sustain the premium charge not authorized by statute, the English courts considered associations as partnership arrangements and such charge not to be within the usury laws: Silver v. Barnes, 6 Bing. N. C. 180; Burbidge v. Cotton, 8 E. L. & E 57; see, also, Shannon v. Dunn, 43 N. H. 194; Montgomery etc., Association v. Robinson, 69 Ala. 413; Franklin etc., Association, v. Marsh, 29 N. J. L. 225; Concordia, etc., Association v. Read, 93 N. Y. 474; Merrill v. McIntire, 13 Gray, 157; St. Louis, etc., Association v. Augustin, 2 Mo. App. 123; Contra, Reiser v. Wm. Tell, etc., Association v. 39 Pa. St. 137; Mechanic's

etc., Association v. Wilcox, 24 Conn. 147; Baltimore, etc., Society, v. Taylor, 41 Md; Mills v. Salisbury, etc., Association, *supra;* Forrest City, etc., Association v. Gallagher, 25 Ohio St., 208. In Parker v. Fulton, etc., Association 46 Ga. 166, it was held as the scheme involved risk of losing the whole or getting less than the legal rate of interest, there was no usury. See, also, Bibb Co., etc., Association v. Richards, 21 Ga. 592. As the statutes generally authorize the fixing of premium charges, they are taken out of the usury laws and the principles laid down in the above cases have no application. Premiums when authorized by statute are held lawful and recoverable: Jarrett v. Cope, 68 Pa. St. 67; Franklin, etc., Association v. Marsh, *supra;* Hoboken, etc., Association v. Martin, *supra;* Red Bank, etc., Association v. Patterson, 12 C. E. Green, 223; Citizens', etc., Association v. Webster, 25 Barb. 263; West Winsted, etc., Association v. Ford, 27 Conn. 282; Licking Co., etc., Association v. Bebout, 29 Ohio St. 252; Robertson v. American, etc., Association, 10 Md. 397; Bowker v. Mill River, etc., Association, *supra;* Shannon v. Dunn, *supra;* Massey v. Citizens, etc., Association, 22; Kans. 624; McLaughlin v. Citizens Association, 62 Ind 264; Shaffrey v. Workingmen's, etc., Association, 64 Ind. 600; White v. Mechanics, etc., Association, 22 Grat. 233. If there were any precedent conditions to a recovery, as that the borthe cost of money that will involve usury; so, where there was an agreement that retiring members of a building association may take out the money they had paid in, and interest thereon, at a certain rate above the legal rate, it was held that it is not open to the objection of usury. Such addition is not interest on money loaned, but an adjudged profit on the money put in.[1]

Sec. 3. **Premiums Authorized by Statute.** The statutes in nearly all the states, now exempt building associations from usury in charging premium, so that when the cost of the money by the addition of the premium to the interest is increased beyond the legal rate, there is no usury, but this privilege extends only to premiums, and the association has no authority to increase, by any device or system, the distinctively interest charge on the loan, beyond that fixed by statute as the lawful rate. The legislative intention in allowing premiums, was to confer on the association an equitable and profitable method of selecting its borrowers, by requiring of them a bonus. So if the association disregards this intention, and by any form increases the interest, the courts promptly restrain any such practice, and compel it to refund any such over charges.

Sec. 4. **When Interest is not Usurious.** Interest at the lawful rate may be charged on the principal of the loan, without regard to the weekly or monthly reductions,[2] and because the interest is payable monthly or weekly, does not render it usurious.[3] Interest should be on the sum advanced and not upon the par value, where the premium is deducted,[4] as

rower should sign an agreement, it must have been complied with before there can be a recovery: Building Association v. Lyons: 2 Kulp. 409. See Nicely's Estate, 3 Kulp, 47.

[1] Jungkuntz v. Building Association, 6 Bull. 428.

[2] City, etc., Company v. Fatty, 1 Abb. Ct. App. 347.

[3] Red Bank, etc., Association v. Patterson, 12 C. E. Green, 223.

[4] Baltimore, etc., Society v. Taylor, 41 Md. 409; Oak Cottage, etc., Association v. Eastman, 31 Md. 556; Contra: Citizens', etc., Association v. Webster, 25 Barb. 263.

it is unlawful to charge interest upon premiums unless permitted by statute.[1]

**Sec. 5. Illegal Interest not Recoverable by the Association.** Mortgagors are only liable for the true amount due on the mortgage, excluding all excessive interest exacted or paid in the shape of bonus or otherwise.[2] A loan to a person not a member, at a premium, in addition to interest, is usurious,[3] as the legislative privilege is intended to apply to the members only. A borrower paying legal interest and dues, cannot claim usury, because he did not receive his entire loan, but which was ready for him at all times.[4]

**Sec. 6. May be Recovered Back by the Borrower.** If usurious interest is refunded and accepted under an agreement that only legal interest shall thereafter be collected, it frees the note from the taint of usury.[5] Usurious interest paid may be recovered back, not being considered voluntary.[6] The measure of damages depends upon the statutes of the different states; in some, it would be the difference between the debt, with legal interest added, and the amount of payments made thereon, computed as partial payments on such debt,[7]

**Sec. 7. A Personal Defense.** Usury is generally considered a personal defense and the purchaser of mortgaged

[1]Hawkeye, etc., Association v. Blackburn, 48 Iowa, 385; Oak Cottage, etc., Association v. Eastman, 31 Md., 556; Jackson v. Cassidy, 68 Tex. 282; Watson v. Aiken, 55 Tex. 536; Forrest City, etc., Association v. Gallagher, 25 Ohio St. 208. Authorized in Pennsylvania; Association v. Neurath, 2 W. N. C. 95; Association v. George, 3 Ib. 239; Selden v. Reliable, etc., Association, 32 P. F. Smith, 346.

[2]Birmingham v. Maryland, etc., Association, 45 Md. 541.

[3]Mechanics, etc., Association v. Meriden Company, 24 Conn. 159; Joseph, etc., Association v. Thompson, 19 Kans. 321; Vermont, etc.,

Company v. Whithed, 49 N. W. Rep. 318.

[4]Hammerslough v. Kansas City, etc., Association, 79 Mo. 80.

[5]Phillips v. Columbia City, etc., Association, 53 Iowa, 719.

[6]Border State, etc., Association v. Hilleary, 68 Md. 52; Williar v. Baltimore, etc., Association, 45 Md. 546; Bexar, etc., Association v. Robinson, 78 Tex 163; Philanthrophic, etc., Association v. Mc. Knight, 35 Pa. St. 470; Skinner's Estate, 4 Phila. 189.

[7]Bexar, etc., Association v. Robinson, supra.

property, assuming the mortgage debt, cannot set it up in an action to foreclose the mortgage.[1]

SEC. 8. **Rules for Officers.** The officers of the association should be governed in fixing the interest charges on loans by the statute. If premium is authorized, there is no question that such authority takes its charge out of the usury statute. If not authorized, the officers should safely confine the interest rates within those allowed by law.

[1]People's, etc., Bank v. Collins, 27 Conn. 142; Stein v. Indianapolis, etc., Association, 18 Ind. 237.

[2]In Kentucky, no more than statutory interest is allowed, and the charging of more invalidated the contract. Herbert v. Kenton, etc., Association, 11 Bush. 296; Grodon, v. Winchester, etc., Association, 12 Bush 110; Henderson, etc., Association v. Johnson, 88 Ky. 191; see, also Hawkeye, etc., Association v. Blackburn, 48 Iowa, 385; Burlington, etc., Association v. Heider, 55 Iowa, 424; Baltimore, etc., Society v. Taylor, 41 Md. 409; Lucas v. Greenville, etc., Association, 22 Ohio St. 339.

# CHAPTER XI.

## POWER OF THE ASSOCIATION TO BORROW MONEY.

SECTION 1.  A Practical Aspect.

SECTION 2.  English Authorities.

SECTION 3.  American Authorities.

SECTION 4.  Weight of American Authorities.

SECTION 5.  Implied Power to Borrow.

SECTION 6.  Overdrawing Bank Account is Borrowing.

SECTION 7.  Resolution to Borrow.

SECTION 8.  The Effect of Assigning Mortgages.

SECTION 9.  No Power to Sell its Mortgages.

SECTION 1.  **A Practical Aspect.**  In the course of its business, an association will often find itself short of money to supply the demands made upon it.  The applications of borrowers exceed the receipts, both temporary and for some time prospective; or a series should be paid off, or some portion of the stock has matured and should be cancelled. In the building season, the association finds itself financially cramped.  This stringency may be temporary, as in the winter season, money will naturally accumulate.  With these conditions confronting it, should the association borrow money to relieve its embarrassment ?  The original idea was, strictly, that of enforced accumulations of members as the source of revenue.  Borrowers were not so numerous, and were educated to wait, until the loan fund thus created was sufficient to satisfy each member, in the order of pri-

107

ority. But the latter day association, with us, having an enlarged membership, and fluctuating demands, which are at
times beyond its funds, is differently situated. The association should have money to meet these demands. Very often
the member has joined to secure a loan. Some provision
must be made to suppress the discontent of disappointed members. The association is thus threated with a crippling of its
membership and diminution of its profits. An association
surrounded by these conditions, unless prohibited by statute,
may borrow money for the purpose of relieving them. It
may be considered as necessary to accomplish the purposes of
the association, but this disposition to borrow must not conflict with the legislative intention in incorporating the association, and it becomes important to discover that intention.
The legislature rarely defines that right to borrow, as it is
considered incidental to ordinary corporations, and its exercise
is left to the control of the courts. But a building association
is not an ordinary corporation; in fact, it exercises some extraordinary privileges, particularly in not being amenable to
the usury laws. It is created for the declared purposes of accumulating money, and lending the accumulations to its members to build or acquire homes for themselves. The legislature
devised this plan of co-operative accumulations for the purpose of assisting each member to become his own landlord.
The state has a selfish motive in the promotion of a building
association, as through its workings, it is planting deeply the
roots of citizenship. The drifting, thriftless classes are offered
a school of economy, and the earnest and economical classes
are given an opportunity. There is, then, a formation of a
steady, energetic and accumulating citizen. The cares of the
state are lessened by decreasing poverty, and its prosperity is
increased by growing material wealth. We may clearly conceive, then, that the intention of the legislature in the creation
of building associations is, first, to encourage savings; second,
to secure homes for the savers. The accomplishment of these
objects may be dependent, partly, upon the ability to borrow.
Such an assumption is not an undue one, or foreign to the
legislative conception of the association. By its silence, the

creative power left the association with the limited right to
borrow as its legitimate necessities might require. This proposition is sustained by the weight of authority.

SEC. 2. **English Authorities.** In England, the question was frequently before the courts prior to the act of parliament of 1874. Borrowing to a limited extent was held
valid,[1] but when there was no rule of the association authorizing borrowing, it was held illegal to borrow, and a person who
had advanced money to the trustees of a society under such
circumstances, was held not to be a creditor, legal or equitable,
of the society, and, therefore, not entitled to a winding up
order;[2] and if the rule did not fix a limit of the amount to be
borrowed, it was held illegal.[3] So a rule authorizing unlimited borrowing was held *ultra vires.*[4] Where the limit was
exceeded, and the society derived no benefit from the loan, it
was held that it was not liable, but that the directors were
personally liable, as they had held out the treasurer as the
agent of the society, although there was no fraud on their
part.[5]

Where there was a rule authorizing the borrowing of money
for the special purpose of making advances to members who
might have applied for them, and the society having borrowed
a sum of money not actually required, to meet applications at
the time of the loan, it was held that the society had no power
to take the loan.[6] And where the rules authorized the trustee
to borrow money, and spend it in a way that was held not to
be for the legitimate purposes of the society, payment was not
allowed to be enforced against the society.[7] Where there was
no rule authorizing borrowing, there was no power, but money
advanced by a bank which was the depository of the society,

[1] Laing v. Reed, L. R. 5 Ch. App. 4.

[2] *In re* National, etc., Society, ex parte, Williamson, L. R., 5Ch. App. 309.

[3] *In re* Victoria, etc., Society, L. R. 9 Eq. 605.

[4] *In re* Liverpool, etc., Society, 15 S. J., 177.

[5] Chapleo v. Brunswick, etc., Society, L. R., 6 Q. B. D., 696.

[6] Moye v. Sparrow, 22 L. T. Rep. N. S., 154.

[7] *In re* Durham Society, etc., Society, L.R., 12 Eq., 516.

which went to pay legal liabilities of the society, the claim
was allowed.  The rules gave the directors power to arrange
for advances and their payment.[1]  But where a lender has
deeds belonging to some of the members deposited with him,
the court refused to compel him to surrender the deeds without payment of the money for which they were held as security.[2]  Unless the rule containing the power was certified by
the registrar, a person loaning upon the faith of it could not
enforce his claim against the society.[3]

Parliament, in 1874, enacted a statute which expressly
empowers a society to borrow under prescribed limits.  Under
that act, any society may receive deposits or loans at interest
within the limits of the section, from the members or other
persons, or from corporate bodies, joint stock companies, or
from any terminating building society, to be applied to the
purposes of the society.  In a permanent society, the total
amount so received on deposit or loan, and not repaid by the
society, shall not at any time exceed two-thirds of the amount
for the time being, secured to the society by mortgages from
the members.  In a terminating society, the total amount so
received and not repaid, may either be a sum not exceeding
twelve months' subscriptions on the shares for the time being
in force.  This statute gives the society power to borrow
within the limit fixed[4] and is evidently the result of experience among English societies, that their purpose can better be
accomplished by limited authority to borrow; and it is a powerful
argument in favor of the right of a building association to borrow.  As will be observed by the decisions prior to this act, the
courts permitted them under certified rules within a reasonable
limit, to borrow, if the provisions of the rules were strictly observed, but as statutory authority more fully established the confidence of the lender in such securities, the right was incorporated in an express statute, substantially as the courts had been

[1] Liquidator of the Blackburn, etc.,
Society v. Cunliffe, 52 L. J. Rep.
Ch., 92.
[2] Wilson's case, L. R., 12 Eq. 521.

[3] Coetmor, etc., Society 51 L. T.
253.
[4] But if the limits are fixed smaller, they must be observed: Looker
v. Wrigley, L. R., 9 Q. B. D., 397.

holding during the prior half century. And it has been recently held that where a society borrowed money to an extent greater than authorized by statute, which was applied by it as advances to members, who gave the society mortgages to secure repayment of the advances, the persons from whom the society borrowed the money were entitled to follow it into the hands of the members to whom it was advanced, and claim against the mortgages held by the society for the amount secured thereby, notwithstanding the society had deducted premiums from such amounts, when making the advances to the members.[1]

When authorized to borrow, mortgages may be deposited with lenders as security, who, thereupon, are entitled in the winding up, to payment out of the assets, after satisfaction of the outside creditors, and in priority to all claims of members. But the lenders are to have the benefit equally and *pari passu* of a first charge upon the general funds and property.[2]

When the rules authorized borrowing, the lenders are entitled, on the association being wound up, to be first paid out of the assets, in priority, to any of the members.[3]

If borrowing is unauthorized, it cannot be upheld on the the ground that the directors mistook the law, but, where the money went to the legitimate purposes, the lenders could recover.[4] When the society directed the issue of paid up or deposit stock, at a fixed rate of interest, with the right of withdrawing it in preference to all other shares, it was held the stockholders were entitled to be paid before the unadvanced members.[5]

SEC. 3   **American Authorities.**   The principles underlying the English cases are recognized and affirmed in this country. The implied power to borrow, within restric-

---

[1] Neath, etc., Society v. Luce, L. R., 43 Ch. D., 158.

[2] Murray v. Scott, 9 App. Cas. 519, overruling Laing v. Reed, L. R., 5 Ch. 8.

[3] *In re* Mutual, etc., Society 30 Ch. D. 434.

[4] Blackburn, etc., Society v. Cunliffe, 29 Ch. D., 902; Owen v. Roberts, 57 L. T. N. S. 81.

[5] Murray v. Scott, *supra.*

# 112      BUILDING ASSOCIATIONS.

tions, has never been denied, except in a case in Ohio.' In
that case, the court considers that associations are not affected
by the doctrine that corporations possess the power to borrow
money which may be needed in the transaction of necessary
business, but that the money to be loaned by associations can
only be properly accumulated in the manner contemplated by
statute, that is, by dues, fines, premium and interest. In
other courts it has been held that associations have implied
power to borrow money for legitimate purposes.' So that an
association, not being prohibited, either by statute or by
by-law, from borrowing money, may, on maturity of a series
of stock, borrow money to pay the shares of the non-borrowing members of such series, instead of accumulating funds to
pay off such series.' And the association having the implied
power to borrow, has, in the absence of express prohibition,
the implied power to assign its mortgages and bonds as security for the loan.' The association would be estopped by the
receipt and application of the money to a legitimate purpose
of the corporation, from setting up in an action to recover it,
a want of power in the corporation to make the loan. The
corporation cannot reap the benefit of the money loaned, and,
then allege a want of power to make it.' The directors of the
association being, by its by-laws, empowered to manage its
affairs, the corporation cannot defeat the recovery of money
borrowed, by direction of the directors, on the ground that the
directors applied the money to an unauthorized purpose,
unless the lender knew such purpose was unauthorized.'

'State v. Building Association, 35
Ohio St. 258. The opinion in this
case is not founded upon reasoning
or authority, and absolutely ignores
the English cases. It is not entitled
to much weight as an authority.

'Davis v. West Saratoga, etc
Union, 32 Md. 285; Jones v. Building Association, 94 Pa. St.,215; Jackson v. Myers, 43 Md. 452; Muth v.
Dolfield, 43 Md. 466.

'North Hudson, etc., Association,
v. First National Bank, 47 N. W. R.
(Wis) 300.

'Ib. But an assignment of mortgages after proceedings to wind up
is void as against the receiver; Hinman v. Ryan, 3 C. C. (Ohio) 529.

'Ib; Jones v. Building Association, supra; Loan Company v. Conover, 5 Phila. 18.

'North Hudson, etc., Association
v. First National Bank, supra.

It was held in Pennsylvania that when the association is authorized by its charter to receive money on deposit from its stockholders. to bear interest, in case of insolvency, such stockholders are creditors as to their deposits, and are entitled to share *pro rata* with other outside creditors in preference to stockholders. This was also held to be true when money has been received from persons who were not stockholders, though the association had no authority to so receive the money.[1]

In another case it was held that a solvent building association may assign a mortgage in payment of, or as collateral for, a debt; and in an action on a mortgage assigned as collateral, for the payment of an order given to a member on his withdrawal, it is unnecessary to determine whether the consent of the directors to such assignment is legal under the statute, providing that at no time shall one-half of the funds in the treasury be applicable to the demands of withdrawing members without the consent of the directors.[2]

SEC. 4. **Weight of American Authority.** The unquestioned weight of authority in America, is to give building associations the incidental right to borrow. The question of the right to borrow is to be determined by enquiring into its objects and purposes. It has conferred upon it those incidental rights that are consistent and reasonably necessary to carry on its business. The vital question is: Is borrowing necessary to accomplish its objects? If it is, then upon principle and authority, it may borrow.

SEC. 5. **Implied Power to Borrow.** The current of English decisions, prior to the act of 1874, is that it has a restricted right. The American cases, excepting the Ohio case, draw the same conclusions. Those courts consider the borrowing power necessary from the nature of its business, and hold it granted by implication of law. It may be necessary to protect its interests as a junior lien holder, or to satisfy the demands of borrowers. If the association is unable to supply borrowers from its regular fund, a temporary loan will satisfy

[1] Criswell's Appeal, 100 Pa. St. 488.  [2] Queiu vs. Smith, 108 Pa. St. 325.

8

the members, and when idle money accumulates, the association can pay its debt. Borrowing is only intended as an expedient. To become a permanent borrower, is not a part of the corporate plan of an association and is not contemplated by the decisions investing the power to borrow in the association. Under proper limitation, it is sanctioned by the courts. That limitation is, that the money is to be applied to an authorized purpose, yet under the decisions, the association cannot escape its obligation to repay, because it applied the money to an unauthorized purpose, unless it can show that the lender had knowledge of this. The rights of the association to borrow is thus settled upon authority, and it rests further upon sound reasoning. It rests upon the doctrine of implied power, and there is no substantial variance between the application by the courts of that doctrine to building associations and other corporations.

Sec. 6.  **Overdrawing Bank Account is Borrowing.**  Prior to the act of Parliament of 1874, the English courts were disposed to indulge associations in overdrawing their bank accounts, by consent of the bank, without applying the rule of borrowing as limited by the courts, so they uniformly held that overdrawing is not borrowing.[1] This distinction is hardly maintainable. The association thus uses money of the bank and pays interest upon it. The relation of creditor and debtor arises and it is difficut to conceive why overdrawing would be legal, if borrowing is illegal. The truth is, if borrowing is unauthorized, such overdrawing is a mere device and is *ultra vires* and cannot be enforced.[2] So held in a recent English case, but the bank permitted the bank to hold deeds as security for money advanced to pay proper debts of the society, presumably on the ground that the society could not dispute its right to make a contract from which it had reaped benefits.[3]

---

[1] *In re* German Mining Company, 22, L. J. Ch., 956. *In re* Cein Cilcen, etc , Company, 38 L. J. Ch. 78; Waterlow v. Sharp, L. R. 8 Eq. 501, doubted in Liquidators of Blackburn, etc., Society, v. Cunliffe, 52 L J. Rep. Ch 92.

[2] Brooks v. Blackburn, etc., Society, L. R., 9 App. Cas., 857.

[3] Ib.

**Sec. 7. Resolution to Borrow.** In making loans by
the association, the directors of course are to be governed by
the creative statute. If there is no prohibition upon borrowing, the directors may borrow for the legitimate purposes of
the association. If the by-laws or rules make no provision for
borrowing, the directors at a legal meeting, with a quorum
present, should pass a resolution authorizing the loan. That
resolution may read as follows:

"Whereas the ...... Association is in need of money to
.. state object of borrowing—therefore; Be it resolved, that
the President and Secretary of this association are authorized
and empowered to borrow the sum of $.... for .... at the
rate of — per cent. per annum, and to deposit with the lender,
bonds and mortgages of the association, as collateral security
for such loan."

**Sec. 8. The Effect of Assigning Mortgages.** As
heretofore cited, the decisions both in this country and England, authorize the assignment of mortgages as collateral
security for the repayment of a loan, or even to secure a withdrawing member, who, by that act, has become a creditor.
Such assignments extend only to the association's interest in
the security. No right of the mortgagor can thereby be affected.
The security, as any other security, is not available so long as
the mortgagor complies with his contract. As he complies
with his contract, by paying his weekly dues, he is decreasing
the association's interest in the mortgage and consequently,
diminishing the security. If the mortgagor thus continues
in compliance with his contract and the association still owes
the debt, it will have to supply other mortgages as collateral,
in which its interest is large enough to be sufficient for purposes of security. And so, if the mortgagors in the collaterals
carried out their agreements, the association is bound to
mature their stock, but if their loan still remains unpaid, the
payment and cancellation of the stock cannot take place until
their debts are paid to the association. The mortgagors may,
however, pay those debts by their matured stock. They have
the right to apply their matured stock in full satisfaction of
their mortgage debts. While the loan in that event has lost

its specific security by these continued weekly mutations and the maturity of the stock, yet the assets which have come out of the mortgage into the general fund for distribution, are subject to the lien of the debt, and must satisfy it before cancellation of the members' stock can take place.

Thus, it is readily seen that the assignee of a building association mortgage can only claim the society's interest, which in in the process of time may be reduced to nothing. To make such mortgages available as collateral security, the association must replace those when its interest has become extinguished, by others where its interest is sufficient for the purposes intended.

SEC. 9  **No Power to Sell its Mortgages.**  The contract of the mortgagor being in a sense personal, and not to be defeated by any assignment by the association, it would be beyond the power of the association to sell absolutely his mortgage. So long as the association has an asset in the mortgage, it may assign it as collateral, so long as it does not conflict with its corporate objects, but it cannot infringe upon the rights of the mortgagor, and if the association undertakes to absolve itself from the contract and not only part with its interest in the mortgage, but transfer rights therein in favor of the mortgagor, and against itself, it is doing a wrong for which the injured member may obtain redress against the association, in whatever amount he has been damaged by the action of the association, in placing beyond its power its ability to keep its contract with him. The courts uphold an assignment as collateral security, upon the theory that it is only the association's interest in the mortgage that is affected. The assignee can in no way interfere with the mortgagor's interest. So that if the mortgagor defaults, he is entitled to credit the value of his stock and if he does not default he is entitled to continue his payments and cancel his mortgage,[1] disregarding the assignment, for he has extinguished the association's interest in the mortgage. The assignee's lien as against the mort-

[1] Barton v Enterprise, etc., Association, 114 Ind. 226.

gage is *eo instanti* extinguished, but it then attaches to other corporate assets.

In selling outright his mortgage, the association undertakes not only to sell its own interest, but to transfer the rights of the mortgagor. It is plain, upon principle, that it cannot do this without his consent. And, as the association is a mutual affair, it becomes a question whether or not such a sale would not require the unanimous consent of the shareholders, as all are interested in any final disposition of its assets, or any part of them.

# CHAPTER XII.

## DISSOLUTION AND SETTLEMENT.

SECTION 1. Dissolution when all stock is matured.

SECTION 2. Other methods of dissolution.

SECTION 3. What acts will not dissolve.

SECTION 4. Dissolution by unanimous agreement.

SECTION 5. Effect of appointment of a receiver.

SECTION 6. Final settlement with members and creditors.

SECTION 7. Settlement before maturity.

SECTION 8. Assignment for creditors.

SECTION 9. Appointment of receiver and winding up.

SECTION 10. Marshalling of assets.

SECTION 11. Liability of stockholders.

SECTION 12. Liability of borrower for debts.

SECTION 13. No liability for losses under the mortgage.

SECTION 14. Liability of withdrawing member.

SECTION 15. Assets to be distributed among borrowers and non-borrowers alike.

SECTION 16. Consolidation of associations.

SECTION 1. **Dissolution When all Stock is Matured.** When the association has matured all of its stock, it then dissolves. The old terminating society, with its one series, entered voluntary dissolution when it had paid off the series. Under the present systems, the serial and the permanent, there is no dissolution by the maturing of a series or part of stock. The association is constantly receiving a new infusion of blood and continues its corporate existence by reason thereof. But

118

the dissolution of the association may take place from other causes.

Sec. 2. **Other Methods of Dissolution.** The dissolution of a corporation may be brought about by reason of (a) the forfeiture of its franchises by the adjudication of a court, (b) the loss of its charter by a charter provision to the effect in case the corporation fails to do certain things within a certain time, (c), the repeal of its charter under the reserved power of the state, (d) the voluntary surrender of the franchises by the stockholders, or (e) the expiration of the time limited for its existence in the charter.[1]

Sec. 3. **What Acts will not Dissolve.** Except when the charter is lost by reason of the second provision, the corporation does not dissolve of itself. For instance, neglect to elect officers while the capacity remains in the members to elect, will not dissolve it,[2] nor by a cessation of all corporate acts and business,[3] nor by mere nonuser of its franchise, nor by insolvency,[5] nor by death of its stockholders.[6] Only the state by its proper officer can sue to forfeit the charter, and whenever it misuses its powers, the state has this right. A stockholder cannot maintain the suit.[7]

Sec. 4. **Dissolution by Unanimous Agreement.** The stockholders may, by unanimous agreement, wind up the association before the time prescribed by statute, and such agreement is binding, not only on the member, but on the assignee of such member,[8] but an agreement to suspend operations and close up the affairs of the company is not in any fair

[1] Cook Stock, etc., sec. 628.

[2] Commonwealth v. Cullen, 13 Pa. St. 13; St. Louis, etc., Association v. Augustin, 2 Mo. App. 123.

[3] Kansas City, etc., Company v. Sauer, 65 Mo., 279.

[4] Folger v. Columbian, etc., Company., 96 Am. Dec. 757, note.

[5] Valley Bank, etc., Institution v. Sewing Society, 28 Kan. 423.

[6] Boston, etc., Company v. Langdon, 24 Pick. 49.

[7] North v. State, 107 Ind. 356.

[8] Building Association vs. Kelley, 1 Kulp, 9. A majority cannot force the rest against their will to wind up before the time of maturity. So held in a case where borrowers tried to compel non-borrowers to accept a sum per share less than the amount fixed by charter; Pfaff v. Building Association, 6 W. N. C. 349.

sense, either a present forfeiting or laying down of the franchises
or corporate rights of the association.[1]  If the members unanimously agree to cease business before maturity of the stock,
the assets should be reduced to a distributive basis.  The non-
borrowing members should pay their dues to the date of dissolution as should the borrowing members, while the latter
should repay their loans, less the surrender value of their
stock, if they choose to so apply it.[2]  Unless there has been an
intention to dissolve the corporation, accompanied by the surrender of the charter, the association will not by this distribution of assets, be considered defunct so far as its chartered
existence is concerned.  Sometimes, the association in times
of depression or misfortune, may determine to suspend until
its condition is determined, and this the members may do; but
a borrower is not thereby relieved from the payment of interest on the loan during the suspension.[3]

SEC. 5.  **Effect of Appointment of a Receiver.**
However, when the association goes into the hands of a
receiver, the borrower is not chargeable with weekly dues and
interest, for this is equivalent to a dissolution as to him[4]

The appointment of a receiver to wind up the association and distribute its assets, operates as a discontinuance of

---

[1] City Loan etc. Association **v.**
Goodrich, 48 Ga. 445.

[2] The following holding as to
computation was made in a Maryland case:

When the affairs of a building
association are in course of liquidation, the original purposes having
been abandoned by mutual consent
the proper mode of stating an account between such association and
a shareholder who has obtained advance on his shares of stock, on a
mortgage, is to charge the mortgag-
or with the sum actually advanced
to him by the association, and interest thereon at the rate of six per
cent. (the legal rate) per annum, deducting from time to time, the pay-

ment made by the mortgagor, according to the rule applicable to
an account between debtor and
creditor; Hempstead, etc., v. King,
58 Md. 279.

[3] Thomson v. Ocmulgee, etc., Association, 56 Ga. 350.

[4] Peter's etc Association v Jaecksch,
51 Md., 198; Bowker v. Mill River
etc., Association, 7 Allen, 100; Cook
v. Kent 105 Mass., 248; In Hinman
v. Ryan 3 C. C. (Ohio) 529, it was held
that while the dues stop, the mortgage remains in force, and interest
continues.  As to the continuance
of interest, the court took a different view.  See also Hekelnkaemper v. German, etc. Association, 22
Kans. 549.

all future payments; or, if the association be not actually dissolved, if there can be no chance of paying the unredeemed shares their par value, and the association be unable to carry out its contract with the mortgagor, so as to enable him to get a release of the mortgage, according to the terms of its covenants, then the contract as originally contemplated is terminated, and the mortgagor occupies the same position as if the association were dissolved[1]

SEC. 6. **Final Settlement with Members and Creditors.** Final division and distribution of the assets of the association are required to be made when the accumulated fund is sufficient to pay the par value of the shares after the payment of all debts and liabilities of the association.[2] The shareholders must wait until the debts and liabilities are discharged before taking the assets. Any agreement for a contrary arrangement will be held void by the courts as to creditors.[3] Unless the association has distributed all of its assets and matured all of its stock, there is no dissolution of the corporation, merely a termination of the membership of those holding cancelled and retired stock. In the old societies issuing but one series, or all of their stock at one time, there was no settlement with the members until dissolution, but under the plan of associations as existing in the United States, they issue stock in series, one after the other, or as it is applied for, so that the effect is to continue the existence of the association. Whenever the payments on stock, together with its pro rata share of profits above debts, equal its face, the association is bound to retire it, and thereupon the association sets to work to retire the next issue and so on. If the stock is issued in classes or series, the entire series is retired; if it is issued at different times, as in the permanent, each issue is retired separately. In the former, the profits are credited to each series on the books of the association, as it may be entitled to them, and in the latter, the profits are credited each divi-

---

[1]Hampstead, etc., Association v. King, 58 Md. 279; Windsor v. Bandel, 40 Md. 172; Low Street, etc., Association, v. Zucker, 48 Md. 448.

[2]White v. Mechanics etc., Association, 22 Grat. 233.

[3]Heggie v. Building Association, 107 N. C. 581.

dend day, on the member's stock, in his pass book.  When the
maturity is reached in the serial, it is determined by a division
of the profits, attaching to that series, by the total number of
shares in the series, and in the permanent, it determines itself
by adding together the payments and credited dividends.  If
in its computation, the association made an error in extin-
guishing stock, the shareholder may maintain a bill in equity
to correct the error,[1] or, if the association made a settlement
contrary to its constitution, by which a stockholder received
more than his share, he may be made a party to a bill in
equity, for the purpose of having all questions arising in the
transaction adjudicated, one of which is their liability to refund
such excessive amount,[2] and though such settlement is in good
faith, the overpaid members will not be released, where it turns
out that there will be a deficiency as to non-retiring members.[3]
In assuming a basis for the distribution of its earnings, the
association should not regard so much the time of its issue of
stock, or its series, as the amount of dues received on the stock.[4]
The association has been able to realize a profit on account of
money paid into its treasury by the members, and the profits
thereon justly attach to those paying.  If a member is delinquent in his payments for a short period, and the association
is compensated for such delinquency by the fines, the member's share of profits should attach notwithstanding, but if the
default is long, without any prospect of removal, the association
should in its by-laws provide for some disposition of such
stock.  It may be by forfeiting it after a long continued
default, but the more equitable method is to retire it, and after
deducting the proper charges, place it at the member's disposal
in the treasury.  The association has been, in this way, protected and receives the use of the money.

SEC. 7.  **Settlement Before Maturity.**  The members may agree unanimously to wind up the association, before
maturity of the stock, and any fair and equitable agreement

[1]Building Association's Appeal,
33 P L. J. 324.
[2]Goodrich v. City, etc., Association, 54 Ga., 98.

[3]McKeown v. Building Association, 5 Bull. 52.
[4]Seibel v. Building Association,
43 Ohio St., 371.

made between them, as to the mode of settlement and dissolution, will be upheld. Thus, an agreement to wind up an association by paying the owners of the unredeemed shares the sums they had advanced, with interest, and that the owners of the redeemed shares who had given mortgages for the price of the redemption, should be discharged upon paying the amount of their mortgages with interest, was held valid and enforceable[1]

In order to make any such agreement valid, there are two cardinal points to be observed, to-wit: The discharge of all of the society's debts and, the equal distribution of all the remaining profits among the stockholders, according to their stock-holdings.

SEC. 8. **Assignment for Creditors.** When a building association has become insolvent, it has been held in Pennsylvania, it may make an assignment for the benefit of its general creditors,[2] but not for the benefit of its members,[3] but if an assignment has been made for general creditors, the treasurer of the association is entitled to be reimbursed as a general creditor, for moneys paid by him on orders drawn before the assignment, in priority to the claim of withdrawing stockholders.[4] The fact, that an association has made an assignment for the benefit of creditors does not prevent the recovery of a judgment against it.[5] The usual method is for a receiver to be appointed for an insolvent association, and the rights of creditors and members are protected and adjusted through the receivership.

SEC. 9. **Appointment of Receiver and Winding up.** In regard to the appointment of a receiver, it is under the control of the statutes of the state, and, to some extent, within the discretion of the court, considering the application for the receiver. Insolvency of an association is seldom, and so rarely do the assets shrink, so that creditors are unable to

[1]Hoboken, etc., Association v. Martin, 2 Beas., 428.

[2]*In re* Estate National, etc., Association, 9 W. N. C., 79.

[3]Ib.

[4]Christian'sAppeal, 102 Pa. St.,184.

[5]Connolly v.Building Association, 6 W. N. C. 176.

enforce their claims without a receiver, that the courts have not often been called upon to exercise that authority.

A member, when he believes the assets are sufficient to discharge the stock, may invoke the aid of a court of equity to compel a settlement, if it is established one should be made. But in order to have the right of such aid, the petitioner must be a full member and not a creditor.[1]

SEC. 10. **Marshalling of Assets.** When there is insolvency and dissolution, the adjustment of the rights of borrowers, non-borrowers and creditors, becomes a question of nicety and importance. Equity must be done to all,[2] and this is true, no matter what preferences as to payment are made by the charter and by laws among different classes of stockholders.[4] If the parties unanimously agree upon an equitable settlement upon dissolution, it will be upheld in a court of equity.[5]

The rights of the different classes will be considered in the inverse order as stated.

The creditors, whether lien holders or general, are entitled to be first paid in full, before any distribution is made to the stockholders. And, while payments on stock are not considered, *ipso facto*, payments on mortgages, to such an extent that any one except the parties can make such application of them yet the rule is varied, so a junior mortgagee may, in equity compel the association, as holder of the first mortgage, to resort first to stock held by it as collateral security, before enforcing the mortgage lien,[5] and the association must sell the stock or retire it, in either case crediting the proceeds or value on the debt. The association has the right to sell or apply this stock on the mortgage debt, as against any subsequent purchaser of

[1]Lister v. Log Cabin, etc., Association, 38 Md. 115; Edelin v. Pascoe, 22 Grat. 826.

[2]Bowker v. Mill River, etc., Association, 7 Allen, 100.

[3]Strohen v. Association, 115 Pa. St. 273.

[4]Criswell's Appeal, 100 Pa. St. 488.

[5]Goodrich v. City, etc., Association, 54 Ga. 98.

[6]Herbert v. Mechanics, etc., Association, 2 C. E. Gr. 497.

the stock. He takes it subject to the lien and cannot prevent its enforcement.[1]

Giving the junior mortgagee the right to compel the association, as a first mortgagee, to resort to collateral security, in the shape of stock, before reaching the land held as common security, is but an expression of the equity rule, that if one party has a lien on, or interest in, two funds for a debt, and another party has a lien on, or interest in one only, of the funds, for another debt, the latter has the right, in equity, to compel the former to exhaust the other fund in the first instance for satisfaction, if that course is necessary, for the satisfaction of the claims of both parties, whenever it will not trench upon the rights, or operate to the prejudice of the party entitled to the double fund.[2]

While this right of the junior mortgagee would more often be called into exercise in foreclosure proceedings, it is likely in any settlement of the corporate affairs where the security is of questionable sufficiency for all liens.

In the event of the application of stock payments, under such circumstances, to the mortgage debt, the simplest manner is for the association to give the borrower credit on his debt to the amount of the withdrawal value of his stock. But the right to require application of stock does not extend to a judg-

---

[1] Weiss's Appeal, 5 W. N. C. (Pa.) 423 It would seem upon principle that when the mortgagor sold his stock as against him, the assignee could compel the association to first resort to the mortgage before resorting to the stock.

[2] Redbank, etc., Association v. Patterson, 12 C. E. Gr. 223; Washington, etc., Association v. Beaghen, 12 C. E. Gr. 98. Contra: Economy, etc., Association v. Hungerbuehler, 93 Pa. St. 258; Springville, etc., Association v. Raber, 33 Leg. Int. 329; Building Association v. Eshelbach, 7 Phila. 189; Selden v. Reli-

able, etc., Association, 32 P. F. Smith 336; Kremer v. Springfield, etc., Association, 6 W. N. C. 267; Association v. Wall, 7 Phila. 240; Kingsessing, etc., Association v. Roan, 9 W. N. C. 15; North America, etc., Association v. Sutton, 35 Pa. St. 463; Spring Garden, etc., Association v. Tradesmen's, etc., Association, 46 Pa. St. 493; Link v. Germantown, etc., Association, 89 Pa. St. 15. The Pennsylvania cases are out of harmony with other courts and conflict with principles of equity.

ment creditor.[1] When the rights of a second mortgagee and the assignee of stock must be adjusted, the doctrine of marshalling assets applies, and the repayments by the mortgagor to the society must be apportioned ratably between the mortgaged property and the stock.[2] But the doctrine will not be applied in any case where third parties, over whom the person seeking benefit of the doctrine has no superior equity, will be injured.[3] Any subsequent incumbrancer to compel the association to make the application of stock payments, must notify it of his claim,[4] and, unless so notified, the association will not, by releasing one of its funds, prejudice its right as to the other.[5] The recording of a subsequent encumbrance, is not notice,[6] but where there was actual notice of a subsequent mortgage, and the association released stock held as collateral security, its mortgage was deemed satisfied to the extent of the stock as against the second mortgage.[7]

In the event of insolvency, or dissolution of the association, the creditors must be paid in full, or the assets exhausted,[8] before the rights of the members to participate can be exercised.

[1] Herbert v. Mechanic's, etc., Association, 2 C. E. Gr. 497.

[2] Moxon v. Berkeley, etc., Society 59 L. J. Ch. 524.

[3] Reilly v. Mayer, 1 Beas. (N. J.) 55.

[4] Uniontown, etc., Association's Appeal, 92 Pa., St. 200.

[5] Quakertown, etc., Association v. Sorver, 33 Leg. Int. (Pa.), 359; Patty v. Pease, 8 Paige, 277; Stuyvesant v. Hone, 1 Sandf. (N. Y.), 419; Cheesebrough v. Millard, 1 Johns Ch. 409.

[6] Ib.

[7] Washington, etc. Association v. Beaghen, 12 C. E. Gr. 98.

[8] Mortgages of advanced members, it has been held, cannot be treated as assets for the purpose of paying the liabilities of the association. The revenue from them is an available asset. This revenue, with other revenues of the association, creates the assets, the common fund which is used to pay off the stock of all shareholders: Lister v. Log Cabin, etc., Association, 38 Md. 115. It seems to the writer that, in a sense, a mortgage to the extent of the amount due thereon is an asset. It represents a part of the accumulations of the society, in fact it is a loan and subsisting debt in the society's favor. Until application is made of stock payments, it is a debt for the full amount. It is not an available asset however, so long as the mortgage contract is in force. In case of insolvency, the amount due on the mortgage is available as a paying or distributing asset.

Sec. 11. **Liability of Stockholders.** If the assets do not pay out the debts to outsiders, the stockholders must respond to the extent of the deficiency, and the limit of their iability is the amount of their stockholding. Building association stock, just as stock in any other corporation, must be paid for, and the distinguishing difference between it and other corporations, is the manner of payment. The building association undertakes to make a profit by use of its accumulations, to be applied in reduction of the member's subscription. It requires partial payments up to the period when these profits upon a *pro rata* division among the members will make the stock worth face. The stock is then paid for. If it contracts debts in excess of the earnings and stock payments, the receiver, just as in ordinary corporations, would be entitled to enforce a *pro rata* assessment against each member to cover the debt. The assessment, so long as it did not exceed the amount of the association's assets, would only have the effect of postponing so long the maturity of the stock, but if it exceeded the assets, then each member would be liable to an assessment, not exceeding an amount equal to the difference between his dues paid in and the amount of stock held by him.

In distributing the assets or in assessing liabilities, there is no distinction between investor and borrower, so far as their stock is concerned. Whatever profits accrue to the investor's stock, attach in the same proportion to the borrower's stock. If the society dissolves before maturity, the investor is relieved from further payments and this is true of the borrower. The association has placed itself beyond the power of performing its part of the contract, and the courts will not require either class of shareholders to longer perform their agreements.

Sec. 12. **Liability of Borrower for Debts.** But this does not release the borrower from the payment of his debt The association settles with the investor by paying him the value of his stock; it settles with the borrower by collecting the amount of the loan, less the value of his stock. In the event of loss, the borrower must bear his proportion with the investor.[1] This is the rule established by the American cases, but in England, it is held the borrower cannot be held to that liability,[2] unless the rules imposed it.[3]

SEC. 13. **No Liabilities for Losses under the Mortgage.** The liability against the borrower for losses, as has been stated, is a personal one, just as that of the investor is, and cannot be enforced against the mortgaged property, unless the mortgage clearly includes it. So, that when the mortgagor has paid off his mortgage, he is entitled to have it released, although he may be liable for debts of the association. His personal liability continues. That is a matter arising out of his stock transaction and an entirely separate contract.

SEC. 14. **Liability of Withdrawing Member.** When a member gives notice of withdrawal, his membership ceases and he is creditor of the association, so that he cannot be held to losses from bad investments made after he withdrew.[4] But if any shareholder has been illegally released, as by receiving an amount which should have been subject to a loss, his liability can be enforced in a proceeding to wind up, by making him a party.[5]

---

[1] Hinman v. Ryan, 3 C. C. (Ohio) 529; Edelin v. Pascoe, 23 Grat. 8?6; Windsor v. Bandel, 40 Md. 172; Strohen v. Franklin, etc., Association, 115 Pa. St. 273; Laurel Run, etc. Association v. Sperring, 106 Pa. St. 334; Booz's Appeal, 16 W. N. C. 365; People v. Lowe, 117 N. Y. 175 reversing 47 Hun, 577. In the 117 N. Y. case, it was held that each member for each share held by him was entitled to the same amount, i. e., a proportionate share of the assets, if a debtor, and if he owed more than his distributive share, he was bound to pay the balance and upon such payment was entitled to a discharge of his mortgage; see also, Everman v. Schmitt, 24 Bull. (Ohio) 56; McGrath v. Hamilton, etc., Association,

44 Pa. St. 383; Knobiauck v. Robert Blum, etc., Association, 25 Pitts L. J. O. S. 39; Wittman v. Building Association, 7 W. N.C. 80; Seibel v. Building Association, 43 Ohio St. 371.

[2] Buckle v. Lordonny, 56 L. J. Ch. 437; Brownlie v. Russell, L R., 8 App. Cas. 235; Tosh v. North British, etc., Society L. R., 11 App Cas 489.

[3] Rosenberg vs. Northumberland, etc., Society, L R., 22 Q B. 373, But see the case of *In re* West Riding society, L. R., 43 Ch. Div. 407, where it was held that borrowers and non-borrowers must contribute equally to losses.

[4] Christian's Appeal, 102 Pa. St. 184.

[5] Cason vs. Seldner, 77 Va. 293.

SEC. 15. **Assets to be Distributed Among Borrowers and Non-Borrowers Alike.** After the creditors are satisfied, or if there be none, and the payment of all expenses, the method of distribution of the assets of an association, solvent or insolvent, is to pro rate them among the shareholders, borrowers and non-borrowers alike. If the association is insolvent and the winding up is voluntary or involuntary, so that the distribution will not mature the stock and discharge the mortgages, the payment of the difference may . be enforced against the mortgagors and the sum thus realized passes to the common fund for like distribution. Confusion will be avoided in these matters, by holding fast to the fact that the borrowing has no effect on the membership of the borrower, and its only effect upon his stock, is to subject it to a collateral lien. The debt remains in law undiminished, although the stock may have reached maturity, and then the member of the association has the privilege of applying it in satisfaction of the debt. Until such application is made, it remains in full force, unaffected, except by the lien, and it is subject to all liabilities and rights accorded any other stock.

SEC. 16. **Consolidation of Associations.** It sometimes happens, in the management of associations, that by union of their interests, two associations can accomplish more than either can do singly. But how to unite their interests when it is wise, is a question of some difficulty. Without legislative authority, they have no power to consolidate, and if they had such power, the actual union would be full of unadjustable points. The clearest way is for the stockholders of one association to unanimously agree to dissolve. This right is vested in them.[1] The manner of dissolving should be by agreement to that effect signed by each stockholder, and a resolution duly entered on the minutes record of the association reciting that as it is the expression and consent of each stockholder that the corporation dissolve, such action be taken, and that the value of the assets of the association be ascer-

---

[1] Barton v. Enterprise, etc., Association, 114 Ind., 226.

9

tained, and a pro rata distribution thereof had. If there are borrowers, their debts should be repaid and such repayment should go into the common fund. The assets realized from the various sources are then divided up among all the members *pro rata*, and the society is dissolved. This is the way it is done theoretically, but in case of practical amalgamation, the surviving society receives the applications of the borrowing members of the other society, for loans in amount as held by them in such society, and if the security and titles are satisfactory, the surviving society grants loans upon the properties in the full amount as theretofore held, and then ascertains the value of the stock of such society, and issues stock to all the members of the old society, according to their old holdings, entering credits on their passbooks as entered by the old society, and the stockholders become members of the surviving association. The absorption is then complete. A serial may be changed into a permanent, or *vice versa*, by the unanimous action of the stockholders. If a serial is changed to a permanent, the only changes to be made would be to issue stock at any time, instead of in classes, and then to credit upon the pass books the profits of the entire preceding time, or in other words, divide the profits after all proper deductions as expenses, the amount carried to the reserve fund and other charges. Thereafter, the profits are divided up every six months and stock is issued at any time. These are the two important distinguishing characteristics of the permanent. It virtually makes a division of profits every six months, or annually, instead of at the maturity of the stock as with the serial. If the change is from the permanent to the serial, the profits credited as dividends are withdrawn from the division and lumped in the treasury, to be held until they aggregate sufficient to pay off the stock. The difficulty in this part of the change would be to throw the separate issues of stock into different classes. It could only be done if some of the issues were near enough to each other to form classes. It would not matter as to the size of the classes, as such division is only for convenience of issuing stock, and does not create an independent and distinct part of the association. It is a part of the association entitled to its share of the entire profit. If the shares issued in the permanent can be so classified, the change is then easily effected as indicated.

If permitted by statute, the association, upon paying off stock, may provide for reissuing the same as new stock. Thus, when a share is paid off, a new certificate therefor may be issued to a new member, upon his entrance into the association.

# CHAPTER XIII.

## PRACTICAL RESULTS.

SECTION 1. The character of a building association.

SECTION 2. Method of loans.

SECTION 3. Some results.

SECTION 1. **The Character of a Building Association.** Having considered the building association in various phases, it remains to look at its results.

The simplicity and comparative certainty of the scheme, inspire confidence, and its successful growth and substantial achievements have enlisted a very strong support. The scheme is simple, as a proposition, to receive and loan money for the common profit of all members, and to return the receipts with the accumulations, to the members, whenever they reach a certain amount. The principle of co-operation has but received another application. The only element of uncertainty in its business is in its securities. Unless they are depressed by unforeseen causes, so as to impair them, or render them worthless, the association can foretell with almost mathematical accuracy what it can do. And whatever would affect its securities, consisting of real estate, would, unless it were some local trouble, disturb directly or indirectly all securities. The assets of the association are in the hands of the earning classes of the land, the wageworkers, who are contributing daily to the substantial and material wealth of the country. There is no element of speculation or hazard to be considered, as in most large moneyed interests. The successful mastery of those elements have built up large financial institutions, but talents

132

of that character find no field in the operations of building associations. So simply, and yet so certainly, are they constructed, that they almost carry themselves. They do not deal with men whose financial security is their personal responsibility, which may be lost in a day. Whatever financial disaster closes the factories, shops and stores, and stops the railroads, threatens the future usefulness of the associations, but not their solvency, so long as real estate is not greatly depressed. But when this result is reached, larger but less stable securities have been impaired before the building association has been reached. Besides the ordinary security, the association has bound its borrower by the strong tie of home interests. A member will give his best energies to save his home. It is the instinct of self preservation. All his capital outside of his home may be involved, his note in bank may be protested and he philosophically regards these things as culminations of misfortunes, but he does not look so calmly upon the creditor of his home. The building association mortgage, resting upon it, is protected, if possible. With the home maker, all energies bend to its payment. Thus, it becomes apparent why the building association is prosperous and secure.

SEC. 2. **Method of Loans.** It loans its money upon first mortgage on real estate. In addition, it requires the borrower to be a member, to take an active interest and hold stock. It pledges the stock as additional security and appeals to his sense of accumulation by offering him a share of the profits. The borrower, in addition to interest, pays a premium, which generally increases the interest at least two or three per cent. This would seem oppressive, were it not for the fact that he shares in all the profits, which, when applied on the debt, decrease the interest. The source of the great profit to associations, by which they are enabled to show great earnings, compared with other money lenders, is the weekly repayments.

A borrower pays in a certain amount each week or month, as the case may be, on his stock, which is pledged. These amounts are reloaned at once and are being repaid in the same manner, and so on, that one dollar loaned to A, is partly repaid and reloaned to B, who repays part of it, which is loaned to C, and each loan is earning for the full amount, as no credit is made upon repayment to stop interest. A as a borrower has, in fact, repaid part of his debt, and the society has reloaned it to B for the benefit of A and the other members. Thus, money by this method, assumes a manifold earning capacity, attainable nowhere else. The burden on the borrower is not heavy, for while he is paying interest on his full debt and making repayments, those repayments are earning a good profit and his accumulations, secured in this way, are making a sure sinking fund to discharge his debt. The security of the association is thus weekly being increased. The debt is growing gradually smaller by the weekly repayments. The borrower has obligated himself to make them or the whole debt becomes due and collectible. He understands this, and that by his payments he is substituting for a rent cost, on most favorable terms to himself.

The money paid in as dues, as it accumulates to a size large enough, is at once loaned. The experience of associations is an inability to supply the demand. The home-getters are not limited to any particular business or locality, so the field of building associations is, almost, as wide as humanity itself. So long as other businesses thrive, this institution's operations are practically unlimited.

Several methods have been tried in loaning money, but there are three generally recognized systems. Nearly all associations charge a premium in addition to interest. In some, the premium charge is deducted from the face of the loan and interest is charged on the full amount. Suppose the shares are $200 each and the member owns five shares. He desires to borrow $1,000, and his bid is 25 per cent. The association pays to him $750 and charges him interest on $1,000, to be paid quarterly,[1] and takes an assignment of his shares as col-

---

[1] While this is generally done, it has been held, as has been stated, usurious. See pp. 104, 105.

lateral security, besides a mortgage on real estate, to secure all the payments. Some associations modify this plan by only charging upon the amount received by the borrower. The borrower continues his payments until his stock has matured, when the association will cancel his mortgage and retire his stock, by applying the latter to the former. If he withdraws before maturity, a per cent of the premium is refunded to him. This introduces a great element of uncertainty in the association's profits. These systems of loaning are practiced in some of the oldest societies.

In Massachusetts, building associations known as co-operative banks, may, by law, provide instead of bids for premium, a rate of annual interest upon the sum desired, payable in monthly instalments. In New York, the premium is charged as a bonus, and is deducted at the time of the loan without any rebate on withdrawal. Interest is charged on the full amount.

The most popular and prevailing system is to loan the member the full amount of each share held by him and make the payment of premium and interest in instalments with the dues. For instance, a borrower of $1,000 holding five shares of $200 each, bids twelve cents premium per share per week. He would be required to pay with his dues of fifty cents on each share, a premium of twelve cents and interest. If the latter were six per cent per annum, his total payments would be, dues $2 50, premium 60 cents, interest $1.20, making a total weekly payment of four dollars and thirty cents, of which one dollar and eighty cents is a profit to the association. The other $2.50 is a credit on his stock payments. The borrower on this basis pays 9.36 per cent interest for the first year, but on his payments he receives a profit. Assuming that the association is receiving on an average the same premium, and is able to make an annual net profit of 8 per cent, which would be a conservative estimate, the borrower's interest is net 8.84 per cent for the first year of his loan. The method of the computation is: He pays to the association during the year in weekly instalments $130. The association has the use of all of it for half the time, and would, therefore,

pay to him a profit of $5.20, or 8 per cent on $65.00. The
second year, his net interest would be 7.8 per cent; the third
year, 6.7 per cent; the fourth year, 5.72 per cent; the fifth
year, 4.68 per cent; the sixth and last year, 3.64, or an average
of 6.23 per cent for the whole time. During that time he has
paid in $780, which, with his dividends, will mature his stock
calling for $1,000. The amount he has paid weekly exceeds
but slightly the rent cost, and he is thus enabled to discharge
a debt he probably never could have met if he had to pay it
all at one time. By distributing the payments over a series
of years, the borrower is able by constant and successive efforts
to dispose of a task, that were he to confront at one time would
render him discouraged and hopeless. If he were to discharge
the entire debt at one time in the future, its maturity would
find him as unprepared as when it was contracted. The building association marshals his forces for him and conducts him
through to a place of safety. He becomes trained in his
observance of its laws, and he is regular in his payments. The
association has involved his greater interests and his watchful
and persevering thrift strengthens it.

In some associations the premium is charged as a whole
and divided into a certain number of instalments, generally as
many months as the estimated maturity of the association, and
each fixed instalment is payable each month.

There is still another manner of lending, originating with
an Ohio association, the Dayton Mutual Home. This association has many imitators throughout the country and has itself
achieved wonderful success. The shares in associations of this
type are usually $100 and the dues are 25 cents on each share.
The profits are distributed semi-annually, by crediting them on
the pass-books of the members. Loans are made upon interest and premium payable weekly. The chief distinction
between it and other associations is the opportunity of a member to extend the time of repaying his loan as he may desire
from a period of six years to approximately fourteen years.
The association gives him the privilege of paying the amount
named as dues only, instead of adding thereto the premium
and interest. That is, if his interest amounts to 12 cents per

week and his premium to 6 cents per week, 18 cents will be deducted from the 25 cents for the cost of the loan, and the balance will be credited on his stock. The advantage to the member is that he can regulate his payments according to his income, and may, if he choose, take the longest time, about 14 years, by paying only the amount required as dues.

SEC. 3 **Some Results.** Building associations have become enormous accumulators of money. Their growth is marvelous and attention is everywhere attracted to them. It is safe to say their assets exceed the combined capital stock of the National banks of the country. Their profits are large and safe. People who have not investigated them are surprised at these statements, yet the facts support them. To give some idea of the workings and profits of associations in different states, the following figures collected from some of the sssocia tions will serve:

The report of the Ohio state inspector of building associa-tions, just issued, states that there are 465 associations in the state. The total deposit of these associations on December 31, 1891, aggregated $59,690,236. Of this sum $59.302,299 has been invested in mortgages. The total earnings of the associations for the year were $2,905,755, and the average of dividends declared, was 6.88 per cent. The total member-ship in the state is 233,100.

One of the largest associations in the country is the Mutual Home and Savings Association, of Dayton, Ohio. It was organized April 19, 1873, with an authorized capital stock of $10,000,000. According to its report of December 31, 1891, it had mortgage loans of $1.489,980.26. The association earns 6 per cent interest for its paid up stockholders and 7 per cent for its running shares. It has had $5,628,200 of its capital stock subscribed, and now has $3,056,500 in force, the difference having been retired or withdrawn.

The Equitable Co-operative Building Association, of Wash-ington, D. C., was organized in 1879, and its total receipts to March 15, 1892, were $7,403,899.50. with assets, October 15, 1891, of $1,272,311.01 and 5,138 shareholders, owning 15,371

# 138 — BUILDING ASSOCIATIONS.

shares. The association has had but two foreclosures since organization, without any losses. It has matured considerable stock at a handsome profit. There are are about 45 associations in the District.

The Erie Savings and Loan Association, of Buffalo, New York, was organized in 1884, and, at the close of December, 1891, its receipts had been $1,276,193.67; 14,301 shares are in force, held by 1,673 shareholders. No dividends are declared, the stock being retired as it is matured. Three series have been paid since organization, showing a large profit. The association reports assets of $462,133.35 to mature the other 13 series. It has had but one foreclosure and no losses. The Homestead Savings and Loan Association, of Albany, New York, incorporated May 7, 1888, has assets of $261,324.39 and pays six per cent interest on paid up stock certificates. The other members receive a larger per cent.

In Pennsylvania, there are invested in building associations, upwards of $65,000,000, and the outstanding shares number more than $1,000,000. In a recent report of secretaries to the Chicago Building Association News, and the Building Association and Home Journal, of Philadelphia, the folllowing profits are shown:

| | | | |
|---|---|---|---|
| Norris Square, Philadelphia | ...... 8 | per cent per annum. | |
| The Phoenix, | " ...... 9 | " | " |
| The Solar, | " ......11 2-3 | " | " |
| German Central, (2d) | " ...... 6.22 | " | " |
| Allegany Avenue, | " ......10.76 | " | " |
| The Daniel O'Connel | " ......14.38 | " | " |
| The Lessing, | " ......12.95 | " | " |
| Richmond Mutual, | " ...... 9.5 | " | " |
| West End, | " ...... 9.84 | " | " |
| Carpet and Hosiery, | " ......10.46 | " | " |
| Union, McKeesport, Pa., | ......13.67 | " | " |
| North Star, Philadelphia, | ......11 | " | " |
| The Republic, | " ......10.5 | " | " |
| The Active, | " ...... 8.15 | " | " |
| Ark, | " ...... 7.96 | " | " |
| The Ben Franklin, | " ...... 7.57 | " | " |

Energetic,    Philadelphia ...... 11.23 per cent per annum.
Northern National,    "     ...... 8.76     "         "
The Joseph B. Clausen,"    ...... 9.73     "         "
Philadelphia,    "    ...... 8.5     "         "
Model, Roxborough, Pa.,    ...... 9.58     "         " .

In New Jersey there are over 200 associations, and their average profit is 9.5 per cent. The Artisans, of Camden, reported net assets in its eighteenth statement, issued in May, 1891, of $110,087.98. Its profits are 9 per cent per annum on the investment.

Tennessee Building Associations average 20 per cent profit. The Tennessee Mutual Building and Loan Association is one of the leading associations in the state, and has mortgage loans of $50,000 as the result of one year's operations, and realized a profit of 22.8 per cent on the total capital paid in to the association.

The associations in Maryland are generally good and working very successfully. One of the largest, is the Provident Building Association of Baltimore, which was organized in October, 1887. Its trial balance of April 19, 1892, showed assets of $562,255.47, and it has paid 6 per cent cash each year during its existence.

Building Associations in Massachusetts are known as Co-operative Banks, and number about 110, with shares in force 353,069, and 49,441 members. The sum of $3,980,475.00 were paid in last year as dues, and the net profits were $605,-129.09. They have accumulated assets of $11,874,530,14, representing loans on real estate of $10,791,168,62 and on shares of $520,800.67. In handling their loans, they have acquired real estate by foreclosure of $67,556,86. They have a surplus of $41,314,44 and a guaranty fund of $39,195,51. The average dividend is about 6½ per cent.[1]

There are large banks in Boston, Malden, Worcester, Camp bells, Taunton and Fitchbury. The Guardian Co-operative Bank of Boston began business August 6th, 1886, and has

[1]The figures were taken from October last report by the state inspector.

assets of $169,749.04. The Homestead, began September 12, 1877, and has assets of $333,172.82. The Pioneer started August 6, 1877, and has assets of $355,112.74.

The Malden Co-operative Bank commenced May 9, 1887, and has assets of $126,580.67. It pays 7 per cent dividend and has never had any losses or a foreclosure.

The Equitable Loan Association, of Wilmington, Delaware, was organized February 22, 1878, and has assets of $183,729.09. Its receipts have been $191.510.46 and it has matured three series. The last series represented a profit of of $51.41 on a share of $200.00.

In Michigan, the associations earn about 20 per cent per annum for the average time. The Marquette Building & Loan Association, organized in 1889, has assets in the sum of $118,677.49 without foreclosures or losses. The Northern Michigan Building and Loan Association of Hancock, organized in the same year, has assets of $131,116.05, its real estate loans consisting of $121,342.00.

There are fifteen associations in New Hampshire, and their combined assets, $1,287,000. They have about 13,500 members. The profits are about 20 per cent. The Granite State Provident Association of Manchester, organized in 1888, has $813,000, invested in loans, with 11,000 shareholders, no losses and two foreclosures. The Concord Building & Loan Association begun in 1887, has real estate loans of $79,200, with 2,922 shares issued.

Building Associations have grown very rapidly in Illinois in the past eight or nine years. The associations were confronted with constitutional objections that threatened their existence, but these were finally and favorably disposed of by the Supreme Court,[1] and these obstacles removed, they have a prosperous career.

The Equitable Savings and Loan Homestead Association of Chicago, organized seven years, reports March 31, 1892, assets of $411,812.00. Its profits are about 11 per cent. The Dan-

[1] Holmes v. Smythe, 100 Ill. 413; Freeman v. Ottawa, etc., Association, 114 Ill. 182; Winget v. Quincy, etc., Association, 128 Ill. 67.

ville Building Association received last year $220,754.85. It
has been organized eleven years and represents the new growth
of associations in the state. Its assets are $362,431.74 and it
pays a fraction above 9 per cent profit.

Associations are not numerous in Wisconsin, but they are
steady earners. There are in the neighborhood of 100 associations in the state. The Home Building and Loan Association of Milwaukee, in four years, has accumulated assets of
$105,334.81, and makes a profit of 12 per cent per annum,
paying 10 per cent cash, and carrying 2 per cent to the reserve
fund. During its fourth year, to October 24, 1891, its receipts
were $141,143.37.

Associations are of recent development in Maine. The
York Loan & Building Association of Biddeford, was organized January 21, 1889, and has $31,295.02 in assets. It has
had no foreclosures or losses and pays 8 per cent on the
investment.

A large association in Rhode Island is the Roger Williams
Building and Loan Association. The other associations are
at Newport, Westerly and Woonsocket. The Roger Williams
has been organized eleven years and reports assets of $582,
974.64. It has met with no losses and has had three fore-'
closures. Its profits have averaged a trifle over 7 per cent.
The Homestead Association under the same management, is
the second one in the City of Providence, and has been in
business nine months and has received and loaned about
$10,000.

In North Carolina, the Wilmington Daily Review says:
"We have seen here in Wilmington, some of the excellent
effects derived from the establishment here of building
associations. There are six in operation. The consequence
has been that real estate has held its own, even in stringent
times, and that new dwelling houses are going up continuously
in every section of the city." The Wilmington Homestead
and Loan Association, starting August 14, 1886, has assets of
$104,809.61, with no losses or foreclosures, and a profit of
10 2-5 per cent net. The Mechanics' has had no losses or
foreclosures and began 3 years ago. According to its second

annual statement, it had assets of $37,613.62 and paid a profit
of 11¾ per cent net.

In West Virginia, the Eagle Building Association of Wheeling, is in its fourth year, and has assets of $83,672.31, showing
a profit of about 10 per cent.

In Minnesota, the assets of building associations reach into
the millions of dollars, the great bulk being in St. Paul and
Minneapolis. The state law requires a rigid inspection. The
associations are prosperous and earn heavy profits. The
Rice Street, of St. Paul, organized 9 years, has assets of $103,-
385.34, with no losses and a profit of 17 per cent for the average time. The Seven Corners, organized in 1884, has assets of
$66,790.39. The Globe organized in 1887, has assets of $31,-
567.32. The Columbia, starting November, 1880, has assets of
$70,167.01. These associations are all under one management
and show about the same results. In Minneapolis are located
what are known as "National" Associations, i. e. associations
making loans in the different states. They have accumulated
enormous amounts of money, as for example, The Pioneer,
organized six years, reports $1,632,400.60 assets and a profit
of 8 per cent on the investment for the paid up shareholder
and a larger return for its other members.

In Mississippi, the Vicksburg Building Association is one
of the largest. It was organized in 1870, and up to date has
retired eleven series. Its monthly receipts are about $10,000,
and it now has assets of $519,900.74, to help mature the
remaining sixteen series. Its last year's profits were about 20
per cent. It has had no losses and not a foreclosure in the
last ten years.

Missouri associations are growing with great rapidity. The
Prudential Building and Loan Association, of Kansas City, in
three years has received deposits of $73,651.31 and has
averaged a profit of 10 1-2 per cent per annum.

In Kansas, their early history was a disappointment to their
friends, and their prospects were discouraging, but since they
have become better understood, their advantages are receiving
appreciation. The Leavenworth Mutual Building, Loan and
Savings Association, organized three years, reports $68,218.72

of assets. The profits average about 15 per cent per annum.

Iowa associations, while not large, are successful. One of the oldest is the Council Bluffs Savings, Loan and Building Association, incorporated in 1877. It has never suffered a loss and has accumulated assets of $130,311.68, realizing a profit of about 12 per cent per annum.

Building associations in Colorado are a growth of the past ten years. A few institutions had been working quietly prior to that time, " but to-day they have," so says the Republican, of Denver, "an acknowledged place, like the banks, among the financial institutions of the city." In Denver, there are about 15,000 shareholders in 31 associations, with combined resources of $5,500,000, and undivided profits approximating $2,000,000. During 1891 they loaned $1,750,000 in spite of a stringent money market. The profit realized is from 8 to 10 per cent. The Denver Home and Savings Association, incorporated July 1, 1890, has assets of $108,013.65. The People's Building and Loan Association, four years old, reports assets of $462,871.25. The Capital, of the same duration, has assets of $240,241.11. The Standard, during the same time, has accumulated $564,564.82 for its stockholders. The Home Mutual, organized in 1880, has assets of $403,082.43. The serial plan is the one usually adopted, and the instalment premium is growing in favor, although most of the older associations use the gross premium plan, and consequently, deduct the entire premium at the time of the loan, with a rebate on withdrawal. This has led to the " unearned premium," which unsatisfactorily creates uncertainty in the ultimate profits. The first of the above named associations is on the " Dayton plan," called such from the Mutual Home, Dayton, Ohio. There are a number of smaller associations outside of Denver, probably a dozen, all prospering.

The Wyoming associations are not numerous, but profitable. Interest rates are high, and when premiums are tacked on, the profit is enormous, as is shown by the results of the Home Building and Loan Association, of Cheyenne, which, after one year of operations, accumulated $18,540.02 and paid its stock. holders 41 1-2 per cent.

In Oregon, in the principal cities and towns, building associations are becoming established. Their net profits average 14 per cent. per annum. The Franklin Building and Loan Association, of Portland, is eight years old, has assets of $448,352.-95, with 1,000 shareholders and has sustained no losses.

There are about 135 associations in California, with assets of about $4,000,000. Six per cent. interest is paid on paid up stock, while running stock averages 10 per cent. The Home Security Building and Loan Association, of San Francisco, inincorporated July 20, 1875, has assets of $573,804.87. The Home Mutual, organized six years, has assets of $170,171.-95. The Commercial, five years old, has $95,347.05. The Homestead, six years old, has $206,568.60 and the Citizen's, in its seventh year, has assets of $409,901.40.

The Pioneer association, of Omaha, Nebraska, is the Omaha Loan and Building Association, organized in April, 1883. In about nine years it has handled $337,636.30 and paid off its first series, wherein the shareholder received $200 for $105 paid in.

In Texas, the Dallas Homestead and Loan Association, organized in December, 1879, has assets of $400,000, without a loss and has averaged $18\frac{1}{2}$ per cent per annum profit. The Mutual Building Association, of the same place, started in October, 1887, and has assets of $300,000, no losses, and has made 15 1-2 per cent.

In North Dakota, The Fargo Building Association, commenced business in March, 1880, and has assets of $49,308.39 and realizes a profit of about 10 per cent per annum. There are other associations at Grand Forks and Lisbon, all prospering.

In Indiana, the greater number of the associations are in the city of Indianapolis, there being about 120, with total weekly deposits of about $36,600. There are about 35,000 shareholders, and the associations have loaned, within the past four years, it is estimated, $4,243,344, having collected $4,210,901. The deposits, last year alone, it is estimated, were $1,600,000. The profits vary from 8 to 18 per cent. The Star Savings and Loan Association has assets of $144,169.26 and realizes an average profit of $15\frac{1}{2}$ per cent per annum.

The Aetna Saving and Loan Association, four years old, has assets of $179,284.52 and pays 18 per cent per annum. The German American Building Association, twenty months in business, has assets of $120,691.49 and pays eight per cent to paid up shareholders and a larger profit to installment stock. The Indiana Savings and Investment Company, three years old, has assets of $108,771.73 and pays its paid up sharehold-holders 8 per cent. per annum. Its running shares receive additional profit.

Foreclosures are comparatively few and losses trifling. The same record is borne by associations throughout the state. They have the confidence of the people and are building up solidly. The variance in the profit showings, in the foregoing illustrations, is explainable where it is less by such causes as accumulated idle money or a dull demand for funds; however, some associations adopt low premiums as a policy and discourage high bidding.

The figures above given do not include all the large and profitable associations in the different states. There are many others equally or more prosperous. The results illustrated by these associations were available and have been used to show the growth, security and profit of the building associations in the different parts of the country.[1]

To readily understand the quick and increasing profits of an association, through the compounding of its interest, a glance at the four following tables will serve.

[1] The above figures are taken from reports of the various associations, procured with care, but in a few states requests for reports were refused. Building associations should be compelled by law to publish at least annual reports of their condition.

## TABLE No. 1.

Showing the accumulations of one dollar per month at 10 per cent interest, compounded monthly, for any number of months, from one to one hundred and twenty :

| No. Months. | Amount. | No. Months. | Amount. | No. Months. | Amount. | No. Months. | Amount. |
|---|---|---|---|---|---|---|---|
| 1 | 1.01 | 31 | 35.50 | 61 | 79.74 | 91 | 136.49 |
| 2 | 2.03 | 32 | 36.80 | 62 | 81.41 | 92 | 138.64 |
| 3 | 3.05 | 33 | 38.12 | 63 | 83.10 | 93 | 140.80 |
| 4 | 4.08 | 34 | 39.44 | 64 | 84.80 | 94 | 142.98 |
| 5 | 5.13 | 35 | 40.78 | 65 | 86.52 | 95 | 145.18 |
| 6 | 6.18 | 36 | 42.13 | 66 | 88.25 | 96 | 147.40 |
| 7 | 7.24 | 37 | 43.49 | 67 | 89.99 | 97 | 149.64 |
| 8 | 8.31 | 38 | 44.86 | 68 | 91.75 | 98 | 151 89 |
| 9 | 9.38 | 39 | 46.24 | 69 | 93.52 | 99 | 154.17 |
| 10 | 10.47 | 40 | 47.64 | 70 | 95.31 | 100 | 156.46 |
| 11 | 11.57 | 41 | 49.04 | 71 | 97.11 | 101 | 158.77 |
| 12 | 12.67 | 42 | 50.46 | 72 | 98.93 | 102 | 161.10 |
| 13 | 13.78 | 43 | 51.89 | 73 | 100.76 | 103 | 163.45 |
| 14 | 14.91 | 44 | 53.33 | 74 | 102.61 | 104 | 165.82 |
| 15 | 16.04 | 45 | 54.78 | 75 | 104.47 | 105 | 168.21 |
| 16 | 17.18 | 46 | 56.24 | 76 | 106.35 | 106 | 170.62 |
| 17 | 18.33 | 47 | 57.72 | 77 | 108.25 | 107 | 173 05 |
| 18 | 19.49 | 48 | 59.21 | 78 | 110.16 | 108 | 175.50 |
| 19 | 20.67 | 49 | 60.71 | 79 | 112.08 | 109 | 177.94 |
| 20 | 21.85 | 50 | 62.23 | 80 | 114.03 | 110 | 180.47 |
| 21 | 23.04 | 51 | 63.75 | 81 | 115.98 | 111 | 182.98 |
| 22 | 24.24 | 52 | 65.29 | 82 | 117.96 | 112 | 185.51 |
| 23 | 25.45 | 53 | 66.85 | 83 | 119.95 | 113 | 188.07 |
| 24 | 26.67 | 54 | 68.41 | 84 | 121.96 | 114 | 190.64 |
| 25 | 27.90 | 55 | 69.99 | 85 | 123.98 | 115 | 193.24 |
| 26 | 29.14 | 56 | 71.58 | 86 | 126.02 | 116 | 195.86 |
| 27 | 30.39 | 57 | 73.19 | 87 | 128.08 | 117 | 198.50 |
| 28 | 31.65 | 58 | 74.81 | 88 | 130.16 | 118 | 201.16 |
| 29 | 32.92 | 59 | 76.44 | 89 | 132.25 | 119 | 203.84 |
| 30 | 34.21 | 60 | 78.08 | 90 | 134.36 | 120 | 206.55 |

## TABLE No. 2.

---

Showing the accumulations of sixty cents per month at 10 per cent interest, compounded monthly, for any number of months, from one to one hundred and twenty:

| No. Months. | Amount. | No. Months. | Amount. | No. Months. | Amount. | No. Months. | Amount. |
|---|---|---|---|---|---|---|---|
| 1 | .61 | 31 | 21.30 | 61 | 47.84 | 91 | 81.89 |
| 2 | 1.22 | 32 | 22.08 | 62 | 48.85 | 92 | 83.18 |
| 3 | 1.83 | 33 | 22.87 | 63 | 49.86 | 93 | 84.48 |
| 4 | 2.45 | 34 | 23.67 | 64 | 50.88 | 94 | 85.79 |
| 5 | 3.08 | 35 | 24.47 | 65 | 51.91 | 95 | 87.11 |
| 6 | 3.71 | 36 | 25.28 | 66 | 52.95 | 96 | 88.44 |
| 7 | 4.34 | 37 | 26.09 | 67 | 53.99 | 97 | 89.78 |
| 8 | 4.98 | 38 | 26.92 | 68 | 55.05 | 98 | 91.13 |
| 9 | 5.63 | 39 | 27.75 | 69 | 56.11 | 99 | 92.50 |
| 10 | 6.28 | 40 | 28.58 | 70 | 57.19 | 100 | 93.87 |
| 11 | 6.95 | 41 | 29.42 | 71 | 58.27 | 101 | 95.26 |
| 12 | 7.60 | 42 | 30.27 | 72 | 59.36 | 102 | 96.66 |
| 13 | 8.27 | 43 | 31.13 | 73 | 60.46 | 103 | 98.07 |
| 14 | 8.94 | 44 | 32.00 | 74 | 61.57 | 104 | 99.49 |
| 15 | 9.62 | 45 | 32.87 | 75 | 62.68 | 105 | 100.93 |
| 16 | 10.31 | 46 | 33.75 | 76 | 63.81 | 106 | 102.37 |
| 17 | 11.00 | 47 | 34.63 | 77 | 64.95 | 107 | 103.83 |
| 18 | 11.70 | 48 | 35.53 | 78 | 66.09 | 108 | 105.30 |
| 19 | 12.40 | 49 | 36.43 | 79 | 67.25 | 109 | 106.78 |
| 20 | 13.11 | 50 | 37.34 | 80 | 68.42 | 110 | 108.28 |
| 21 | 13.82 | 51 | 38.25 | 81 | 69.59 | 111 | 109.79 |
| 22 | 14.54 | 52 | 39.18 | 82 | 70.78 | 112 | 111.31 |
| 23 | 15.27 | 53 | 40.11 | 83 | 71.97 | 113 | 112.84 |
| 24 | 16.00 | 54 | 41.05 | 84 | 73.17 | 114 | 114.38 |
| 25 | 16.74 | 55 | 41.99 | 85 | 74.39 | 115 | 115.94 |
| 26 | 17.48 | 56 | 42.94 | 86 | 75.61 | 116 | 117.51 |
| 27 | 18.24 | 57 | 43.91 | 87 | 76.84 | 117 | 119.10 |
| 28 | 18.99 | 58 | 44.88 | 88 | 78.10 | 118 | 120.70 |
| 29 | 19.75 | 59 | 45.86 | 89 | 79.35 | 119 | 122.31 |
| 30 | 20.52 | 60 | 46.85 | 90 | 80.62 | 120 | 123.93 |

## TABLE No. 3.

Showing the accumulations of one dollar per month, at eight per cent interest, compounded monthly, for any number of months, from one to eighty:

| No. Months. | Amount. | No. Months. | Amount. | No. Months. | Amount. | No. Months. | Amount. |
|---|---|---|---|---|---|---|---|
| 1 | 1.01 | 21 | 22.42 | 41 | 46.92 | 61 | 74.88 |
| 2 | 2.04 | 22 | 23.58 | 42 | 48.23 | 62 | 76.38 |
| 3 | 3.04 | 23 | 24.75 | 43 | 49.54 | 63 | 77.88 |
| 4 | 4.07 | 24 | 25.90 | 44 | 50.87 | 64 | 79.41 |
| 5 | 5.10 | 25 | 27.08 | 45 | 52.22 | 65 | 80.94 |
| 6 | 6.14 | 26 | 28.24 | 46 | 53.57 | 66 | 82.47 |
| 7 | 7.19 | 27 | 29.46 | 47 | 54.94 | 67 | 84.03 |
| 8 | 8.24 | 28 | 30.64 | 48 | 56.27 | 68 | 85.78 |
| 9 | 9.31 | 29 | 31.86 | 49 | 57.66 | 69 | 87.12 |
| 10 | 10.37 | 30 | 33.04 | 50 | 59.02 | 70 | 88.72 |
| 11 | 11.45 | 31 | 34.27 | 51 | 60.62 | 71 | 90.32 |
| 12 | 12.53 | 32 | 35.49 | 52 | 61.85 | 72 | 91.90 |
| 13 | 13.62 | 33 | 36.76 | 53 | 63.24 | 73 | 93.52 |
| 14 | 14.72 | 34 | 38.07 | 54 | 64.65 | 74 | 95.14 |
| 15 | 15.83 | 35 | 39.24 | 55 | 66.09 | 75 | 96.78 |
| 16 | 16.94 | 36 | 40.47 | 56 | 67.55 | 76 | 98.43 |
| 17 | 18.06 | 37 | 41.76 | 57 | 69.00 | 77 | 100.20 |
| 18 | 19.18 | 38 | 43.05 | 58 | 70.45 | 78 | 101.73 |
| 19 | 20.32 | 39 | 44.31 | 59 | 71.91 | 79 | 103.43 |
| 20 | 21.46 | 40 | 45.61 | 60 | 73.40 | 80 | 105.00 |

# TABLE No. 4.

Showing the number of months required to mature shares of $100 or $200, at rates of interest indicated at head of each column, with monthly payments designated in first column:

| MONTHLY PAYMENTS. | 5 per ct. $100 | 5 per ct. $200 | 6 per ct. $100 | 6 per ct. $200 | 7 per ct. $100 | 7 per ct. $200 | 8 per ct. $100 | 8 per ct. $200 | 9 per ct. $100 | 9 per ct. $200 | 10 per ct. $100 | 10 per ct. $200 | 11 per ct. $100 | 11 per ct. $200 | 12 per ct. $100 | 12 per ct. $200 | 13 per ct. $100 | 13 per ct. $200 | 14 per ct. $100 | 14 per ct. $200 | 15 per ct. $100 | 15 per ct. $200 | 16 per ct. $100 | 16 per ct. $200 |
|---|---|---|---|---|---|---|---|---|---|---|---|---|---|---|---|---|---|---|---|---|---|---|---|---|
| 50 cents.. | 146 | 236 | 139 | 220 | 133 | 207 | 127 | 195 | 123 | 186 | 118 | 177 | 114 | 169 | 110 | 162 | 107 | 156 | 104 | 150 | 101 | 144 | 98 | 139 |
| 55 " .. | 135 | 222 | 129 | 208 | 124 | 196 | 119 | 184 | 115 | 176 | 111 | 169 | 107 | 161 | 104 | 154 | 101 | 148 | 98 | 143 | 95 | 138 | 93 | 133 |
| 60 " .. | 127 | 209 | 121 | 193 | 117 | 185 | 112 | 175 | 109 | 168 | 105 | 160 | 102 | 155 | 99 | 147 | 96 | 142 | 93 | 137 | 91 | 132 | 88 | 128 |
| 65 " .. | 119 | 193 | 114 | 187 | 110 | 177 | 105 | 167 | 103 | 160 | 100 | 154 | 96 | 147 | 93 | 141 | 91 | 136 | 89 | 131 | 86 | 127 | 84 | 123 |
| 70 " .. | 112 | 188 | 108 | 178 | 104 | 169 | 100 | 160 | 97 | 153 | 95 | 147 | 92 | 141 | 89 | 136 | 87 | 131 | 85 | 126 | 82 | 122 | 80 | 119 |
| 75 " .. | 106 | 180 | 103 | 170 | 99 | 161 | 96 | 153 | 93 | 147 | 90 | 141 | 87 | 136 | 85 | 131 | 83 | 126 | 81 | 121 | 79 | 118 | 77 | 115 |
| 80 " .. | 101 | 171 | 97 | 163 | 94 | 155 | 91 | 147 | 89 | 141 | 86 | 136 | 84 | 131 | 81 | 126 | 79 | 122 | 78 | 118 | 76 | 114 | 74 | 111 |
| 85 " .. | 96 | 161 | 93 | 156 | 90 | 148 | 87 | 142 | 85 | 136 | 83 | 131 | 80 | 126 | 78 | 121 | 76 | 118 | 74 | 114 | 73 | 110 | 71 | 107 |
| 90 " .. | 92 | 158 | 89 | 150 | 86 | 143 | 83 | 137 | 81 | 131 | 79 | 126 | 77 | 122 | 75 | 118 | 73 | 114 | 72 | 110 | 70 | 107 | 69 | 104 |
| $1.00.... | 84 | 146 | 81 | 139 | 79 | 133 | 77 | 127 | 75 | 123 | 73 | 118 | 71 | 114 | 70 | 110 | 68 | 107 | 67 | 104 | 65 | 101 | 64 | 98 |
| 1.20.... | 72 | 127 | 70 | 121 | 68 | 117 | 66 | 112 | 65 | 109 | 64 | 105 | 62 | 102 | 60 | 99 | 59 | 96 | 58 | 93 | 57 | 91 | 56 | 88 |

# APPENDIX.

# STATUTES AND CONSTRUCTION.

The following references show where the statutes, and decisions construing them, which relate to building associations in the different states, may be found.

Alabama. See Code 1886, sections 1553, et seq.; Statutes 1888-9, p. 31.

Arkansas. Organized under general stock company statute of 1869; Digest Stat. 1884, secs. 960, et seq.; See Acts 1883, p. 227; Statutes 1884, sections 5644, et seq.

California. See 2 Deering's Codes, sections 283, 571, 579.

Colorado. See Laws 1889. p. 41, et seq.

Connecticut. See Gen. Stat. 1888, sec. 1, where it is provided that the term "saving banks" shall include savings societies, and see chapter CX., concerning "Savings Banks." Construction of the act of 1850; Mutual Savings, etc., Association v. Wilcox, 24 Conn. 147, 154; Id. v. Meriden, etc., Company, 24 Conn. 159; and see West Winsted, etc., Association v. Ford, 27 Conn. 282; Id. v. Rice, Ib. 293; Babcock v. Middlesex, etc., Bank, 28 Conn., 302.

Dakota. See Compiled Laws, 1887, sections 3166, et seq.

Delaware. See Laws 1875, p. 188; Special Incorporations, see Acts 1877, 1891.

Florida. See Act of May 31, 1887; also Acts 1889, p. 115.

Georgia. Incorporated by decree of court; See Code 1882, sections 1674, 1676; Construction; See Redwine v. Gate City etc., Association, 54 Ga. 474; see also In re. Deveaux, Ib. 673; See R. S. 1882, section 3968; Acts 1888, p. 47; Acts 1889, p. 180; Acts 1890-1 part 1, p. 176; Construction; See McGowan v. Savannah, etc., Association, 80 Ga. 515.

Illinois. See Starr & Curtis, Ann. Stat.. Vol 1, pp. 629, et seq. ib., Vol. 3, p. 282. Former Statutes; Laws 1869, p. 105; 1871, p. 173; 1879, p. 83.

Indiana. See Elliott's Supp. Sections, 840, et seq.

Iowa. See McClain's Ann. Code, Sections 1290, 1784-87.

Kansas. See General Statutes 1889, sections 1424, et seq. Statutory Construction; see Salina etc., Association v. Nelson, 22 Kans. 751.

Kentucky. Incorporation by special enactment.

Lousiana. See Acts 1888, pp. 177, 212.

Maine. See R. S. 1883, p. 435, sec. 132; Acts 1889, p. 146; Acts 1891, p. 64.

Maryland. See Pub. Gen. Laws 1888, p. 312; Statutory Construction; See Border State, etc., Association v. Hayes, 61 Md. 597.

Massachusetts. See Pub. Stat. 1882, pp. 134, 572, 667, 1004. Suppl. Publ. Stat. 1888, pp. 63, 64, 103, 276, 548, 549; Acts 1889, pp 893, 1177; Acts 1890, pp. 60, 71, 213, 262; Acts 1891, pp. 722, 1010. Statutory Construction; See Baxter v. McIntire, 79 Mass. 168; Manahan v. Varnum, 77 Mass. 405; Cook v. Kent, 105 Mass. 246.

Michigan. See Howell's Ann. Supl. Statute 1890, Sections 3981, et seq.

Minnesota. See Statutes 1891, sections 1421, et seq., and 2409 et seq. Statutory Construction; see State v. Redwood Falls, etc., Association, 45 Minn. 154.

Mississippi. Incorporation by special enactment; see Acts 1886 pp. 20, 35; Acts 1888, p. 17; Acts 1890, p. 10.

Missouri. See R. S. 1889, Sections 2808, et seq.; Acts 1891, p. 74. Statutory Construction; See Maguire v. State, etc., Association, 62 Mo. 344; State v. McGrath, 95 Mo. 193.

Montana. See Comp. Statutes 1888, pp. 795, et seq.

Nebraska. See Comp. Statutes 1887, p. 258; Stat. Laws 1891, Chap. 14, p. 200.

New Hampshire. See Public Statutes, 1891, pp. 204, 205, 459, 460, 472, et seq.

New Jersey. See R. S. Suppl. 1886, pp. 69, 70, 138, et seq. R. S. 1877, pp. 92, et seq. and p. 1272; Acts 1887, p. 62; Acts 1888 p. 36; Acts 1889, p. 299; Acts 1890, pp. 420, 427, 441. Statutory Construction; Savings Association v. Vandervere, 3 Stock, 382; People's, etc., Association v. Furey, 20 Atl. Rep. 890; Vanneman v. Swedesboro, etc., Association, 15 Stew. 263; Newton Tp., etc., Association v. Boyer 15 Stew. 273; Washington Association v. Creneling, 10 Vr. 465; Id. v. Hornbaker 12 Vr. 519; For bill in equity held defective, see McNeal v. Florence, etc., Association, 13 Stew. 351.

New Mexico. See Acts 1887, pp. 22, et seq., also amendatory act of 1889; Acts 1889, pp. 266, et seq.

New York. Authorized by manufacturing acts 1879, 1880, 1884. See R. S. 1889, pp. 1587, et seq.; See also R. S. 1890, (Birdseye Ed.) pp. 342, et seq.; Laws 1891, p. 318. Statutory Construction; see Franklin etc., Association v. Mather, 4 Abb. Pr. 274; Second Manhattan etc., Association v. Hayes, 2 Keyes 192; Remington v. King, 11 Abb. Pr. 278.

North Carolina. See Code, Vol. 2, Chap. 7, Sec. 2,294, et seq; Battle's Revisal, pp. 105, et seq. Laws 1881, p. 604; Laws 1891, p. 1,041.

Ohio. See 1 R. S. 1890, sections 3,817, 3,883, et seq and 3,935.; Laws 1891, pp. 469, et seq. Statutory Construction; Windhorst v. Building Association, 7 Bull. 29; Licking County, etc., Association v. Bebout, 29 Ohio St. 252; Forrest City, etc., Association v. Gallagher, 25 Ohio St. 208; State v. Building Association, 35 Ohio St. 258; Bates v. People's, etc., Association, 42 Ohio St., 655.

Oregon. For incorporation, see general statute for private corporations, 2 Hill's Ann. Laws, secs. 3,217, et seq; also, Laws 1891, p. 131.

Pennsylvania. See Brightley's Purdon's Digest, pp. 223, et seq. Acts 1891, p. 174. Statutory Construction; See Cooper v. Association, 100 Pa. St. 402; O'Rourke v. Building Association, 8 W. N. C. 176; Houser v. Herman, etc., Association, 41 Pa. St. 478; Marble, etc., Association v. Hocker, 3 Phila. 494; Building Association v. Eshelbach, 7 Phila. 189; Spring Garden Association v. Tradesmen's, etc., Association, 46 Pa. St. 493; Springville, etc., Association v. Raber, 33 Leg. Int., 329; Snider's Estate, 34 Leg. Int. 49; Schober v. Accommodation, etc., Association, 35 Pa. St. 223; Building Association v. Seemiller, 35 Pa. St. 225; Philadelphia, etc., Association v. Moore, 21 Leg. Int., 109; Flounders v. Hawley, 78 Pa. St. 45; Wolbach v. Lehigh, etc., Association, 4 W. N. C. 157; Jarrett v. Cope, 68 Pa. St. 67; Rhoads v. Hoernerstown, etc., Association, 82 Pa. St. 180; Building Association v. Building Association, 100 Pa. St; 191; Commonwealth v. Association, 2 Chest. 189; Association v. Commonwealth, Ib. 546; Building Association v. Commonwealth, 98 Pa. St. 54; Abbott v. Building Association, 1 Del. 397; Building Association v. Robinson, 46 L. I. 5; Hansbury v. Pfeiffer, 35 L. I. 395; Heckman v. Building Association, 11 L. Bar. 110; Link v. Building Association, 89 Pa. St., 15; Rowland's Estate, 1 Del. 98; Fredericks v. Corcoran, 100 Pa. St. 413; Building Association v.

Hanlen, 7 Luz. L. Reg. 165; Beckct v. Building Association, 88 Pa. St. 211; Selden v. Building Association, 32 P. F. Sm. 336; Building Association v. Iloary, 8 Luz. L. Reg. 180; Saving Fund v. Longshore, Ib. 199; Sherman, etc., Association v. Rock, 9 Phila., 75; Building Association v. Coleman, 89 Pa. St. 428; Miller's Estate, 2 Pears. 348.

Rhode Island. Incorporated by special enactment.

South Carolina. Special incorporations; see Acts 1883, 1886, 1887, 1888, 1889; General Statute, Acts 1885, p. 40, Acts 1888, p. 46.

Tennessee. Incorporation by special enactment. See Code 1884; Sections 1742 et seq., Acts 1891, p. 17.

Texas. Incorporated under Clause 17, Article 566, Sayle's Civil Statute concerning "Corporations."

Utah. See Acts 1890, p. 7.

Virginia. See Statues 1852, pp. 81-3; see also Code 1887, Secs. 1145, et seq. The Richmond Perpetual Building, Loan, and Trust Company was incorporated by special enactment. See Act of March 30, 1875, amended March 2, 1888. Statutory Construction; Davies v. Creighton, 33 Grat. 696.

Wisconsin. See Sanborn & Berryman's Ann. Stat., pp. 1,204, et seq., Statutory Construction; Wood v. Union Gospel, etc., Association, 63 Wis. 9; Wood v. Iloskin, 63 Wis. 15.

Washington. See Acts 1891, p. 199.

West Virginia. See Chapter 26, R. S. 1879; Code 1891, pp. 514, et seq.
Statutory Construction; see Pfeister v. Wheeling, etc., Association, 19 W. Va., 676.

Wyoming. For incorporation of Saving Associations, see Laws 1888, pp. 193, et seq. The association contemplated is of a savings bank character.

## FORMS.

### PRELIMINARY AGREEMENT FOR INCORPORATION.

We, the undersigned, do each of us hereby agree to form ourselves into a building association, under the laws of the State of ......, and to take the number of shares in said association set opposite our respective names, and pay the dues thereon, as may be required by said association. In the event such association is not incorporated, we and each of us, agree to bear our proportionate part of the proper expense incurred in the effort to organize and incorporate such association.

### APPLICATION FOR MEMBERSHIP.

No. of Shares........                              No......

I ........ being desirous of obtaining ...... shares in the ............ Association, of ......, ...., each of the maturing face value of $......, do hereby make application therefor. I do hereby agree to abide by all the terms and conditions contained or referred to in the certificate of shares, and I hereby certify that I have carefully read the printed literature of the Association, and make this application to become a member from the facts set forth in said literature, and from said facts only, and I hereby agree to abide by the same.

¹I hereby appoint ............, or his successor in office, to vote in my place and stead, as my proxy, and authorize him in my name and during my absence, to vote at any election of officers and directors, and on any and all matters which, at any meeting of the members may properly come before them; said appointment is made and such proxy is to be held and vote to be cast in all respects in accordance and conformity with Section .... of the By-Laws of the Association. I will also comply with all the Articles of the Association, By-Laws, Rules and Regulations of said Association, and hereby make the same a part of this contract with said Association.

Name in full.............................................................

Age.........Married or single.........Occupation.......................

| | STREET AND NUMBER | TOWN OR CITY. | COUNTY. | STATE. |
|---|---|---|---|---|
| Residence, | | | | |
| Post-Office Address' | | | | |

IF TRUSTEE, FOR WHOM.
{ Name in full................................................
{ Residence..................................................
{ Relationship and Age.......................................

Kind of shares desired, whether installment or paid up................
Are you a member of this Association?.................................
If so, How many shares do you hold?..................................

IF APPLICATION IS MADE FOR TRANSFER FROM WHOM.
{ Name.......................................
{ Number of book or certificate.............
{ Number of shares transferred.............

Dated at..................this............day of...........189

Signature of applicant.................................

...............................Witness.

## FORM OF ARTICLES OF ASSOCIATION.

The form of the incorporating articles will depend, to some extent, upon the statute of the state. It must be consulted to conform with it, but the general character may be seen from the following articles, incorporating an Oregon association:

ARTICLES OF INCORPORATION OF THE FRANKLIN BUILDING AND LOAN ASSOCIATION, OF PORTLAND, OREGON,

KNOW ALL MEN BY THESE PRESENTS, that we, the undersigned, John A. Child, Robert Newcomb, J. H. Lyon, William Stokes, W. M. Gregory, N. Versteeg, Alfred Thompson, have this day associated ourselves together for the purpose of establishing a private corporation, under the general laws of the State of Oregon, and for that purpose do hereby make and subscribe in triplicate the following articles.

## ARTICLE I.[1]

The name assumed by this corporation, and by which it shall be known, is " THE FRANKLIN BUILDING AND LOAN ASSOCIATION;" and the duration of the said corporation shall be unlimited.

## ARTICLE II.

The enterprise or business in which the said corporation proposes to engage is—

1. To raise a capital fund in shares of two hundred dollars each, payable by monthly installments; such payments to accumulate at interest and profit until the par value shall be attained, when the amount shall be paid to the shareholders and the stock revert to the Association.

2. To grant loans of money to members, upon the security of freehold or leasehold properties, upon United States bonds, or upon the shares of this corporation only.

3. To buy, improve, and sell real estate.

4. To receive money on deposit, at interest or otherwise, repayable at call or fixed periods.

## ARTICLE III.

The said corporation shall have its principal office and place of business in the city of Portland, in the county of Multnomah, and State of Oregon.

## ARTICLE IV.

The capital stock of the incorporation shall be the sum of four hundred thousand dollars, divided into two thousand shares.

## ARTICLE V.

The amount of each share shall be two hundred dollars.

## ARTICLE VI.

The sums to be paid by shareholders on their respective shares, the time when such payments shall be made, the penalties for delay or neglect in making such payments, and also the manner and terms upon which shareholders shall be

[1] The part following the formal parts should adhere closely to the statute.

entitled to withdraw their shares from the Association, shall be determined by the By-Laws, which the stockholders shall have power to make, in accordance with the Constitution and Laws of the United States and of the State of Oregon.

## ARTICLE VII.

The number, titles, functions and compensation of the officers of this corporation, the time and manner of their election, and the time for the periodical meetings of this corporation shall be determined by the said By-Laws.

## ARTICLE VIII.

The officers of this corporation shall hold stated meetings at which the money in the treasury of the corporation, or such portion thereof as they shall deem advisable, shall be offered for loan, upon such terms and conditions as shall be directed in the said By-Laws.

In WITNESS WHEREOF, we have hereunto set our hands and seals this seventh day of April, one thousand eight hundred and eighty-three.

| | |
|---|---|
| JOHN A. CHILD, | [SEAL.] |
| R. NEWCOMB, | [SEAL.] |
| J. H. LYON, | [SEAL.] |
| WM. STOKES, | [SEAL.] |
| W. M. GREGORY, | [SEAL.] |
| N. VERSTEEG, | [SEAL.] |
| A. THOMPSON, | [SEAL.] |

Signed and sealed in presence of
    J. B. SCOTT,
    W. A. GRADON.

STATE OF OREGON,   ⎱ ss.
  COUNTY OF MULTNOMAH, ⎰

Be it remembered, that on this seventh day of April, A. D. 1883, before me, the undersigned, a Notary Public, in and for said county of Multnomah, and State of Oregon, personally appeared the within named John A. Child, Robert Newcomb, J. H. Lyon, William Stokes, W. M. Gregory, N. Versteeg and A. Thompson, to me known to be the identical persons described in and who executed the foregoing Articles of Incor-

11

poration, and severally acknowledged to me that they executed the same freely and voluntarily and for the uses and purposes therein mentioned.

In testimony whereof, I have hereunto set my hand and affixed my notary seal.

Done in triplicate, on the day and year in this certificate above written.

J. B. SCOTT,

[L. S.]                    Notary Public in and for Oregon.

OFFICE SECRETARY OF STATE, )
SALEM, April 10, 1883.    )

Articles of Incorporation of the "Franklin Building and Loan Association," of Portland, Oregon, were recorded and filed in this office on the 19th inst.

R. P. EARHART,
*Secretary of State.*

If the incorporation is by special enactment of the Legislature, the following act incorporating the "Guardian," of Wilmington, Delaware, may be consulted.


## ACT OF INCORPORATION.

AN ACT TO INCORPORATE "THE GUARDIAN SAVINGS AND LOAN ASSOCIATION."

*Be it enacted by the Senate and House of Representatives of the State of Delaware, in General Assembly met, (two-thirds of each branch concurring herein.)*

SECTION 1. That Daniel H. Kent, James H. Semple, Robert McCaulley, Henry R. Pennington, John H. Simms, B. Frank McDaniel, Henry P. Scott, Samuel C. Pierce, Henry F. Pickels, John B. Price, Edwin W. Jackson, Henry Evans, Samuel C. Penrose, Solomon H. Staats, Samuel H. Baynard, and William E. Harkins, and such other persons, as are now or hereafter may be associated with them, and their successors, be, and they are hereby created a body politic and corporate, by the name, style, and title of "The Guardian Savings and Loan Association," for the purpose of accumulating a fund from monthly contributions and fines, premiums on loans and interest on investments, for the benefit of its members, and by the said name, style and title, shall have succession for twenty years, and be able and capable in law to sue and be sued, plead and be impleaded in all courts of law and equity in this State and elsewhere; to have and use a common seal, and the same to alter and renew at pleasure; to ordain, establish, and enforce by-laws not repugnant to the Constitution and Laws of the United States, and of this State; and, generally, to exercise and enjoy all the powers, privileges, and franchises of a corporation aggregate, except banking powers.

SEC. 2. The said corporation shall, by the name, style and title aforesaid, be able and capable of purchasing, receiving, having, holding, and enjoying to itself and its successors and assigns, lands, tenements, hereditaments, annuities, money, securities, goods, chattels and effects, of what nature or kind soever, real, personal, and mixed; provided, the same shall not exceed the sum or value of six hundred thousand dollars; and the same, from time to time, at pleasure to sell, grant, demise, bargain, alien, and dispose of; and, also, to make such laws, rules, regulations, and contracts, and the same to alter, amend or repeal as the said Corporation shall deem proper and expedient, for conducting the affairs and business of said Corporation; and, generally, to do all and singular the matters and things necessary and proper for the good government and well being of said Corporation; provided, the same be not contrary to the provisions of this Act or the Constitution and Laws of the United States, and the State of Delaware.

SEC. 3. The affairs and business of said Corporation shall be conducted by a President, Vice President, Secretary and Treasurer, and nine Managers, who shall constitute a Board of Directors, seven of whom shall be a quorum. The President, Vice President, Secretary and Treasurer, shall be elected

annually.   At the first regular meeting, after the passage of
this Act, there shall be nine Managers elected, who shall,
within ten days thereafter, meet and divide themselves into
three classes, and draw lots, for one, two or three years, and
at every annual meeting thereafter, three managers shall be
elected to serve three years.   The said Board of Directors
shall have power to fill all vacancies that may occur in their
own body during the year.

Sec. 4.   The funds of said Corporation, as they accumulate
in the Treasury, shall be offered and loaned by the Board of
Directors, to the highest bidder among the stockholders.   In
case no stockholder offers to borrow said funds at the rate
fixed by law, then the Board of Directors shall have power to
loan to persons not members or stockholders of the said Corporation, at a rate of interest not exceeding that fixed by law.

Sec. 5   This act shall be deemed and taken to be a private
Act, and the power to revoke the same is hereby reserved to
the Legislature.

*Passed at Dover, Del.,* Feb. 20, 1883.


GEO. H. BATES,

*Speaker of the House of Representatives.*


SAMUEL B. COOPER,

*Speaker of the Senate.*

## FORM OF STOCK CERTIFICATE.

Certificate No.....
For ....... Shares
Issued to
................ ........
................ ........
Date ........ 18..
Received this
Certificate
............. 18..
............ ... ....
Tranferred from
............. ... ....
to
............. ....
Date........ 18..
Reissued ........
See Certificate
No.....

STOCK CERTIFICATE—NON-FORFEITABLE.
No.....                     Shares, $100.00
............
Building Association.
This Certifies, that...... of the County
of......State of......is the owner
of.... Shares of the Capital Stock of
the.... Building Association, of the
par value of One Hundred dollars
each, subject to the provisions
of the by-laws of the said Association. Transferable on the
[SEAL.] books of the Association only
on the surrender of this Certificate.
Given under the seal of the
......... ....Association, at.......... this
........ day of........18..
...... Secretary.      ....... President.

## ASSIGNMENT.

For value received, I hereby assign the within Certificate of Stock to........of the County of........State of........ this........day of........., 18.., and I hereby authorize the Secretary to transfer the same on the books of the Association.

Witness my hand and seal this........day of ............18..

Witness............

The following by-laws incorporate the essential points to be observed by the association and have been prepared with special reference to the avoidance of legal contentions.

## BY-LAWS.

SECTION 1. The name of this association shall be the.... ....association of................

Sec. 2.   The object of this association is to provide for its members a safe and profitable investment of their savings, and to loan money on easy terms to its members in manner provided by law.

Sec. 3.   The capital stock of this association shall be.... ....dollars, divided into shares of $........ each, to be issued (whenever applied for, or (in series of...... shares), at discretion of the board of directors.

Sec. 4.   Every share of stock shall be subject to lien for the payment of unpaid instalments and other charges incurred thereon.

Sec. 5.   No member in arrearages to the association in any manner whatever, shall be allowed to vote at the meetings of the association, until all such arrearages shall have first been paid.

Sec. 6.   No member who is indebted to the association as a borrower shall be allowed to vote upon any matter affecting the claim of the association against himself.

Sec. 7.   Any person taking shares in any series after the same has been started, shall pay in addition to dues thereon to the beginning, interest on such dues at the rate of.... per cent for the average time.[1]

Sec. 8.   Whenever the shares of stock, (in any given series),[2] of this association, shall have been redeemed by loans or advances thereon, or whenever the funds and property of the association in any given series shall be sufficient to pay all of the debts of the association, and to pay upon the unredeemed shares of such given series the par value thereof,........ hundred dollars, then the debts of the association shall first be paid and the deeds of trust or mortgages of borrowers in such series shall be released of record, and their bonds or other evidence of indebtedness delivered to them, and their stock shall be cancelled, and the free or unborrowed shares shall be redeemed or paid off.   When all the stock of a series (or share if the association is a permanent) is matured, then each holder of stock shall be notified thereof, in writing, by mail, to the

[1]Omit if permanent.                    [2]Insert this clause if the association is a serial one.

residence of such stockholder, as shown by the books of the association. Payment of unpledged stock, shall be in the order of presentation of notice from such holders, that they desire to be paid. The holders of matured stock, not desiring to be paid, may leave the amount thereof, with the association, if the directors so elect, and receive thereon such interest as the directors may see fit to allow, and the amount so left by any series, shall be considered a debt against the series, having the use of the money, which may be paid whenever the directors elect. Such holder shall be considered a creditor, and not a member of such association, from the time of notice by the association of the maturity of his stock.

New shares of stock may be issued in lieu of all shares redeemed, forfeited or matured.

SEC. 9. 'Should any member desire to pay in the full face value of his shares at the time of subscribing for the same, or at any time thereafter, or should any member whose shares have become paid up, as provided in section 8, prefer to allow the money due thereon to remain in the association, the Board of Directors, may, if they think best, and upon such terms as they may prescribe, accept said money, and issue to such member a certificate of paid up stock, for the shares so paid up.

SEC. 10. Each and every shareholder, for each and every share he or she may take, shall pay the sum of........... into the treasury, on the........ in every........ until each share (of the series) shall reach the value of........... hundred dollars, and dues not paid in before............... shall become delinquent, and fines accrue on the same. The payments of dues on a series of stock shall commence at the date of the issue of the same.

SEC. 11. Each member shall be entitled to a certificate of the stock for each share held by him or her, to be issued in the name of and under the seal of the association.

Each shareholder shall also be entitled to a pass book, marked

---

'If authorized by statute this section is proper.

with his name and residence, also numbered, and designating the number of shares owned, the number of series and date of issue in which all payments of dues, interest and fines shall be entered; and no money shall be received without the pass book.

Any stockholder may sell or transfer his share or shares, or any number of them, to any stockholder or any other person, the said person to have the right and obligations of the person from whom he purchased, and said purchase shall make him a stockholder and every person purchasing shall pay...... cents for each and every share so transferred. Shares are transferable only on the books of the association and in the presence of the secretary. Transfers of stock, to enable the holder to vote, must be made, at least, thirty days previous to an election. Holders of certificates authorized to be so issued, shall be members of the association, enjoying the rights and privileges thereof and participating in all the profits and losses, on the same *pro rata*, from the date of the certificate, whether borrowers or non-borrowers.

SEC. 12. All dues, premiums, interest, fines and other charges must be promptly paid off by the shareholder when due, and payments made shall be applied in the following order: first, upon charges; second, upon fines; third, upon premiums; fourth, upon interest, and fifth upon dues.

SEC. 13. Stock on which the holder shall fail to pay the monthly payments of dues, fines or charges, for six months, may be declared forfeited by the board of directors, and if such dues, fines or other charges shall remain delinquent and unpaid for the space of twelve months, then such shares shall *ipso facto* be cancelled, and such delinquent shareholder, whether at the expiration of six or twelve months, shall be credited with the same amount as if he had voluntarily withdrawn, less all dues, premiums, interest, fines, or other charges that may be due to the date of cancellation, and the stockholder, whose shares shall have been thus cancelled, shall at once cease to be a member of the association.

The amount so placed to his credit, either at six or twelve months, shall be paid to him or his legal representative on demand, but shall not bear interest.

SEC. 14. All stock shall be voted by shares, one vote being allowed each member, without reference to the number of shares held by him; any member, may authorize another person by written proxy to vote his stock, provided, that all proxies shall be filed with the secretary, at or before the hour of the meeting at which they are to be used, provided, that no person shall be allowed to vote more than........proxies.' (See sections 5 and 6).

At the annual meetings, the election shall be by written or printed ballot. All other questions at such meetings, or any weekly or special meeting, shall be decided by a *viva voce* vote, unless a ballot be demanded by ten shareholders present, entitled to vote, in which event the question shall be decided by ballot.

SEC. 15. Upon the death of a stockholder, his legal representatives shall be entitled to receive the full amount paid in by him on all shares not borrowed upon or pledged to the association as collateral security, and legal interest thereon, first deducting all charges that may be due on the stock; but no fines shall be charged to a deceased member's account, from and after his decease, unless the legal representatives of such decedent assume the future payment of the dues on the stock.

SEC. 16. The officers of this association shall consist of a President, Vice-President, Treasurer, Attorney and........ Directors. They shall be stock-holders, and be elected at the annual meeting to be held on the first..........after...... ...., and every succeeding year thereafter.

SEC. 17. At the first annual meeting for the election of directors, held on the........day of........18........there shall be elected three directors to serve for one year, three directors for two years, and three directors for three years; and annually thereafter, on the........day of ......of each year, there shall be elected three directors, to take the place of those retiring for that year.

'This last clause should only be used in case proxies are intended.

SEC. 18. The directors shall at the close of each annual meeting, or as soon thereafter as a full board has been elected, choose from their number, by ballot, a president and vice-president, and shall in a like manner choose from the stock-holders or from their own number, a secretary, treasurer, attorney and abstracter, all of whom shall serve for one year or until their respective successors are elected and qualified; provided, that any officer may be removed for neglect or malfeasance in his duties, by a two third vote of the board of directors.

SEC. 19. The board of directors shall have the general management of the affairs of the association, including the granting of loans and the acceptance of securities therefor. They may employ the money of the association, subject to the control of the stockholders, in any way consistent with the objects of the association. The board of directors may establish rules, with regard to loans, and with regard to the payment, by the association, of money to borrowers, upon mortgage securities, which rules shall be printed and furnished by the secretary to stockholders, on application. Such rules shall be binding upon all. Compensation for services, excepting those provided for, shall be fixed by the board of directors.

SEC. 20. The directors shall fill all vacancies in their number.

SEC. 21. A majority of the directors shall constitute a quorum of the board. The office of any director who shall be absent for four successive meetings of the Board, without sufficient excuse, may be declared vacant.

SEC. 22. It shall be the duty of the president, or in his absence, the vice-president, or in the absence of both president and vice-president, any director who may be elected *pro tem*, to preside at the meetings of the stockholders and of the board of directors, and to sign all orders for the payment of money authorized by the board.

SEC. 23. The president shall represent the association in the execution of all deeds, mortgages and other contracts in writing, and also in the release of mortgages made to the association. He shall have the custody of all bonds given to the association by its officers, except his own, if any, which shall be deposited with the treasurer. In the absence of the president, all his duties shall devolve upon the vice-president. In the absence of the president and vice-president, the directors may select one of their number to preside, with all the powers of the president.

SEC. 24. It shall be the duty of the secretary to attend all stockholders' meetings and meetings of the board of directors, and enter minutes of such meetings in a book of records kept for that purpose, and to receive all moneys due to the association, and pay over the same to the treasurer, taking his receipt therefor.

He shall keep a correct account between the association and the stockholders, draw and sign all orders on the treasurer, and attend to all publications. He shall be the custodian of all papers and documents pertaining to the business of the association, except the bonds of its officers. He shall make, to the board of directors, a statement of the affairs of the association, quarterly, and to the stockholders annually. He shall keep insured, for the benefit of the association, its interest in any building or property liable to loss by fire, and for this purpose is authorized to draw on the treasurer, without awaiting the action of the directors. Upon retiring from office, he shall turn over to his successor, within one week, all moneys, books and papers in his possession, belonging to the association. The secretary shall give to the association such bond as the board of directors may require.

SEC. 25. It shall be the duty of the treasurer to receive from the secretary all moneys paid into the association, giving his receipt therefor, and pay the same out only upon orders signed by the president and secretary, or in absence of the president, the vice-president, or president *pro tem*, except as provided in Section 24. He shall keep a correct account of all money received and paid by him. At the close of each semi-annual term, and at each annual term, and at each annual meeting of the stockholders, or oftener, if requested by the board of directors, he shall render a full statement of the business of his office. His books shall be open to inspection

by the board of directors at all times.  At the expiration of
his term of office, he shall, within one week, turn over to his
successor, all moneys, books, papers and other documents in
his possession belonging to the association.  .He shall execute to
the association such bond as the qoard of directors may require.

SEC. 26.  It shall be the duty of the attorney to examine all
abstracts of title to real estate offered to the association by
way of mortgage, as security for loans, and after such examination, to certify to the board of directors, his opinion in writing as to the title of such real estate, and in his certificate to
state any facts within his knowledge, touching the acceptabil-
ity of the security offered.

He shall prepare all bonds, notes, mortgages and other
papers incident to the making and securing of loans, and
cause them to be properly executed and to deliver the same to
the secretary.  He shall represent the association in all its legal
proceedings in which it is a party or is interested, and shall
have power to enter the appearance of the association therein.
In general, it shall be his duty to counsel and advise with the
directors and officers of the association therein, and give
proper attention to all its business of a legal nature.  His compensation shall be such as may be agreed upon by him and the
board of directors.

SEC. 27.  The annual meeting of the stockholders of the
association shall be held on the . . . . . . . . . . . ., and annually
thereafter, at 7:30 p. m., at the office of the association.

Special meetings of the stockholders may be called by the
president or the board of directors, or by the secretary, upon
the application of ten (10) members of the association in writing, stating the time and object of such meeting, provided that
none of said ten members are in arrears on any account, and
provided further that each of them shall have been shareholders one month.  Shareholders representing not less than one
tenth (1-10) of the subscribed capital stock of the association,
shall constitute a quorum at any meeting of the stockholders,
for the transaction of business.

SEC. 28.  The regular meetings of the board of directors
shall be held on the . . . . . day of every month, special meet-

ings may be called by the president, whenever the business of
the association may require. Upon the request of any three of
the directors, the president shall call a special meeting of the
directors at any time.

Sec. 29. On the first and third Monday nights of each
month, the moneys of the association shall, so far as any otherwise needed, be loaned to its members, at the rate of six per
cent. interest per annum, payable weekly in advance, the loan to
be secured by first mortgage on real estate in ...... county,
state of ......, and by the transfer to the association, as collateral of, one share of stock for each three hundred dollars, or
fractional part thereof, loaned, and by a transfer of any insurance to the association, that the board of directors may
require, or on pledge of stock alone.

The order of preference in granting loans shall be determined by auction sale, the person bidding the highest premium per share, to be paid weekly,* during the continuance of
the loan, to secure the preferance, and be entitled to have a
loan, to the aggregate face value of the number of shares
named in his bid.

Sec. 30. Bidders for preference in loans must state the
number of shares they are bidding upon and the premium per
share they are willing to pay.

Sec. 31. Loans may be made to stockholders in sums not
exceeding the par value of the stock held by the borrower.
Special loans may be made to others than members, on first
mortgage security, but loans to members shall have the preference. No loans will be made on personal security except as
provided in section 36.

Sec. 32. The directors may require from successful bidders
for loans, a deposit of money, in amount sufficient to meet the
probable expenses incident to meet the examination of the
security offered and consummation of the loan. The securities
must be submitted to the board of directors by the proposed
borrower, within two weeks from the date of the acceptance of
the bid, unless the time be extended by the board of directors.

*In some associations the pre-
mium is deducted at the time of the loan. In such associations a change
to that effect should be made.

SEC. 33. In case any successful bidder for a loan shall refuse to perfect the same, he shall pay, as fine for such refusal, $2 per share, and all expenses that may have been incurred, and such fine and expenses shall be a lien upon such member's stock. All the expenses incident to the making of abstracts of title, the examination of the same, appraisement of property, execution and recording of instruments, etc., shall be paid by the borrower, and shall constitute a lien upon his shares.

SEC. 34. Shareholders obtaining loans from the association must regularly and punctually pay to the secretary, all fees, instalments, fines and interest that shall accrue upon the shares pledged to the association, and if the same, or any portion thereof, shall remain unpaid for the period of .... months, it shall be the duty of the board of directors either to sue for the recovery of such fees, instalments, fines and interests, or such portion thereof as shall be unpaid, or to compel payment of all principal, interest to date, fees and fines due; and in either case the delinquent shareholder shall pay all expenses incurred by the Board in relation thereto. No shareholder, who is in arrears for instalments or fines, shall be entitled to a loan. And in the event of suit upon such loan, the amount recoverable shall be the amount of the loan, together with all arrears and costs, less instalments paid on the member's stock, which shall be applied on said debt. No interest shall be paid on such instalments.

SEC. 35. Borrowers on improved real estate must insure the said improvements to an amount satisfactory to the board of directors, (unless the real estate, irrespective of the improvements, be sufficient security,) at their own expense and have all policies of insurance endorsed with a mortgage clause to the association, and deliver said policies to the secretary, and also the receipts for the current year's premium thereon. Such policies must be filed with the secretary, at least three days prior to the expiration of the same, and if not so filed, the association shall renew such insurance, and the cost thereof shall be charged to the borrower, and shall also operate as a lien against the property loaned upon, and bear interest at the rate of .... per cent. per annum until paid.

Sec. 36. Any member may borrow on his stock its surrender value, the association deducting the interest and premium in advance. Such loans to be made for such time as
the directors may see fit.

Sec. 37. Any stockholder wishing to withdraw from the association, may do so by giving .. months notice in writing to the
secretary, and the liabilities to pay further dues, and the right
to dividends shall cease with said notice, and he shall be
entitled to receive the amount of dues paid in on the stock
withdrawn, together with....per cent. interest, for the average
time accruing from the date of such notice. Provided, however, he shall not be released from any liability as a stockholder,
for losses accrued at the date of such notice. Provided further, that at no time shall more than one-half of the funds in the
treasury of the association be applicable to the demands of withdrawing stockholders, without the consent of the board of directors, and further, that no stockholder be permitted to withdraw,
whose stock is held in pledge as security. The board of
directors shall have the power to provide for involuntary
withdrawals of stock, whenever, in their opinion, the best
interests of the association require it, but the stockholders
thus compelled to withdraw, shall receive the full profits, as
shown by the statement of the association next preceding
such action, with all instalments of dues on stock. This shall
not apply to pledged stock.

Sec. 38. Upon the death of a stockholder, his legal representatives shall be entitled to receive the full amount paid
in by him as dues on his stock, and such dividends as may
have been declared upon such stock, first deducting all charges
that may be due on the stock. No fines shall be charged on a
deceased member's account, unless the legal representatives of
such decedent assume the future payment upon such stock.

Sec. 39. A borrowing stockholder, who is not in arrears
for dues, interest, fines or assessments, may repay his loan at
any time, and at the same time withdraw from the association,
upon paying the amount of his loan, less the surrender value
of his stock, as fixed in section 37, and upon surrendering to
the association for cancellation, the stock held by him. And

thereupon he shall receive from the association the surrender of his note and mortgage, or other evidence of his loan, and a satisfaction and release of mortgage.

Sec. 40. The president shall appoint an appraising committee from among the stockholders, consisting of three members. It shall be the duty of the committee to visit property offered to the association as security for loans, to acquaint themselves with the cash value of such property, and make report thereof in writing, to the board of directors, at their next meeting.

The appraisers shall receive such fees as the board of directors may determine upon. No fee shall be paid to an appraiser who has not personally visited the property.

Sec. 41. The president shall appoint two persons, who shall constitute an auditing committee, who shall make an examination of the books, accounts and affairs of the association, semi-annually, and whose services, in making the examination, may be properly compensated.

Sec. 42. The president shall appoint a building inspector. It shall be the duty of this inspector to exercise a general supervision over all buildings erected with funds borrowed from the association, and to make such reports to the board of directors as may be required by the board. The building inspector may be paid such fees by the association as may be fixed by the board of directors.

Sec. 43. Every member neglecting to pay regularly the dues shall pay a fine of.... cents per share for each.... week (or month) of such neglect.

Sec. 44. ¹The secretary shall, at the end of every six (or twelve) months, calculate the earnings of the association, and said earnings shall be used as follows:

---

¹ This section is proper if the        Otherwise omitted.
association is a permanent one.

(a) For the payment of all expenses.

(b) Such an amount as the board of directors shall determine to be placed in the reserve fund.

(c) The balance shall be credited to the account of the members, according to their average investment, whether they have drawn money or not, and shall be paid upon withdrawal.

(d) No dividends shall be declared on dues paid in advance.

[1] Sec. 45. When, and so soon as the shares of any series shall have attained the value of two hundred dollars, the Directors shall call a meeting of the stockholders of that series, at which meeting stockholders who have not pledged their shares shall receive the value thereof, after deducting any fines that may be due thereon, and stockholders who have borrowed shall have their securities released and returned to them and shall surrender their stock to the association : Provided that no stockholder shall be entitled to have his or her securities released, or liens against him or her satisfied until he or she has fully paid all fees, instalments, fines and interest, and all charges that he or she may owe to the association.

[2] Sec. 46. Any member of this association who shall make a loan with the association for the purpose of building or purchasing improved property, and who shall pass a satisfactory examination for life insurance, in a life insurance company named by this association, by paying as a part of the monthly premium upon his loan, the amount necessary to pay the premium upon his policy of life insurance on his life, and in favor of the association, shall receive from the association

[1] Used if association is serial; otherwise omitted.

[2] If life insurance is desired, this section is proper. In some places life insurance for borrowing members on the instalment premium plan is popular and it presents strong advantages of security for the family of the borrower and the association.

12

an agreement or guarantee, that in case he shall keep up his
monthly payment of dues, premiums, interest, fines and other
charges, from month to month, when due, including the
amount necessary to keep up his policy of life insurance as
stated herein, that if he shall die before the repayment of the
loan or the maturity of the shares loaned upon, the association
will pay off the loan upon his shares, and will cancel the
mortgages or deeds of trust securing the same, leaving to the
estate the share or shares of stock owned by such shareholder
at the time of his death, unpledged and continuable, or withdrawable at the option of the heirs, said loan not to be cancelled, however, until such proof of death has been made as
shall be satisfactory to the life insurance company holding the
policy of insurance upon the life of the shareholder aforesaid.

The conditions of the foregoing section are to be embodied
in the mortgage or deed of trust, given by the borrower to
secure the loan made to him, and the faithful fulfilment of
all of the conditions of same on his part, to be made a condition precedent to the guarantee of the association.

Sec. 47.   The expenses shall be .... cents per week per
share (or shall be deducted from the profits before any division is made), and shall be incurred only by authority of the
board of directors.

Sec. 48.   The seal of the corporation shall consist of the
name and location of the association, and the date of its charter, the whole to be surrounded by an ornamental circular
border.   It shall be produced by a single impression of an
embossing press.   It shall be in the custody of the President,
and he shall see that it is affixed to all official papers that require it.   The president may delegate custody of the seal to
the secretary.

Sec. 49.   In case a deposit book is lost or stolen, immediate
information of the same must be given to the secretary.   As
the officers of this association may be unable to identify every
shareholder, when the shareholder fails to notify the officers
that his deposit book has been lost or stolen, the association

will not be responsible for loss sustained, if his shares shall be fraudulently withdrawn by another, provided, that in case of the alleged theft or loss of a deposit book, the Executive Committee may at their discretion authorize the issue of a duplicate, or may authorize the payment of the shares without the deposit book, if withdrawn in full, but shall in either case require a bond to indemnify the association for any loss it may sustain on account of the lost or stolen deposit book.

Sec. 50. The by-laws may be amended by a two-thirds vote of the directors present and voting at a regular or special meeting, provided that the proposed amendment shall have been submitted by the association in writing, at a meeting held at least four weeks previous to action on the same. Notice of each amendment given to each member at his last place of residence, as shown on the books of the association, by mail, shall be sufficient.

The following application completely presents a loan before the directors. The vital point in the life of the association is in its securities, and too much care cannot be exercised in guarding all points, one of which is the application. Too many societies are careless in this matter, and if trouble follows, it is often traceable to this as its source.

## Application for a Real Estate Loan from the ..............Association.

I........do hereby make application for a loan of...... Dollars, to bear interest at the rate of....per cent per annum, and a premium of........payable on or before the......day of..........; all payments to be at such place as the lender may direct; and to secure the same....hereby agree to assign and transfer......shares of the capital stock of said association, owned by......as collateral security, and to give a first

mortgage on the real estate set forth in the following questions and answers:

1.  Name of applicant (State surname and christian name
in full)..........................

2.  What is your Post Office address?............

3.  Are you married?............

4.  Give full name of husband or wife............

5.  What is your occupation?............

6.  How long has this been your occupation?........

7.  What was your occupation previous to this time?....

8.  State age of each husband....wife........

9.  What is your regular monthly income, and from what
source do you obtain it............
State full particulars as to source and amounts.

10.  How many persons are dependent upon you for
support?....................

11.  In whom is the title to the real estate on which the
loan is asked?...............

12.  What is the description of the property according to
the deed?...............

13.  What is the size of the ground?....ft. by.....ft., on
........Street, between........Street and........Street.

14.  Is the ground above or below grade?........

15.  How much?...............

16.  What is the distance from the business center of the
town?....................

17. **Improvements now on the premises.** Foundation, wood, brick, or stone?........Solid wall or pillars? ........Building on foundation; frame, brick or stone?.... Stories high?....How long built?......How many rooms? ........Bath room?........Hard or soft wood finish?.... Size of house on the ground?....ft by....ft.....Well?.... Cistern?........City water?......Sewer?........Furnace? ........Gas?........Grates?........Shutters?....Kind of roof?........Size and description of cellar?........Is house all finished?........In what repair?..........Is the house painted?........How many coats?....Fence?....Side-walk? Out house?........Stable?.......Value?.......Other improvements?........Give date of last improvement and what they were........For what purpose is the property used? ........In what direction does the house front?........

18. **Improvements to be built.** Kind of foundation. Wood, brick or stone?........Solid walls or pillars?........ Building on foundation; log, frame, brick or stone?........ stories high?........Is the house painted?......How many coats?....Plastered?......No. coats and skim coat?........ No. of rooms?........Bathroom?........Hard or soft wood finish?........Well?........Cistern?........City water? ........Sewer?........Furnace?........Shutters?....... For what purpose is the property to be used?..........Gas? ......Grates?........Size of cellar?........Kind of walks? ........Good fence?........Size of house on ground?..... ft. by....ft....................

19. What kind of flues in the house?..........In what direction does the house front?............

20. Have you a barn?........Size on the ground?...... Height of corner posts?............

21. Value in cash of the barn? $........

22. Of what material and in what repairs are the fence?..

23.  Side walks?...........

24.  What other buildings or improvements are there besides those already mentioned?........

25.  Give date of last improvements and what were they?.....................

26.  State particulars as to trees and shrubbery?........

27.  How long have you owned the property?........

28.  How much did you pay for it?........

29.  Did you pay cash or did you trade for it?........

30.  Is it all paid for?................

31.  If not, state how much is unpaid?.........

32.  Do you agree to carry approved fire insurance equal in amount to the loan?............

33.  Is the property rented?...........

34.  How much per month?........

35.  Have you ever applied for a loan on this property? If so, from whom?........What result?........

36.  If occupied by a tenant how much would it bring per month?....................

37.  What is the value of the ground without the improvements?..........What is the value of the improvements in their present condition?....   .......

38.  What is the estimated cost of the improvements to be made?....................

39.  Is the title perfect in applicant?........

40.  The property is assessed for taxes; ground $........

Improvements $......... Are taxes all paid to date?........

41.   Is the sidewalk in front of the property curbed and paved?...................

42.   Is the bed of the street paved?........

43.   Are gas pipes laid in the street?........

44.   Are water pipes laid in the street?..........

45. Is the property incumbered in any way by mortgage or mechanic's liens, unpaid taxes, judgments, suits pending or liens of any kind?   If so, state the nature, date, maturity, and amount of incumbrance and by whom held.

46. Can the liens on the property be paid now?

47. For what purpose is the money borrowed?

48. Do you wish this loan to be made in installments as the building progresses or on completion of the improvements?

49.   Does your wife consent to join in the bond and mortgage?

50.   What could the property be sold for now in cash?

51.   What would it bring at forced sale now?

52.   What is the cash value of all the property owned by you?   Real estate.............personal.................

53.   What are your total liabilities at this time?

If this application is accepted, I will furnish, at my own expense, a complete abstract of title to the land proposed as security, and have the same certified to be correct by the proper party, which abstract shall be brought down to a date subsequent to the approval of my application for the loan, and show a clear and perfect title in the applicant. I agree to pay the expenses of examination and appraisement of the property and for examining the title and recording the mortgage and making of the papers.

The secretary of the association is hereby authorized to procure an abstract of the property herein offered, as security, and a policy of insurance on the buildings thereon, unless the same shall be furnished by me as soon as required by the board of directors, or the rules of the association, and to deduct the cost of the same from the proceeds of the loan, together with all other costs or indebtedness connected therewith, and to pay therefrom any judgments, taxes, liens or incumberances of any kind whatever, which may exist against the property at the time of closing the loan; and if this is a building loan, I agree, before any payments are made on the same, to furnish the secretary a complete list of all contractors, or sub-contractors, or parties furnishing material or work for the said buildings, together with the amounts of their several claims, and their signatures, waiving all senior rights of lien, for any amounts, in excess of the same, unless my contractor furnishes a satisfactory idemnifying bond to the said association. I also agree to be governed by rules in force, concerning loans, a copy of which I acknowledge receipt.

The applicant herein warrants that the representations above made are true, and agrees that they shall form a part of the consideration of a mortgage, which may hereafter be executed by said applicant to said association, to secure such loan as may be granted, and if there is any misrepresentation in said application, it shall operate as a default in conditions of said mortgage, and render the debt due and the mortgage may be foreclosed.

### APPRAISER'S REPORT.

STATE OF ........,  } ss.
......County }

We, the undersigned, do solemnly swear that we are all well

acquainted with the value of real estate, described in said application, and with the property described in the within application, and that the ground without improvements is worth in cash $...., and the buildings are worth in cash $...., and the improvements to be made will cost ...... dollars. The property would bring at forced sale, in cash, at the present time, $....... We are also personally acquainted with ............, mentioned in the within application, and believe him to have good standing and credit. We regard .... as a prompt, upright, reliable person, pecuniarily responsible for ...... contracts, and we believe that he will promptly meet all payments of principal and interest on the loan herein applied for. We believe this property is adequate security, with improvements, present and proposed, for a loan of $....... We are not interested in said premises, nor in the result of this application for a loan.

Signed,

............, [SEAL.]

(Notarial Certificate.)
............, [SEAL.]

**Rules of Saving and Loan Association,** governing the bidding for loans, the manner of making payments to builders and other information for borrowing stockholders.

1. The regular periods for the sale of money are the nights in each month, prescribed in the by-laws.

2. Bidders for preference in loans must state the number of shares they are bidding upon and the amount per share they are willing to pay.

3. Immediately upon the acceptance of his bid, each applicant shall pay into the hands of the secretary the sum of .... dollars, to be paid to the members of the appraising committee, for services in appraising property within the corporate limits of ....or ....dollars for like services outside of said limits: The proposed borrower should promptly call at the office of the attorney of the Association, taking with him his abstract to title to the real estate to be offered as security;

in case he has no abstract of title he should take his deed; at the attorney's office a written application and all necessary legal papers will be prepared.

4.  The fees of the attorney, notary, abstracter, county recorder, and insurance premiums, shall be noted on the first warrant drawn in favor of the borrower, and be retained for, and paid to them by the treasurer from the amount so drawn, unless sooner paid from the private funds of the borrower.

6.  The payment of premium and interest shall begin with the date of execution of bonds and mortgages to the Association.

5.  On the receipt of the written certificate of the attorney, that title to security offered for a loan is perfect, and all legal requirements having been complied with by the borrower, the secretary shall draw warrants in favor of the person to whom the loan is made, for amount not exceeding cash in hands of the treasurer, and be subject to the conditions preceding and following this rule.

7.  Should the borrowing member desire to build upon or improve his property, the money may be advanced in install-ments as the work progresses; but no money shall be paid until the plans and specifications for the work have been submitted and approved, and a contract or contracts have been made with responsible parties, said parties in all instances to execute a good and satisfactory bond, conditioned to indem-nify the Association' from any and all loss that may arise from said improvements, by reason of mechanics or other liens.  Should the borrowing member however, desire to make more extensive improvements than called for by the amount of money borrowed, he will be at liberty to do so by paying the said extra improvements, *prior* to any payment made by the board of directors, and shall furnish receipts showing proper expenditure of the same to the secretary.

8.  The money shall be advanced in installments as follows: The first payment when the property is secured and foundation

completed and the contract or contracts are signed as above, and indemnifying bond given as above provided. The second payment when the frame is up and the building enclosed. The third payment when the plastering is on. The last payment when the house is finished.

9. No building shall be considered finished until a good supply of water is provided.

10. The manner of making payments, however, may be changed by the board of directors so as to meet the requirements in special cases.

11. The payments must be so arranged that at least *one fourth* of the whole amont of the loan shall be retained for the last payment.

12. A bidder failing to perfect his loan for a period of thirty days after the date of his bid, shall incur the penalties provided for in Section 33 of the by-laws of this Association.

13. Borrowers on stock securities will be governed in all respects by the provisions of Sec. 36, of the by-laws of this Association.

14. Loans shall not in any case exceed $66\frac{2}{3}$ per cent of the value of the security offered, after completion of all contracts on the part of the borrower.

15. The board of directors reserve the right to strike out, amend, modify or change any of their rules, whenever deemed by it advisable so to do.

## MORTGAGE NOTE.

...........................189..

For value received, I, we, or either of us, promise to pay to the............ Association, of .........., the sum of ........... dollars, with interest at the rate of .... per cent per annum, from date until paid, and attorney's fees.

The said interest and premiums to be paid in ...... instalments, on or before the .... day in each ...., from and after
this date. And as collateral security for this note, .. hereby
transfer and assign .... shares of the capital stock of said
association and agree to pay dues, fines and other charges on
said stock, as provided in the by-laws of said association.

This note to be due when such stock matures, as provided
in the by-laws of said association, and such matured stock may
be applied in full payment thereof.

## BOND. GENERAL FORM.

This form of bond may be used in those states where a form
is not herein given for a state, and has been prepared after consulting bonds used in different states.

Know all men by these present, that ...................
...... ..., of ........ county, in the State of ..........,
held and firmly bound unto the.............Association, of
........, in the sum of .... hundred dollars, together with
ten per cent attorney's fees, which well and truly to be paid,
.... bind .... heirs, executors and administrators firmly by
these presents.

Sealed with .... seal and dated this .... day of ....
189...

The conditions of this obligation are such; That whereas,
the above bounden obligor, ................, has subscribed
for .... shares of the capital stock of $......, each in said
association, for which share.. of stock.. he received from said
association the sum of ........ hundred dollars, as a loan,
which shares of stock are hereby transferred as collateral
security for the payment of this bond, with agreement on....
part that .. he .. will continue to pay .... dues on the said
shares of stock, at the rate of .... cents per .... on each
share, together with a premium of ........ per .... on each

share of stock,[1] and interest on said loan at the rate of ....
per cent per annum, all payable on or before the .... day of
..., until such share.. mature, as provided by the by-laws of
said association; also, pay all fines and assessments on such
shares, as provided for in said by-laws. All payments of
money hereunder shall be made at the office of the association,
in the city of ........

Now, if the above bounden obligor shall, well and truly
keep and perform said bond in every part, without fraud
or delay, then the above obligation to be void and of no
effect, but if default be made in any part thereof, then the
above bounden obligor is to forfeit all the premiums, fines,
assessments and interest so paid into said association, and pay
back said loan, less all such dues credited[2] thereon.[3]

All payments of money hereby secured, shall be made without relief, from valuation or appraisement laws.

## MORTGAGE. GENERAL FORM.

The following form of mortgage may be used in the states,
other than those where the forms are hereinafter given. It has
been prepared after consulting the forms in use in the different states:

This indenture witnesseth; That ......................

[1] In associations in New York, where the premium is deducted at the time of making the loan, this clause is omitted.

[2] Or the surrender value of the stock.

[3] In Delaware the following clause is added:

And .... do hereby authorize and empower any clerk, prothonotary or attorney of any court of record, in America, or elsewhere, in case of default in the conditions of said bond, to appear for .... the said... ............ heirs, executors or administrators, at the suit of the said corporation, its successors or assigns, on the above obligation, as of any term prior or subsequent to the date hereof, and thereupon to confess judgment for the above sum of ............. dollars debt, besides cost of suit, by *non sum informatus*, *nihil dicit*, or otherwise, with stay of execution until the day of payment.

(or do grant, bargain, sell, convey and confirm unto)[1] of
............county, State of.. ....., mortgage and warrant to the ............ Association, a corporation incorporated and existing, by virtue of the laws of the State of ....,
the following real estate, situated in ........ county, State
of ........, and described as follows, to wit:

................................................ ................
together with all and singular the tenements, hereditaments
and appurtenances thereunto belonging, or in any wise appertaining, for its own use, benefit and behoof forever.

This mortgage is intended and executed as security for the
performance of the stipulations and agreements of a certain
bond[2] of even date, herewith executed by said ............,
as obligor to said association, in the sum of ........ hundred
dollars, which is a just and full loan, made to said ........,
under the rules and by-laws of said association, at an authorized meeting of the board of directors, upon a certain written
application therefor, by said ...., which application is made a
part of this mortgage. Conditioned, that the said..........
shall continue to pay monthly dues upon .... share.. of
$......, each of the capital stock of said association, at the
rate of .... cents per ...... on each share of stock, and ....
premium per .... on each share of stock, and interest, on
said loan, at the rate of .... per cent per annum, all payable
on or before the .... day of each ....., until such share..
mature, as provided by the by-laws of said association; also
pay all fines and assessments on said shares, as provided in
said by-laws, and to pay all money herein provided for, at the
office of the association, in the city of ........

And it is further agreed, if the said obligor.... shall well
and truly keep and perform said bond in every part, then

---

[1] Instead of "mortgage and war-
rant" this clause is used in the fol-
lowing states: North Carolina,
Kansas, Oregon, North Dakota,
Arkansas, Connecticut, Nebraska,
Wisconsin, Maine, Florida, Rhode
Island and Wyoming.

[2] If a note is used as in California,
Oregon and New Mexico, the clauses
identifying the bond should be
omitted and the note (see form) incorporated in full.

said bond to be void and of no effect, and this mortgage shall
be cancelled: but if default be made in any part thereof, the
above obligor....to forfeit all the premiums, fines, assessments and interests so paid into said association and pay back
said loan, less all dues credited thereon.

The mortgagor.., further agree..to keep such mortgaged
premises in good repair, to pay all taxes, assessments and
charges thereon as the same become due, not commit or suffer
any waste of said property, and to keep the improvements on
said real estate insured in some responsible insurance company, to the satisfaction of the board of directors of said
Association, in the sum of $........for the benefit of said
association, and to transfer such insurance to said association,
and deliver the policies for said insurance to said association,
to be held as collateral security until the loan is fully paid.
In the event said mortgagor... fail..to pay said taxes or assessment, or keep said property insured, said association may do
so, and the cost thereof, with....per cent interest, shall be
collectible under this mortgage.

The mortgagor....further agree....that upon default of
any of the conditions of this mortgage, or of said bond, in any
part thereof, for a period of............,said bond shall without notice (notice being hereby expressly waived), at the option
of the board of directors of said association, be and become
due and collectible, either by suit upon said bond, or by the
foreclosure of this mortgage; and upon such default occurring, it is agreed that the mortgagee shall have possession of
the said premises during the redemption year, and a receiver
may be appointed to take possession of the said premises, for
the purpose of applying the rents and profits thereof to the
payment of the debt secured by this mortgage, which receivership shall continue from date of such default until the said
premises shall be redeemed according to law, or until such
year expires.

It is further agreed, that all of said payments herein mentioned, shall be made without relief from valuation and appraisement laws, waiving and releasing homestead exemption

laws. All moneys payable under this mortgage may at any time be required in gold coin of the United States. No failure to exercise this right by the mortgagee shall operate as the waiver thereof.

¹And the said mortgagor....for....heirs, executors and administrators, covenant....and agree....that.... he.... well seized of the premises conveyed, as of a perfect, absolute and indefeasible estate of inheritance in fee simple absolute, and ha....good right, full power, and lawful authority to grant, bargain, sell and convey the same in manner and form aforesaid, and that the same are free and clear of all incumbrances, and that....he...will forever warrant and defend said land, unto said mortgagee or its assigns, against all claims to the same.

The said............... wife of said mortgagor, by joining in this mortgage, relinquishes all her interest in said property, as against the said association.

In witness whereof, said mortgagor.. ha.. hereunto set .....hand.. and seal.. this........day of........18 .

The acknowledgment by the mortgagors should follow, and, as its form depends upon the law of each state, governing acknowledgments to instruments for record in such state, and differs in many states, no form is here given.² It is easily ascertainable from any conveyancer.

---

¹This clause is added in the forms used in the following states: North Carolina, Kansas, Oregon, North Dakota, Arkansas, Connecticut, Nebraska, Wisconsin, Maine, Florida, Rhode Island and Wyoming.

²In the following states and territories the signing of a mortgage must be attested by witnesses, in addition to acknowledgment, before it can be recorded: New Hampshire, Minnesota, South Carolina, Oregon, Ohio, Georgia, New York, North Carolina. (Alabama and Pennsylvania, where party is unable to write), Colorado, Connecticut, Florida, Idaho, Lousiana, Michigan, Nebraska, Rhode Island, for married woman, Utah, Vermont, Virginia, Washington, Wisconsin and Wyoming.

In the following states and territories, North Carolina, Alabama, Arkansas, Montana, Rhode Island, Wyoming, Michigan, Maryland, New Mexico and California, this clause is to be added:

It is further understood and agreed, that if any default, as aforesaid, shall be made by said............ or his grantee, then it shall be lawful for said association to sell said real estate at public (or private)¹ sale in said county, for cash or upon such other terms as said association may deem best, after ............notice, by publishing in a proper newspaper, published in said county, and thereafter said association may convey in fee simple, such land to the purchaser or purchasers thereof, freed from any claim, title or right of redemption of said mortgagors, or either of them; and out of the proceeds of such sale to retain the amount due said association, on account of said loan, together with all costs incident to such sale and conveyance, and the balance, if any, remaining, shall be paid to said................

---

The association may loan its shareholders on their stock up to its surrender value. In such cases, the following form is used:

.....................Association.

### Collateral Transfer for Loans.

I, the undersigned, shareholder in the above named Association, do hereby assign, transfer, and set over to the said Association, all my right, title and interest in and to the number of shares (in the particular series) of the capital stock of said association, indicated below, said shares to be held by said association as collateral security, (in addition to note given) for payment of loan made to me by said association. I hereby bind myself to continue to pay the monthly dues upon each of the several shares, and all fines, if any, and to be governed in all respects by the by-laws of said association.

13          ¹Just as the statute may provide.

## Loan.

Book No........Shares of Series........On Shares $....
........Shares of Series........Monthly Interest........
:........Shares of Series........Monthly Premium.......
Dated.

Signature of Witness.        Signature of Shareholder.

........................      ........................

## Note.

$..............          ................18....

Having this day pledged and transferred to the....a corporation duly established by law........shares of its capital stock, said shares being....in the ....series as collateral security, for the payment of the sums herein mentioned, upon which shares the sum of........dollars ($.......) has been advanced to me, by said association, for value received, on demand after date, I promise to pay to said association, or order, the sum of............dollars ($......) and until the payment of said sum of............dollars ($........), to pay to said association, or order, the sum of............ dollars ($........) at or before the stated..... meetings of the board of directors of said association on the second......of each and every........hereafter, being the amount of the........dues on said shares of the......... interest and premium upon said loan or advance of........ dollars ($........) for which said shares are pledged and this note given, together with all fines chargeable by the by-laws of said association, upon arrears of such (monthly) payments.

Signed in the presence of

........................

........................

........................

## Form of Trust Deed.

Trust deeds are used in the following States and Territories: Missouri, Mississippi, Utah, Tennessee, Virginia, West Virginia, New Mexico, and also District of Columbia.

This indenture made and entered into this........day of
................, A. D., 18....by and between..........
..............of the County of..........State of......
....part....of the first part, and.................County
of............, State of...........part....of second part,
and the....................Association, a corporation duly
organized under the laws of the State of.............part
of the third part.

Witnesseth: That the said part....of first part, in consideration of the debt and trust hereinafter mentioned and created, and the sum of One Dollar to......paid by said part ....of the second part, the receipt of which is hereby acknowledged, do by these presents grant, bargain and sell, convey and confirm, (or convey and warrant), unto the second party of second part, the following described real estate, situated in the County of.........., State of..............
................and possession of said premises, now deliver unto said party of second part.

To have and to hold the same, with the appurtenances to said party of the second part, and to his successors hereinafter designated, and to the assigns of him and his successors forever; in trust, however, for the following purposes:

Whereas, the said..................part....of the first part, by..........certain bond (or note) duly executed and delivered, bearing even date herewith, are bound unto said association, party of the third part, in the sum of.......dollars ($......) lawful money of the United States of America, loaned by said association to said part......of the first part, on...........shares of stock owned by..............(in series...........) of said association, being at the rate of ........dollars on each share, conditioned that said part.... of the first part........heirs, executors and administrators, do..well and truly pay or caused to be paid, unto the said association, its successors or assigns, in lawful money, the interest to accrue on said sum of........dollars; at the rate of....per cent per annum, payable. ..........on the....

........of each and every........hereafter, and shall also well and truly pay, or cause to be paid, unto said association or assigns, the sum of..........dollars...... .on the...... day of each and every..........hereafter, for the.......... contribution or dues on...............shares of the capital stock of said association now owned by said............... until the value of said stock shall be sufficient to divide to each and every share thereof, the sum of two hundred dollars, ($200.00), and shall also well and truly pay, or cause to be paid, to the said association, its successors or assigns, the sum of.. ....dollars on said............of each and every........ hereafter, for the premium upon the amount of said loan, and shall fully indemnify and save said association from all losses by reason of said loan, according to the by-laws, rules and regulations that are or may be made by the said association, and also that............will promptly pay all taxes or liens of whatsoever nature, levied or assessed upon said real estate, described in this deed of trust, within the limited time by law for the payment thereof, and also that..........will keep the buildings upon said real estate as herein described, con- stantly insured in some responsible insurance company or companies, to be approved by the directors of said association, in a sum not less than...............dollars, and the policy or policies of such insurance duly assigned and de- livered to said association; and also pay all fines and assess- ments against said shares. Said bond further contains an express covenant and agreement on the part of said part.... of the first part to and with said association, that if, at any time, default shall be made in the payment of said interest on said sum of...............dollars, or in the payment of the monthly contributions or dues on said stock, or in any monthly payment of the sum provided in said bond, and herein to be paid as premium on said loan, or fines or assessments, the same or either of said sums shall remain unpaid for the space of six months after any payment thereof shall fall due, then, and in such case, the whole principal debt aforesaid shall, at the option of said association, their successors and assigns, immediately thereupon become due and payable and recoverable; and the payment of said principal sum and all interest thereon, as well as contributions on said.............shares of stock, whatsoever due, may be recovered by sale, under said deed of trust, or other legal proceedings, as provided by law, and also if any taxes or liens whatsoever lawfully levied or assessed on said real estate remain due and unpaid, or if said real estate shall be advertised for sale for the payment of taxes, or if the said................shall fail or neglect to keep said buildings constantly insured, and the policy or policies of insurance duly assigned to the said association, then the said association, may at its option, proceed to recover the whole amount due by the provisions of said bond; or the said association may pay said taxes or liens, or redeem said real estate from sale for taxes or liens, and cause said buildings to be insured for the amount above specified, and the amount of taxes or liens paid and amount of premiums paid for said insurance, by said association, shall be added to the record as a part of the amount secured by said bond in this deed of trust; and the same shall bear interest at the rate of...... per cent per annum, until repayment shall be made to said association, and also that the part......of the first part, shall pay all necessary and proper costs and expenses of whatsoever nature, incurred about the collection of this trust, including a reasonable attorney's fee, costs of sale, or other legal proceedings thereunder.

Now, therefore, if the said part....of the first part shall fully and faithfully comply with the conditions, provisions and agreements contained in said bond, and, in this deed of trust, according to the true tenor and effect thereof, then this deed shall be void, and the property hereinbefore conveyed shall be released at the cost of said part....of the first part.

But should the said part....of the first part, fail or refuse to comply with such conditions, provisions and agreements contained in said bond, and in this deed of trust, then this deed shall be and remain in full force and effect, and the said party of the second part, or is case of his absence or death, or refusal or disability to act in anywise, the then acting sheriff

of........County........at the request of said association, its successors and assigns, may proceed to sell the property hereinbefore described, or any part thereof, at public vendue, to the highest bidder, at.....................in.............
County............for cash, first giving........day's notice of the time, place and terms of sale, and all the property to be sold, by advertisement in some newspaper, printed and published in........County..........and upon such sale shall execute and deliver a deed of conveyance of the property sold to the purchaser or purchasers thereof, and any statement or recital of fact in such deed, in relation to the nonpayment of money hereby secured to be paid, existence of the indebtedness so secured, notice of sale by advertisement, sale, receipt of money, and the happening of any of the aforesaid events, whereby the sheriff may become successor as herein provided, shall be *prima facie* evidence of the truth of such statement or recital; and the said trustee shall receive the proceeds of said sale, out of which he shall pay, first, the cost and expenses of executing this trust, including compensation to the trustee for his services, and legal expenses to the attorney for his services; and next he shall apply the proceeds thereof, remaining over, to the payment of said debt and interest, and the premium and so much thereof as remains unpaid, and the remainder, if any, shall be paid to the said part....of the first part or....legal representatives.

The said party of the third part may become the purchaser at the sale of said land, made by said........as trustee, or any person acting in his stead as trustee, as aforesaid, just as if such sale were made by a trustee in whose trust said association had no interest.

In witness whereof, the said part....of the first part, ha....hereunto set....hand....and seal...., this day and year first above written.

Executed in the presence of......................[SEAL]
.......................            ....................[SEAL]
.......................            ....................[SEAL]
                                 ....................[SEAL]

## Form of Insurance Clause.

The following insurance clause should be used. Under the ordinary "loss if any payable" clause, the rights of the association may be jeopardized by some act of the mortgagor.

## Union Mortgage Clause.

Loss, if any, payable to........mortgagee or trustee, as hereinafter provided.

It being hereby understood and agreed, that this insurance, as to the interest of the mortgagee or trustee, only herein, shall not be invalidated by any act or neglect of the mortgagor or owner of the property insured, nor by the occupation of the premises for purposes more hazardous than are permitted by the terms of this policy. Provided, that in case the mortgagor or owner neglects or refuses to pay any premium due under this policy, then, on demand, the mortgagee or trustee shall pay the same. Provided, also, that the mortgagee or trustee shall notify this company of any change of ownership, or increase of hazard, which shall come to his, or their knowledge, and shall have permission for such change of ownership or increase of hazard, duly endorsed on this Policy. And, provided, further, that every increase of hazard not permitted by the policy to the mortgagor or owner, shall be paid for by the mortgagee or trustee, on reasonable demand, and after demand made by this company upon, and refusal by the mortgagor or owner to pay, according to the established schedule of rates. It is, however, understood that this company reserves the right to cancel this policy, as stipulated in the printed conditions in said policy; and also, to cancel this agreement on giving ten days' notice of their intention to the trustee or mortgagee named therein, and from and after the expiration of the said ten days, this agreement shall be null and void. It is further agreed, that in case of any other insurance upon the property hereby insured, then this company shall not be liable under this policy for a greater proportion of any loss sustained than the sum hereby insured bears to the whole amount of insurance on said property, issued to or held by any party or parties having an insurable interest therein. It is also agreed, that whenever this company shall pay the mortgagee or trustee any sum for loss under this policy, and shall claim that as to the mortgagor or owner, no liability therefore existed, it shall at once, and to the extent of such payment, be legally subrogated to all the rights of the party to whom such payments shall be made, under any and all securities held by such party, for the payment of said debt. But such subrogation shall be in subordination to the claim of said party, for the balance of the debt so secured. Or said company may, as its option, pay the said mortgagee or trustee the whole debt so secured, with all the interest which may have accrued thereon, to the date of such payment, and shall thereupon receive from the party to whom such payment shall be made, an assignment and transfer of said debts, with all securities held by said parties for the payment thereof.

To attach to Policy No.........of the................
Dated at........this........day of........189....
.....................Agent.

## Form of Bond.

Where the whole premium is deducted from the loan at the time of making it, this form may be used with the general form of mortgage hereinbefore given, identifying it in the body of such mortgage.

Know all men by these presents, that......of....County ......State of............held and firmly bound unto the .....Building and Loan Association, of........a corporation duly organized and doing business under the laws of the State of...............in the sum of................dollars, for the payment whereof, well and truly to be made,....... bind........sel............heirs, executors, administrators and assigns, jointly and severally, firmly by these presents.

Witness........hand and seal, this.......day of...... A. D. 18....

The condition of the above obligation is such, that whereas, on the........day of........A. D. 18...., the said...... being a member of said association, by bidding....per cent premium on the par value of........shares of the.....series of the capital stock of the said association, obtained precedence of an advanced loan, to the amount of........dollars, and has, after deducting the premium bid as aforesaid, received ........dollars, it being the full value and in full payment of said........shares of stock.

Now, if the above obligor,........heirs, executors, administrators and assigns, or any of them, shall well and truly pay, or cause to be paid, unto the above obligee, its successor or assigns, the sum of........dollars, said sum to be paid in monthly installments of........dollars each, the first payment or installment due and payable........A. D. 18 ..., and........dollars monthly thereafter, being the monthly dues on said........shares of stock, together with interest at the rate of .... per cent per annum, on said........dollars, said interest due and payable in monthly installments of..... dollars and........cents, the first of said interest installment, due and payable........A. D. 18....said dues and interest payable on the first day of each month thereafter; said installments of principal and interest to be paid promptly, as they become due, during the existence of said association, or until each shareholder in the........ series thereof, has received on each of his shares one hundred dollars, including any premium which he may have bid on his share or shares, and shall also pay all fines assessed on said stock, and all taxes, insurance or incumbrances of any kind, which may be imposed upon the property conveyed by mortgage deed to secure the above indebtedness, without delay, then the above obligation to be void, otherwise to remain in full force and virtue.

Provided, however, and it is expressly agreed, if at any time default shall be made in the payment of said installments of principal money, when due, or of said interest, or of fines due under the by-laws of said association, for the space of six

months after any payment thereof shall fall due, the said
........shares of stock of........series, on which the said
loan is obtained and herewith transferred, may at any time
thereafter be declared forfeited, as for non-payment of dues,
and therefrom revert to said obligee, its successors or assigns,
as forfeited stock, and the withdrawal value thereof, less one-
eighth of said premium bid for said loan for each year, said
........series of stock shall have run, at the option of the
obligee, its successors or assigns, be applied to the satisfaction
of the above indebtedness, and in such case or cases, the whole
principal debt aforesaid, and interest shall, at the option of the
obligee, its successors or assigns, immediately become due and
recoverable, and payment of said principal sum and all the
interest thereon, as well as any contribution on said........
shares of stock, and all fines and taxes as aforesaid then due,
may be enforced and recovered at once, anything herein contained to the contrary notwithstanding; and it is further
understood and agreed, that all fines and penalties for non-
payment of dues are agreed, assessed and liquidated damages
for such non-payment of installments due on said stock.

.............................[SEAL.]

.............................[SEAL.]

The following is the form of bond in use by associations in
Pennsylvania:

Know all men by these presents, that........(hereinafter
called the obligor), is held and firmly bound unto.....(hereinafter called the obligees), in the sum of........dollars, lawful money of the United States of America, to be paid to the
said obligees, their certain Attorney, successors or assigns.
To which payment well and truly to be made,........do bind
........heirs, executors and administrators, and every one of
them, firmly by these presents. Sealed with........seal....
dated the........day of........in the year of our Lord one
thousand eight hundred and...........

The condition of this obligation is such, that if the above bounded obligor........heirs, executors and administrators, or any of them, shall and do well and truly pay, or cause to be paid, unto the above-named obligees, their certain attorney, successors or assigns, the just sum of........dollars, such as above said, at any time within one year from the date hereof, together with interest,........for the same, and together with all fines imposed by the constitution and by-laws of the aforesaid association, in like money, payable monthly, on the ........of each and every month hereafter, and shall also well and truly pay, or cause to be paid, unto the said obligees, their successors or assigns, the sum of....dollars, on the said ....of each and every month hereafter, as and for the monthly contribution on........share of the capital stock of the said obligees, now owned by the said obligor, without any fraud or further delay; and shall also deliver to the said obligees, their successors or assigns, on or before the........day of ........of each and every year, receipts for all taxes of the current year, assessed upon the premises described in the accompanying indenture of mortgage. Provided, however, and it is hereby expressly agreed, that if at any time default shall be made in the payment of the said principal money when due, or of the said interest, or of the said fines, or the monthly contribution, on said stock, for the space of six months after any payment thereof shall fall due, or in such delivery to the said obligees, their successors or assigns, on or before the........day of........of each and every year, of such receipts for such taxes of the current year, upon the premises mortgaged, or if the said obligor shall not well and truly pay, or cause to be paid, the........and taxes, on the premises particularly described in the mortgage accompanying this obligation, when the same shall become due and payable, and also shall not well and truly pay, or cause to be paid, all and every such sum or sums as shall hereafter be assessed by any public authority upon the said principal debt or sum, or upon the interest thereof, then, and in such case, the whole principal debt aforesaid shall, at the option of the said obligees, their successors and assigns, immediately thereupon become due, payable and recoverable, and payment to said principal sum, and all interest, and all fines, thereon, as well as any contribution on said........share of stock then due, may be enforced and recovered at once, any thing herein before contained to the contrary thereof notwithstanding. And it is hereby further agreed, that if the same, or any part thereof, has to be collected by process of law, that an attorney's fee of ........per cent shall be added to and collected as a part of the costs of such proceedings. And the said obligor, for....heirs, executors, administrators and assigns, hereby expressly waive and relinquish unto the said obligees, their successors and assigns, all benefit that may accrue to........ by virtue of any and every law, made or to be made, to exempt the premises described in the indenture of the mortgage herewith given, or of any other premises or property whatever, from levy and sale under execution, or any part of the proceeds arising from the sale thereof, from the payment of the moneys hereby secured, or any part thereof, and the cost of such action and execution, then the above obligation to be void, or else to be and remain in full force and virtue.

Sealed and delivered, } ........................... in the presence of us, } ...........................

To........Esquire, Attorney of the Court of Common Pleas, at....... in the County of......in the State of.:....
or to any other Attorney, or to the Prothonotary of the said Court, or of any other Court, there or elsewhere.

Whereas,....in and by a certain obligation, bearing even date herewith, do....stand bound unto....in the sum of.... lawful money of the United States of America, conditioned for the payment of the just sum of........dollars, such as above-said, at any time within one year from the date thereof, together with interest,........for the same, and together with all fines imposed by the constitution and by-laws of the aforesaid association, in like money, payable monthly, on the.... of each and every month thereafter, and should also well and truly pay, or cause to be paid unto the said obligees, their successors or assigns, the sum of........dollars, on the....

of each and every month thereafter, as and for the monthly contribution on......share of the capital stock of the said obligees, now owned by the said obligor, without any fraud or further delay; and should also deliver to the said obligees, their successors or assigns, on or before the........day of ........of each and every year, of receipts for all taxes of the current year assessed upon the premises described in the mortgage accompanying said obligation. Provided, however, and it is thereby expressly agreed, that if at any time default should be made in the payment of the said principal money when due, or of the said interest, or of the said fines, or the monthly contribution on said stock, for the space of six months after any payment thereof should fall due, or in the delivery to the said obligees, their successors or assigns, on or before the........day of........of each and every year, of such receipts for such taxes of the current year, assessed upon the mortgaged premises, or if the said obligor shall not well and truly pay, or cause to be paid, the........and taxes, on the premises particularly described in the mortgage accompanying this obligation, when the same shall become due and payable, and also shall not well and truly pay, or cause to be paid, all and every such sum or sums as should thereafter be assessed by any public authority upon the said principal debt or sum, or upon the interest thereof, then and in such case the whole principal debt aforesaid should, at the option of the said obligees, their successors and assigns, immediately thereupon become due, payable and recoverable, and payment of said principal sum, and all interest, and all fines thereon, as well as any contribution on said........share of stock, then due, might be enforced and recovered at once, any thing thereinbefore contained to the contrary thereof notwithstanding. And it is thereby further agreed, that if the same, or any part thereof, has to be collected by process of law, then an attorney's fee of........per cent should be added to the amount so collected, as a part of the costs of such proceedings. And the said obligor for........heirs, executors, administrators and assigns, thereby expressly waived and relinquished unto the said obligees, their successors and assigns, all benefit that

might accrue to........by virtue of any and every law, made
or to be made, to exempt the premises described in the
indenture of mortgage therewith given, or of any other premises or property whatever, from levy and sale under execution, or any part of the proceeds arising from the sale thereof,
from the payment of the moneys thereby secured, or any part
thereof.    These are to desire and authorize you, or any of you,
to appear for........heirs, executors, or administrators, in
the said Court or elsewhere, in an action of debt, there or
elsewhere brought, or to be brought, against....... heirs,
executors, or administrators, at the suit of the said obligees,
their successors or assigns, on the said obligation, as of any
term or time past, present, or any other subsequent term or
time, there or elsewhere to be held, and confess or enter judgment thereupon, against........heirs, executors, or administrators, for the sum of........dollars, lawful money of the
United States of America, debt, besides costs of suit, by *non
sum informatus, nihil dicit*, or otherwise, as to you shall seem
meet; and for your, or any of your so doing, this shall be your
sufficient warrant.    And....do hereby for........heirs, executors and administrators, remise, release, and forever quit
claim unto the said obligees, their certain attorney, successors
and assigns, all and all manner of error and errors, misprisions,
misentries, defects and imperfections whatever, in the entering
of the said judgment, or any process or proceedings thereon
or thereto, or anywise touching or concerning the same.

In witness whereof,....have hereunto set....hand and seal,
the......day of......in the year of our Lord one thousand
eight hundred and....................

Sealed and delivered, ⎫      ............................
in the presence of us,    ⎭      ............................

The following is the form of mortgage used by associations
in Pennsylvania:

This indenture, Made the ........ day of ........ in the
year of our Lord one thousand eight hundred and........
between ........ of the one part (mortgagor),........of the
other part mortgagees).

Whereas, the said mortgagor, in and by ........ obligation,
or writing obligatory, under .... hand and seal, duly executed,
bearing even date herewith, stand bound unto the said mortgagees, in the sum of ........ dollars, lawful money of the
United States of America, conditioned for the payment of the
just sum of ........ dollars, at any time within one year from
the date thereof, together with interest, ....... for the same,
in like money, payable monthly, and together with all fines
imposed by the constitution and by-laws of the aforesaid association, on the .... of each and every month thereafter, and
should also well and truly pay, or cause to be paid, unto the
said mortgagees, their successors or assigns, the sum of..... .
dollars, on the said .... of each and every month thereafter,
as and for the monthly contribution on ........ share of the
capital stock of the said mortgagees, now owned by the said
mortgagor, without any fraud or further delay; and should also
deliver to the said mortgagees, their successors or assigns, on or
before the .... day of .... of each and every year, receipts
for all taxes of the current year assessed upon the hereinafter.
described premises. Provided, however, and it is hereby
expressly agreed, that if at any time default should be made
in the payment of the said principal money when due, or of
the said interest, or of the said fines, or the monthly contribution on said stock, for the space of six months after any payment thereof should fall due, or in such delivery to the said
mortgagees, their successors or assigns, on or before the ....
day of.... of each and every year, of such receipts for such taxes
of the current year, upon the premises mortgaged, or if the
said mortgagor should not well and truly pay, or cause to be
paid, the ........ and taxes, on the hereinafter described
premises, when the same should become due and payable, and
also should not well and truly pay, or cause to be paid, all and
every such sum or sums as should thereafter be assessed by any
public authority upon the said principal debt or sum, or upon
the interest thereof, then, and in such case the whole principal
debt aforesaid should, at the option of the said mortgagees,
their successors and assigns, immediately thereupon become
due, payable and recoverable, and payment of said principal

sum, and all interest, and all fines thereon, as well as any contribution on said ........ share of stock then due, may be
enforced and recovered at once, anything therein before contained to the contrary thereof notwithstanding.  And it was
therein further agreed, that if the same or any part thereof
has to be collected by proceedings at law, then an attorney's
collection fee of .... per cent should be added to the amount
so collected as a part of the costs of such proceedings.  And
the said mortgagor for ........ heirs, executors, administrators and assigns, thereby expressly waived and relinquished
unto the said mortgagees, their successors and assigns, all benefit that might accrue to ........ by virtue of any and every
law made or to be made, exempting the premises hereinafter
described, or of any other premises or property whatever, from
levy and sale under execution, or any part of the proceeds arising from the sale thereof, from the payment of the moneys
thereby secured, or any part thereof, and the cost of such
action and execution, as in and by the said above recited obligation and the condition thereof, relation being thereunto had
may more fully and at large appear.

Now this indenture witnesseth, that the said mortgagor, as
well for and in consideration of the premises, as of the aforesaid debt or principal sum of ........ dollars, and for the
better securing the payment of the same, with interest,
together with all fines, and together with the monthly contribution of ........ dollars, on the said ........ share of
stock owned by the said mortgagor, unto the said mortgagees,
their successors and assigns, in discharge of the said above
recited obligation, as of the further sum of one dollar, lawful
money, unto ....... in hand well and truly paid, by the said
mortgagees, at the time of the execution hereof, the receipt
whereof is hereby acknowledged, ....... granted, bargained,
sold, aliened, enfeoffed, released and confirmed, and by these
presents.. ....grant, bargain, sell, alien, enfeoff, release and
confirm unto the said mortgagees, their successors and assigns.

Together with all and singular the buildings, streets, alleys,
passages, ways, waters, water-courses, rights, liberties, privi-

leges, improvements, hereditaments and appurtenances, whatsoever, thereunto belonging, or in any wise appertaining, and
the reversions and remainders, rents, issues and profits thereof.

To have and to hold the said ........ hereditaments and
premises hereby granted, or mentioned and intended so to be
with the appurtenances,.... unto the said mortgagees, their
successors and assigns, to and for the only proper use and behoof
of the said mortgagees, their successors and assigns forever.

Provided, always, nevertheless, that if the said mortgagor...
heirs, executors, administrators or assigns, do and shall well
and truly pay, or cause to be paid, unto the said mortgagees,
their successors or assigns, the aforesaid debt or principal sum
of ....... dollars, together with interest,....... and together
with the fines aforesaid, on the days and times hereinbefore
mentioned and appointed for the payment of the same; and
shall also well and truly pay, or cause to be paid, to the said
mortgagees, their successors or assigns, the above mentioned
sum of ........ dollars, on the ........ of every month, as
and for the contribution on the said ...... share of stock as
above mentioned; and shall on or before the ........ day of
......of each and every year, deliver to the said mortgagees,
their successors or assigns, receipts for all taxes of the current
year, assessed upon the mortgaged premises, according to the
condition of the said above recited obligation, without any
fraud or further delay, and without any deduction, defalcation
or abatement, to be made of anything, for, or in respect of any
taxes, charges or assessments whatsoever, that then, and from
thenceforth, as well this present indenture, and the estate
hereby granted, as the said above recited obligation, shall
cease, determine, and become void, anything hereinbefore contained to the contrary thereof, in anywise notwithstanding.
Provided further, in case of default in the payment of the
principal, interest or fines as aforesaid, or any part thereof, or
in default of the payment of the monthly contribution on the
said ........ share of stock, as above particularly recited and
mentioned, or any part thereof, for the space of six months
14

after any payment thereof shall fall due, or in such delivery to the said mortgagees, their successors or assigns, on or before the .... day of ..... of each and every year, of such receipts for such taxes of the current year, assessed upon the mortgaged premises, or if the said mortagor shall not well and truly pay, or cause to be paid, the ........ and taxes, on the above described premises, when the same shall become due and payable, and also shall not well and truly pay, or cause to be paid, all and every such sum or sums as shall hereafter be assessed by any public authority, upon the said principal debt or sum, or upon the interest thereof, then, and in such case, the whole principal debt aforesaid shall immediately thereupon become due, payable and recoverable; and it shall and may be lawful for the said mortgagees, their successors or assigns, to sue out forthwith a writ of *scire facias*, upon this present indenture of mortgage, and to proceed at once thereon to recover the principal money hereby secured, and all interest, and all fines thereon, as well as any contribution on said ........ share of stock then due, according to law, without further stay, any law or usage to the contrary notwithstanding.  And it is hereby agreed, that in case the same or any part thereof has to be collected by process of law, that an attorney's fee of .... per cent. shall be added to and collected as a part of the costs of such proceedings.  And the said mortgagor for .... heirs, executors, administrators and assigns, hereby waive and relinquish unto the said mortgagees, their successors and assigns, all benefit that may accrue to .... by virtue of any and every law made, or to be made, to exempt the said above described premises, or any other property whatever, from levy and sale under execution, or any part of the proceeds arising from the sale thereof, from the payment of the moneys hereby secured, or any part thereof.

In witness whereof, the said parties to these presents have hereunto interchangeably set their hands and seals.  Dated the day and year first above written.

      Sealed and delivered    } ..........................
        in the presence of us,  } ..........................

On the .... day of ...... A. D., 18.. before me .......
personally appeared the above named .......... and in due
form of law acknowledged the above or aforegoing indenture
of mortgage to be ...... act and deed, and desired the same
might be recorded as such........

Witness my hand and ....... seal the day and year aforesaid.

Recorded in the office for recording of deeds, in and for....
....in mortgage book .... No. .... page .... &c.

Witness my hand and seal of office, this .... day of......
Anno Domini 18..

## Form of Bond used by New Jersey Associations.

Know all men by these presents:

That ....held and firmly bound unto a ....body corporate,
of the State of New Jersey, in the sum of .....dollars,
lawful money of the United States of America, to be paid to
the said Association, its successors or assigns, for which payment well and truly to be made........bind........heirs,
executors and administrators,........firmly by these presents. Sealed with ........seal, dated the ......day of
........one thousand eight hundred and eighty....

The condition of the above obligation is such that if the
above bounden........heirs, executors or administrators,
shall well and truly pay or cause to be paid, unto the above
named Association, its successors or assigns, the just and full
sum of ........dollars, in the manner following, viz.: by the
payment of dues of........per........on........of each
........on each of........shares of the capital stock of said
Association, owned by said........and standing in....name.
on the books of said Association, and assigned to it as collateral
security for the payment hereof, and on which this loan is
based, during the period of this loan, together with interest on
said sum of........dollars, to be computed from the date

hereof, at the rate of six per cent per annum, and payable as follows, at the expiration of three months from the date hereof, on the whole principal sum aforesaid, and at the expiration of each succeeding three months, on the amount of said principal found to be due at the beginning thereof, after deducting all previous payments made on account of said principal, being the amount of dues paid on said........shares during said three months, as provided for by the constitution and by-laws of said Association, which have been duly assented to by said obligor, and made a part hereof, without any fraud or other delay, then the above obligation to be void, otherwise to remain in full force and virtue.

Provided, however, that when the funds of said Association ........shall equal two hundred dollars per share, over and above all liabilities of the Association, no further payments shall be required hereon, except arrearages, if any, and thereupon a proper satisfaction piece for the cancellation hereof and of the mortgage given to secure this bond shall be duly executed and delivered to said obligor,........heirs, executors, administrators or assigns, and said........shares shall thereupon also be cancelled.

And it is hereby expressly agreed, that should any default be made in the payment of the said interest or any of said dues or installments on said shares, or of any part thereof, on any day whereon the same is made payable, as above expressed, or should any tax, assessment, water-rent, or other municipal or governmental rate, charge, imposition, or lien, be hereafter imposed or acquired upon the premises described in the mortgage accompanying this bond, and become due and payable; and should the said interest or any of said dues or installments on said shares remain unpaid and in arrear for the space of........or said tax, assessment, water rent, or other municipal or governmental rate, charge, imposition or lien, or any or either of them, remain unpaid and in arrear for the space of .......then and from thenceforth, that is to say, after the lapse or expiration of either of the said periods, as

the case may be, the aforesaid principal sum of........or
the balance thereof remaining unpaid, with all arrearage of
interest thereon, shall at the option of the said Association, or
its legal representatives, become and be due and payable
immediately thereafter, although the period first above limited for the payment thereof may not then have expired, anything hereinbefore contained to the contrary thereof, in anywise, notwithstanding.

Sealed and delivered in presence of...........

## Form of Mortgage Used by New Jersey Association.

This indenture, made the........day of.........in the
year of one thousand eight hundred and ninety.........
Between........of the first part and.........a body corporate
of the State of New Jersey, located at........in said State,
party of the second part:

Whereas, the said........justly indebted to the said party
of the second part, in the sum of......dollars, lawful money
of the United States of America, secured to be paid by......
certain bond or obligation, bearing even date with these
presents, in the penal sum of........dollars, lawful money as
aforesaid, conditioned for the payment of the said first mentioned sum of........dollars, lawful money as aforesaid, to
the said party of the second part, its successors or assigns, in
the manner following, viz: by the payment of dues of......
per........on........ of each........on each of.... ...
shares of the capital stock of said association, owned by said
.......of the first part, and standing in........name on
books of said association, and assigned to said party of the
second part, as collateral security for the payment hereof, and
on which this loan is based, during the period of this loan,
together with interest on said sum of........dollars, to be
computed from the date thereof, at the rate of six per cent
per annum, and payable as follows: At the expiration of
three months from the date hereof, on the whole principal
sum aforesaid, and at the expiration of each succeeding
three months, on the amount of said principal, found to

due at the beginning thereof, after deducting all previous payments made on account of said principal, being the amount of dues paid on said.........shares during said three months, as provided for by the constitution and by-laws of said association, which have been duly assented to by said party of the first part, and are made a part hereof.

Provided, however, that when the funds of said association made....shall equal two hundred dollars per share over and above all liabilities of the association, no further payments shall be required hereon, except arrearages, if any, and thereupon a proper satisfaction for the cancellation hereof, and of said bond, shall be duly executed and delivered to said party of the first part,....heirs or assigns, and said........ shares shall thereupon also be cancelled.

And it is thereby expressly agreed, that should any default be made in the payment of the said interest or any of said dues or installments on said shares, or any part thereof, on any day whereon the same is made payable, as above expressed, or should any tax, assessment, water rent, or other municipal or other governmental rate, charge, imposition, or lien be hereafter imposed or acquired upon the premises described in this mortgage, and become due and payable, and should the said interest or any of said dues or installments on said shares' remain unpaid and in arrear for the space of......or said tax, assessment, water rent, or other municipal or governmental rate, charge, imposition or lien, or any or either of them, remain unpaid and in arrear, for the space of........then and from thenceforth, that is to say, after the expiration of either of the said periods as the case may be, the aforesaid principal sum of....... dollars, or the balance thereof, remaining unpaid, with all arrearage of interest thereon, shall, at the option of the said party of the second part, or its legal representatives, become and be due and payable immediately thereafter, although the period above limited for the payment thereof may not then have expired, anything therein before contained to the contrary thereof, in anywise notwithstanding:

as by the said bond or obligation, and the condition thereof, reference being thereunto had, may more fully appear.

Now this indenture witnesseth, that the said part. . of the first part, for the better securing the payment of the said sum of money, mentioned in the condition of the said bond or obligation, with interest thereon, according to the true intent and meaning thereof, and also for and in consideration of the sum of one dollar, to . . . . . . . . in hand paid by the said party of the second part, at or before the ensealing and delivery of these presents, the receipt whereof is hereby acknowledged, ha. . . . granted, bargained, sold, aliened, released, conveyed and confirmed, and by these presents do. . . . grant, bargain, sell, alien, release, convey and confirm, unto the said party of the second part, and to its successors and assigns, forever, all. . . . . . . . . .

## DESCRIPTION.

Together with all and singular the tenements, hereditaments, and appurtenances thereunto belonging, or in anywise appertaining, and the reversion and reversions, remainder and remainders, rents, issues and profits thereof, and also, all the estate, right, title, interest, property, possession, claim, and, demand whatsoever, as well in law as in equity, of the said part. . . . of the first part, of, in and to the same, and every part and parcel thereof, with the appurtenances: To have and to hold the above granted and described premises, with the appurtenances, unto the said party of the second part, its successors and assigns, to its and their own proper use, benefit and behoof forever. Provided always, and these presents are upon this express condition, that if the said part . . . . of the first part, . . . . . . heirs, executors or administrators, shall well and truly pay unto said party of the second part, its successors or assigns, the said sum of money mentioned in the condition of said bond or obligation, and the interest thereon, at the time and times, and in the manner mentioned in the said condition, according to the true intent and meaning thereof, that then these presents, and the estate hereby granted, shall cease, determine and be void.

And the said......for........heirs, executors and admin·
istrators, do........covenant and agree, to pay unto the
said party of the second part,............its successors or
assigns, the said sum of money and interest, as mentioned
above, and expressed in the condition of the said bond.

And it is also agreed, by and between the parties to these
presents, that the said part....of the first part shall and will
keep the buildings erected, and to be erected, upon the lands
above conveyed, insured against loss or damage by fire, by
insurers; and in an amount approved by the said party of the
second part, its successors or assigns,..........and assign the
policy and certificates thereof, to the said party of the second
part; and in default thereof, it shall be lawful for the said
party of the second part to effect such insurance, and the
premium or premiums paid for effecting the same, shall be a
lien on said mortgaged premises, added to the amount of the
said bond or obligation, and secured by these presents, payable
on demand, with interest at the rate of six per cent per annum,
from the time of payment of such premium or premiums.

And the said......the owner of the lands above described,
for........heirs  and assigns, do....further covenant and
agree to and with the said party of the second  part, its successors and assigns, that they will not hereafter apply for any
deduction by reason of any mortgage from the taxable value
of the lands embraced in this mortgage.

And it is further agreed, that in case the said........heirs
or assigns shall claim any deduction from the taxable value of
said lands, in violation of this agreement, then and in that case
this mortgage shall become and be immediately due and payable, and the amount of tax paid by the mortgagee shall be
added to the principal of the debt secured hereby, and recoverable therewith, with interest thereon from time of payment.

In witness whereof, the said part....of the first part ha...
hereunto set........hand and seal, the day and year first
above written

Sealed and delivered in the presence of................

State of....................⎫
⎬ ES.
County of..................⎭

On this........day of........eighteen hundred and....
before me........ personally appeared........who, I am
satisfied,....the mortgagor in the within mortgage named;
and I having first made known to......the contents thereof,
....did........acknowledge that........signed, sealed and
delivered the same as....voluntary act and deed.

And the said......being by me privately examined, separate
and apart from....said husband....did further..........
acknowledge that........signed, sealed and delivered the
same as....voluntary act and deed, freely, without fear, threats
or compulsion of........said husband.

Form of mortgage used by the Mutual Home and Savings
Association, of Dayton, Ohio, which is the parent of a class
of popular associations:

Know all men by these presents, That ............
in consideration of ............ dollars, in hand paid,
by the Mutual Home and Savings Association, of Dayton,
Ohio, ha.. bargained and sold, and do .... hereby grant, bargain, sell and convey unto the said Mutual Home and Savings
Association, its successors and assigns forever, the following
premises, situated in the City of Dayton, County of Montgomery, in the State of Ohio, and described as follows:  ....

To have and to hold said premises, with the appurtenances,
unto the said Mutual Home and Savings Association, its successors and assigns forever. And the said grantor.. for ....
and heirs and assigns, do  ... hereby covenant with the said
Mutual Home and Savings Association, its successors and
assigns, that .. he........ lawfully seized of the premises
aforesaid, and that the premises are free and clear from all
incumbrances whatsoever, and that ....... he .. will forever

warrant and defend the same, with the appurtenances, unto the said Mutual Home and Savings Association, its successors and assigns, against the lawful claims of all persons whomsoever.

Provided, nevertheless, and these presents are upon this condition: That, whereas, the said ...... ha.. entered into contract, in writing, with said association, in the words and figures following, to wit:

$..........                    Dayton, Ohio, ........ 189..
Received of the Mutual Home and Savings Association, of Dayton, Ohio, ........ dollars, as a loan on ........ shares of stock No. ...... owned by ........ in said association.

........ agree to pay to said association weekly, not less than ........ dollars, which shall be applied as follows:

First. To the payment of any fines or other assessments made against .... in pursuance of the by-laws of said association.

Second. To the payment of the premium for precedence due on said loan, amounting to ........ dollars per week.

Third. To the payment of the interest due on said loan, amounting to ....... per week.

Fourth. The balance of said payments shall be credited as dues on said stock. Said payments shall be continued until the dues so credited on said stock, together with the dividends declared thereon, shall equal the amount loaned.

Should .... fail for eight weeks to pay said weekly payments, then the whole amount of said loan shall at once become due and payable.

Now, if the said ........ shall pay to said association, its successors or assigns, the said sums of money when due, as set forth in said contract, then these presents shall be void.

In testimony whereof, the said ........ ha.. hereunto set
...... hand.. this .... day of ........ 189..

Executed in presence of
............................
............................

State of Ohio, Montgomery County, ss:

Before me, a Notary Public, within and for said county,
personally appeared the above named ........ and acknowledged the signing of the foregoing conveyance to be .......
voluntary act and deed, for the uses and purposes therein
expressed.

Witness my hand and notarial seal, this ........ day of
........ A. D., 189..
.................... Notary Public,
Montgomery County, Ohio.

Stock No. ..... Mortgage. ......... to Mutual Home
and Savings Association, of Dayton, Ohio.

Borrowed, $ ...... Date, ...... Received for record,
........ at .... o'clock ........ M. and recorded ........
in book .... page ....
.............................
Recorder of Montgomery County.

Dayton, Ohio...... I hereby release this mortgage.
.......... President Mutual Home and Savings Association, of Dayton, Ohio.

## Co-operative Bank Mortgage used in Massachu-setts.

Know all men by these presents, that I................, in
consideration of........ dollars, paid by the............ Co-
operative Bank, a corporation duly established by law, in
........, in the county of........, and commonwealth of

Massachusetts, the receipt whereof is hereby acknowledged, do hereby give, grant, bargain, sell and convey unto the said corporation, its successors and assigns............  To have and to hold the granted premises, with all the privileges and appurtenances thereto belonging, to the said corporation, and its successors and assigns, to their own use and behoof forever.

And........hereby, for........and........heirs, executors and administrators, covenant with the said grantee and its successors and assigns, that........lawfully seized in fee-simple of the granted premises; that they are free from all incumbrances,............that........have good right to sell and convey the same as aforesaid, and that........will and ........heirs, executors and administrators shall warrant and defend the same to said grantee and its successors and assigns forever, against the lawful claims and demands of all persons............

Provided, nevertheless, that whereas............ha.. this day pledged and transferred to the said corporation....shares of its capital stock, said shares being in the........series as collateral security for the performance of the terms, covenants and conditions of this mortgage, and of the note hereinafter mentioned, upon which shares said sum of.........dollars has been advanced to........by said corporation, now, therefore, if........or........heirs, executors, administrators, or assigns, shall pay unto the said corporation, its successors or assigns, the sum of............monthly, at the stated meetings of said corporation, on the........of each month hereafter, being the amount of the monthly dues on said........ shares, and of the monthly interest and premium upon said loan or advance of............dollars, for which said shares are pledged, and said note and mortgage given, together with all fines chargeable by the by-laws of said corporation, upon arrears of such payments, until said shares shall reach the ultimate value of two hundred dollars each, or if.........or ........heirs, executors, administrators or assigns, shall otherwise sooner pay unto the said corporation, its successors or assigns, said sum of........dollars, together with the said interest, premiums and fines as aforesaid, to the time of such payment, and, until such loan shall be paid, or cancelled by the ultimate value of said shares, if........shall pay without charge to said corporation, all taxes and assessments levied or assessed on the granted premises, including those assessed upon said corporation's interest therein, as holder of this mortgage, and, if said corporation's loans on mortgages of taxable real estate shall not at any time be exempt from a state tax on the amount of its monthly dues, if........shall on demand pay unto said corporation such percentage on the debt hereby secured, as it shall from time to time be required to pay as such state tax, shall keep the buildings thereon insured against fire, in a sum not less than........dollars, for the benefit of the grantee, its successors or assigns, at such insurance office as it or they shall approve, or, in default thereof, shall, on demand, pay to said corporation all such sums as it shall reasonably pay for such taxes, assessments and insurance, with interest, and shall not commit or suffer any strip or waste of the granted premises, or any breach of any covenant herein contained, then this deed, as also a note of even date herewith, signed by........whereby........promise to pay to the grantee, or order, the said sums, at the times aforesaid, shall be void.

But in case of non-payment of the aforesaid monthly dues, interest, premium for fines for the period of six months after any payment thereof shall be due, or upon any other default in the performance or observance of the foregoing condition, the grantee, or its successors or assigns, may sell the granted premises, or such portion thereof as may remain subject to this mortgage, in case of any partial release hereof, together with all improvements that may be thereon, and all benefit and equity of redemption of....or....representatives therein, at public auction, in said........, first publishing a notice of the time and place of sale, once each week, for three consecutive weeks, in one or more newspapers published in said....

....and may convey the same by proper deed or deeds to the purchaser or purchasers absolutely, and in fee simple; and such sale shall forever bar....and all persons claiming under ........from all right and interest in the granted premises, whether at law or in equity.

And......do hereby, for........heirs and assigns, further covenant and agree with the grantee, its successors and assigns, that on such sale,........and they will, upon request, execute and deliver such further deeds and instruments as may be necessary or proper to confirm such sale, and to vest the title to the premises sold in the purchaser thereof, and will execute and deliver to the purchaser an assignment of all policies of insurance on the buildings upon the land covered by this mortgage.

And out of the money arising from such sale, the grantee, or its successors or assigns, shall be entitled to retain all sums then secured by this deed, whether then or thereafter payable, including all costs, charges and expenses, incurred or sustained, by reason of any failure or default on the part of........or of ........representatives to perform and fulfil the condition of this deed, rendering the surplus, if any, to.......or....... heirs or assigns.

And it is agreed that the grantee, or its successors or assigns, or any person or persons in their behalf, may purchase at any sale made as aforesaid, and that no other purchaser shall be answerable for the application of the purchase money; and that until default in the performance of the condition of this deed,......and........heirs and assigns may hold and enjoy the granted premises and receive the rents and profits thereof.

And for the consideration aforesaid, I,.... ...wife of the said...........do hereby release unto the said grantee, and its successors and assigns, all rights of or to both dower and homestead in the granted premises.

In witness whereof,........the said............hereunto
set........hand and seal, this........day of........in the
year one thousand eight hundred and............

Signed, sealed and delivered in presence of

Commonwealth of Massachusetts........ss..........18..

Then personally appeared the above named............and
acknowledged the foregoing instrument to be........free
act and deed, before me,..............Justice of the peace,
..........18.., at......o'clock and......minutes,......M.

Received and entered with........Deeds, libra........folio
........attest:

........................Register.

## Form of Stock Register.

By adding enough weeks downward to constitute a year, the stockholder's account with the association appears in compact form, and like columns may be increased to the right, next to the "Total" column, and the latter will prove the footings. If the accounts are to be cast up but once a year, this form may easily be adapted, by omitting the six months' summary, or, if the association declares no dividends, that much of the form may be omitted. This form is used by permission of Mr. L. G. Dynes, its inventor.

| No. Week. | Month. | Day. | Book No. Ent. and Trans. Fees. | NAME OF STOCKHOLDER. Address Cr. Dues. | Prem | Int. | Fines and Disc'ts | No. Shares Dr. (Loan) (Payments) | Totals. |
|---|---|---|---|---|---|---|---|---|---|
| Balances. | | | | | | | | | |
| 1 | May | 7 | | | | | | | |
| 2 | " | 14 | | | | | | | |
| 3 | " | 21 | | | | | | | |
| 4 | " | 28 | | | | | | | |
| 5 | Jun. | 4 | | | | | | | |
| 6 | " | 11 | | | | | | | |
| 7 | " | 18 | | | | | | | |
| 8 | " | 25 | | | | | | | |
| 9 | July | 2 | | | | | | | |
| 10 | " | 9 | | | | | | | |
| 11 | " | 16 | | | | | | | |
| 12 | " | 23 | | | | | | | |
| 13 | " | 30 | | | | | | | |
| 14 | Aug | 6 | | | | | | | |
| 15 | " | 13 | | | | | | | |
| 16 | " | 20 | | | | | | | |
| 17 | " | 27 | | | | | | | |
| 18 | Sep. | 3 | | | | | | | |
| 19 | " | 10 | | | | | | | |
| 20 | " | 17 | | | | | | | |
| 21 | " | 24 | | | | | | | |
| 22 | Oct | 1 | | | | | | | |
| 23 | " | 8 | | | | | | | |
| 24 | " | 15 | | | | | | | |
| 25 | " | 22 | | | | | | | |
| 26 | " | 29 | | | | | | | |
| Totals. | | | | | | | | | |

Balance, $........   Total, $........

Dividend, --per cent.   Current Term, $.........

The association will only need to keep an expense account in addition to the above.

## Form of Warrant for Payment of Money.

Order No......... Indianapolis, Ind......... 189..

Treasurer Equitable Building and Loan Association,

OF INDIANAPOLIS, IND.,

Pay to............ ..........or order,

.......... Dollars.

Account,

Loan, - - $----

Withdrawal

Book No.....

Class---- Dues

Dividends, $----

Expense, $----

Total, $----

............ President.

............ Secretary.

No.......

Indianapolis, Ind., ----------189

Pay to---------- on account of

Loan, - - $---------

Withdrawal, book----

Class---- Dues $---------

Dividends $---------

Expense $---------

Total, $---------

15

## Bank Check used in Connection with Warrant.

No......... Indianapolis, Ind., ----------189

BANK OF COMMERCE.

Pay to the order of---------- $ ......

............ Dollars,

100 In current funds.

Equitable Building and Loan Association,

Account Order No.. By............ Treasurer.

Secretary ............

President ............

Good only when countersigned by

No......... 189

To----------

Account Order No----

For----

$----

## Form of Building Agreement.

Articles of agreement. It is hereby mutually agreed, this .. day of .... 189 .. by and between ...... part .. of the first part, and .... ... part .. of the second part, all of Marion County, State of Indiana, as follows, to wit:

Part .... of the second part, for ........ heirs, executors and administrators, hereby covenant .... and agree .... to and with said part .... that .... will erect, construct and fully complete in a good, substantial and workmanlike manner, on or before the ...... day of ...... 189 .. for the consideration hereinafter named, the following described improvements upon the real estate described in the specifications hereto attached, to wit: ........ in the manner, in all respects, set forth in the plans and specifications hereunto attached and made a part; that second party shall furnish, at his own expense, all the labor and material used in such erection, construction and completion of said improvements, and will carry a builder's insurance risk on same while in progress; in consideration for all which the party of the first part hereby agrees to pay unto second party the sum of ........ dollars, in the manner following, to wit: ............ Provided, that second part .... shall have fully paid for all material and labor furnished to date of payment, so that there shall not be a lien therefor on the said real estate; that second party shall execute a bond in the sum of ........ dollars, with sureties to the satisfaction of first party and ........ mortgagee, conditioned to idemnify first party and ....... mortgagee from loss by reason of mechanics liens.

It is further mutually agreed by and between the parties hereto, that the said plans and specifications shall co-operate; that is to say, that any work or works set forth in the plans, and not mentioned in the specifications, and *vice versa*, are to be executed as fully as though set forth in both the plans and specifications.

That nothing shall be built, erected, charged and paid for as extras, until after all agreements in relation thereto have been first reduced to writing and signed by the parties hereto; that first party shall not be liable for any damage that shall occur to any part of said work and improvements and to any person or persons employed in or about said premises; that second party ....shall pay unto first party....the sum of........dollars per day for each day the completion of said improvements shall be delayed beyond the date hereinbefore fixed for their completion; that first party....shall have the right to control the location of closets, mantels, shelves, brackets, chandeliers, bracket lights, stove pipe holes in flues, and colors of paint, beyond those mentioned in the specifications; and that first party....shall not be responsible for any material and labor used in the improvements aforesaid................

In witness of all which, the parties have hereunto set their hands on the day and date hereinbefore written.

.................... First party.
.................... Second party.

## Form of Building Specifications.

Specifications for improvements. Specifications for improvements on the following described real estate, situated in...... County, State of........

**Excavation.** a. Outside trenches....inches deep. b. Cellar....by....feet in size, and....feet deep in the clear.

**Foundation.** a. Quality of brick......, ......inches in ground and......inches above ground, ......inches thick; outside walls of cellar to be nine inches thick, and inside walls to be four inches thick. b. The studding shall rest upon timbers placed upon foundation of dimensions and constructed as follows: ........ c. Ventilators of........in foundation shall be used as follows: ........ d. Piers will be used as follows: ........and of following dimensions: .........

**Joists.** a. Quality, and kind of timber......... b. Dimensions of joist shall be.....by.....inches, placed..... inches from center to center, with........rows of truss bridging, and joists shall be accurately sized at the top. c. Second story joists shall be....by....inches, placed....inches from center to center, with....rows of truss bridging, and accurately sized both at top and bottom. d. Joists shall be spiked with....penny nails, and bridging nailed securely with.... penny nails. e. Studding shall be double at all corners and all openings.

**Studding.** a. Quality and dimension of studding. b. How fastened at top. c. Kind of nails and how many used in spiking studding. d. How far from center to center.

**Rafters.** a. Quality and dimensions of rafters. b. Rafters shall be placed..........inches from center to center. c. Pitch shall be.... d. Rafters shall project......inches outside of outer walls, and shall be finished as follows:

**Lining.** a. Paper of........quality, and fastened as follows. b. Timber as follows.......and put on diagonally in following manner, with........penny nails in each studding.

**Weatherboarding.** a. Quality and kind of weatherboarding shall be........and securely nailed to each studding with one....penny nail; free from windshakes, bad knots and placed....inches to the weather. b. Corner boards shall be of......lumber....by....inches. c. The finish around the doors and windows shall be as follows:

**Porticoes.** a. Shall be built, having turned columns resting upon iron stands, piers........by....inches; ...... feet wide, and with....roof, necessary brackets and scroll work, shall be built as follows:

**Roof.** a. Sheathing shall be....inches apart, nailed with ....penny nails in each rafter, and shall be of lumber described as follows. b. Shingles of........quality, placed .....inches to weather, and nailed with two.....penny nails to each shingle. c. Comb boards of following kind and quality:

**Floors.** a. Kind and quality of flooring shall be as follows........ and each plank shall be nailed to each joist with ....penny nails. .

**Windows.** a. Frames shall be of following description. b. Sash of following description will be used. c. Glass shall be of double strength and of following dimensions..... fastened with tin points and well puttied. d. Weights, cords. pullies and locks will be put on all windows, except.........

**Doors.** a. ........outside doors, of....style and of following size and description...... b. ........inside doors of........panels and of following size and description will be used. c. Transoms of following size, and hung on pivots, will be used over each door, (except closet doors). d. Hardware for doors will be of following kind and sizes. e. Bumpers will be provided for each door.

**Plastering.** a. Lath of......quality shall be used. b. ....coats of brown mortar, made of....lime, best hair and sharp sand, shall be put on with true surface and corners. b. One skim coat of white shall be put on the brown coat (when dry), with like accuracy of surface and corners.

**Finish.** a. Kind and quality of lumber for inside finish shall be as follows: b. Style of finish shall be.......... c. Baseboard shall be....by....inches, with......moulding on top and quarter round on floor. d. Finishing shall be ....by....inches round each door and window, with...... moulding as follows............e. Picture moulding shall be put in the following rooms:................

**Closets.** a. Where placed and dimensions. b. Doors of following kinds shall be used for each closet, to wit. c. Shelves shall be placed in each closet as follows. d. Closet hooks of best quality shall be placed in each closet.

**Pantry.** a. Shelving. b. Bread box of following construction shall be provided. c. Other furnishings for pantry shall be as follows.

**Stairways. a.** Location and kind of finish. **b.** Banisters shall be. **c.** Newel posts shall be. **d.** Landings. **e.** Manner of construction shall be. **f.** Stairway for cellar shall be constructed as follows:

**Plumbing.** Shall be put in as follows, and of best material and workmanship:

**Tinwork.** Shall be as follows and of best quality of tin for long wear:

**Paint. a.** ....coats of best boiled linseed oil 'and best brands of lead, of color to suit owner, for outside. **b.** .... coats of......for all inside finish, after finish has been thoroughly sandpapered, except. **c.** Roof, tinwork and comb boards shall be painted with two coats of paint.

**Flue. a.** Shall be located as follows: **b.** Brick shall be of best hard burned where exposed to the weather, with foundation thereof resting on ground, starting........inches below surface, well plastered on the inside, and provided with holes for stove pipe and best sheet iron thimbles and tin caps wherever directed by owner; all flues and chimneys to extent ....feet above roof, and well supplied with tin flashings, to' prevent leaks where they pierce the roof.

**Ventilators.** Shall be made of ornamental scroll work ....by....inches in size and placed as follows:

**Ornamental** Scroll work shall be placed as follows and of following description:

**Outside** steps at each outside door shall be constructed as follows:

**Outside** door and stairway to cellar shall be constructed as follows:

**Fencing. a.** Picket. **b.** Tight boards. **c.** Paint.

**Well.** a. Kind. b. Furnishings.

**Cistern.** a. Size. b. Furnishings. c. Connection with down spout. d. Overflow pipe.

**Sink.** a. Kind. b. Covering.

**Outbuildings.** a. Kind. b. Kind and quality of material to be used therein. c. Size. d. Foundation. e. Roof. f. Paint. g. Vault shall be....feet deep, and walled with whole brick, burned sufficiently hard not to crumble. Its location shall be................

**Extras.........**

Plans for buildings for which the foregoing specifications are made are as follows:

### Form of Indemnifying Bond Against Liens.

Know all men by these presents, that we........of Marion County, and State of Indiana, are held and firmly bound unto the........association of Marion County, Indiana, in the sum of........dollars, to be paid to said association, well and truly, we bind ourselves, our heirs, executors and administrators, firmly by these presents. Sealed with our seals and dated the........day of........A. D., 18....

The conditions of this obligation are such, that whereas, the above bounden..........ha....heretofore entered into a contract with........the owner of certain real estate in..... County, Indiana, to make certain improvements thereon, which real estate is described as follows, to-wit................

And whereas, said association has agreed to lend the owner of said real estate $........with which to make said improvements, such loan to be secured by a first mortgage upon said real estate.

Now, therefore, should said obligors, their heirs, executors, administrators, successors and assigns, construct and fully complete according to contract, said improvements, in all their parts, in a manner satisfactory to the owner of said real estate, and to the board of directors of said association, and furnish and pay for all materials of every description used in improving said real estate, and fully pay all salaries, wages, compensations and moneys, which are or hereafter may be due and owing to any and all employes and laborers, who have been, now are, or hereafter may be employed upon, about or in connection with said improvements, and keep and preserve said premises free from any liens for materials furnished, or work and labor done; or, in case any such lien or liens, be taken against said real estate, should said obligors cause each lien so taken to be satisfied, removed, released and fully discharged, within thirty days from the filing of such lien, and hold and save said association harmless, by reason of such improvement of said real estate, or by reason of any loss, damage or injury growing out of, or, directly or indirectly, resulting therefrom, so that said mortgage shall be and remain a first lien upon said real estate, then this obligation shall be void and of no effect; otherwise, it shall remain in full force.

These obligors hereby agree that changes and additions, if any, in said contract for improvements, shall not operate to release them herefrom, but this bond shall apply to such additions and changes, if any, to the same extent that it would apply were they in existence at this time.

The said obligors hereby agree, jointly and severally, to pay said several sums, and to perform all the conditions of this bond and of said mortgage, and to pay ten per cent attorneys' fees, upon any sum which may be recovered upon this bond, all without any relief from valuation or appraisement laws.

Signed and delivered in presence of }
................................ 
................................ }

........................[SEAL]
........................[SEAL]
........................[SEAL]

State of............... }
                        } ss.
County of............. }

............, being duly sworn upon oath says; that he is the person who signed the attached indemnifying bond as surety thereon; that he is the owner in his own name and right, of unincumbered real estate, situated in......County, State of Indiana, worth double the penalty of the attached bond, over and above all debts, liens and exemptions of law.

Subscribed and sworn to before me, this........day of ........A. D. 189..

.......................Notary Public.

(NOTE.—An exemption as allowed by law should be exclusive of the sworn valuation. The surety should be worth double the penalty of bond. Write in ink.)

## Form of Contractor's Waiver of Liens.

.....................189..
To the............ Association: In consideration of the loan of $........made by you to........on the following real estate in........County, State of........, to wit: .... I, as contractor, for making improvements on said real estate, agree to waive any claim or right I may have to take or hold any mechanic's lien on said real estate, or the building or buildings to be placed thereon, and I agree to idemnify you against any lien for labor done or material furnished to make said improvements.

State of ........ }
                 } ss.
...... County. }

..........being duly sworn, on his oath says that the following is a complete list of the persons who have performed any labor or furnished any material in making the improvements on the real estate belonging to........and described

in the above agreement, and I authorize the ........Associa-
tion to pay said persons, out of the loan made by...........
from said association, the amounts due them severally, to the
extent of said loan:

| NAME. | WHAT FOR. | AMOUNT. |
|---|---|---|
|  |  |  |

Signature................
Subscribed and sworn to before me this........day of
........ 189..

....................N. P.

I authorize said............Association to pay, out of a
loan made by me from it, amounts due contractors, sub-contractors, laborers, or for material as per list furnished by....
as above. Witness........ Signature........

### Form of Sub-contractor's Waiver.

We severally acknowledge the receipt of the amounts set
opposite our respective names, for work done or material furnished for building, on lot................County, State of
........ being on........street........side, between......
and........streets, for........being property upon which
the..........Association has made a loan of $.........
And we hereby certify that no part of the material furnished
or work done was for or on any other property. And we hereby release all our rights to a mechanic's lien on said real
estate, or improvements thereon, for any amount now or hereafter to become due.

| NAME. | WHAT FOR. | AMOUNT. | RECEIPT. |
|---|---|---|---|
|  |  |  |  |

### General form of Bond for Secretary.

Know all men by these presents, That........as principal
and........as surety, are held and firmly bound unto the

APPENDIX. 235

........Association, in the penal sum of........dollars, to pay which they bind themselves, their heirs, executors and administrators, firmly by these presents.

The conditions of this obligation are such, as that, whereas, on the. ......day of........189.., the said........ was duly elected secretary of........Association aforesaid, by the directors thereof.

Now, therefore, if the said........shall faithfully perform his duties as such secretary, during the term for which he was elected, and during any succeeding term, until his successor is duly elected and qualified, as such duties are now, or hereafter may be imposed by the by-laws of said association, and during such time shall faithfully and accurately account for all moneys, books, notes, mortgages and other instruments of indebtedness, in favor of said association, and upon surrendering his said office, deliver to his successor in office, all money or other property of value in his hands, as such secretary, belonging to the said association, then this bond to be void and of no effect whatever; otherwise to be and remain in full force and effect in law.

In witness whereof, we have hereunto affixed our hands and seals, this....day of........A. D., 189..

............[SEAL.]........
............[SEAL.]........

### General form of Bond for Treasurer.

Know all men by these presents, That........as principal and......as surety, are held and firmly bound unto the...... Association, in the penal sum of........dollars, to pay which they bind themselves, their heirs, executors and administrators firmly by these presents.

The conditions of this obligation are such, as that, whereas, on the....day of......189..the said......was duly elected treasurer of the said association.

Now, therefore, if the said........shall faithfully perform his duties as such treasurer, during the term for which he was elected, and for any succeeding term, until his successor is duly elected and qualified, as such duties are now, or hereafter may be imposed by the by-laws of said association, and during such time faithfully and accurately account for all moneys, books, papers and other property belonging to the said association in his hands as such treasurer, and upon the surrendering of his office, deliver to his successor all moneys and other property in his hands as such treasurer, .then this bond to be void and of no effect whatever; otherwise to be and remain in full force and effect.

In witness whereof, the said........and........have hereunto set their hands and seals, this........day of........ A. D. 189..

..............[SEAL.]........

..............[SEAL.]........

*BRADLEY (THOMAS), of the Royal Military Academy, Woolwich—*

## ELEMENTS OF GEOMETRICAL DRAWING. In Two
Parts, with Sixty Plates. Oblong folio, half bound, each Part 16s.

*BRAY (MRS.)—*

## AUTOBIOGRAPHY OF (born 1789, died 1883).
Author of the "Life of Thomas Stothard, R.A.," "The White Hoods," &c.
Edited by JOHN A. KEMPE. With Portraits. Crown 8vo, 10s. 6d.

## MRS. BRAY'S NOVELS AND ROMANCES.
*New and Revised Editions, with Frontispieces. 3s. 6d. each.*

THE WHITE HOODS; a Romance of Flanders.
DE FOIX; a Romance of Bearn.

THE TALBA; or, The Moor of Portugal.
THE PROTESTANT; a Tale of the Times of Queen Mary.

### NOVELS FOUNDED ON TRADITIONS OF DEVON AND CORNWALL.

FITZ OF FITZFORD; a Tale of Destiny.
HENRY DE POMEROY; or, the Eve of St. John.
TRELAWNY OF TRELAWNE; or, a Romance of the West.

WARLEIGH; or, The Fatal Oak.
COURTENAY OF WALREDDON; a Romance of the West.
HARTLAND FOREST AND ROSE-TEAGUE.

### MISCELLANEOUS TALES.
A FATHER'S CURSE AND A DAUGHTER'S SACRIFICE.
TRIALS OF THE HEART.

*BROADLEY (A. M.)—*

## HOW WE DEFENDED ARABI AND HIS FRIENDS.
A Story of Egypt and the Egyptians  Illustrated by FREDERICK VILLIERS.
Demy 8vo, 12s.

*BROMLEY-DAVENPORT (the late W.), M.P.—*

## SPORT: Fox Hunting, Salmon Fishing, Covert Shooting,
Deer Stalking. With numerous Illustrations by General CREALOCK, C.B.
Small 4to, 21s.
A New and Cheaper Edition. Crown 8vo, 6s.

*BUCKLAND (FRANK)—*

## LOG-BOOK OF A FISHERMAN AND ZOOLOGIST.
With numerous Illustrations. Fifth Thousand. Crown 8vo, 5s.

*BURCHETT (R.)—*

DEFINITIONS OF GEOMETRY. New Edition. 24mo, cloth, 5d.

LINEAR PERSPECTIVE, for the Use of Schools of Art. New Edition. With Illustrations. Post 8vo, cloth, 7s.

PRACTICAL GEOMETRY: The Course of Construction of Plane Geometrical Figures. With 137 Diagrams. Eighteenth Edition. Post 8vo, cloth, 5s.

*CAMPION (J. S.).—*

ON THE FRONTIER. Reminiscences of Wild Sports, Personal Adventures, and Strange Scenes. With Illustrations. Second Edition. Demy 8vo, 16s.

ON FOOT IN SPAIN. With Illustrations. Second Edition. Demy 8vo, 16s.

*CARLYLE (THOMAS), WORKS BY.—See pages* 30 *and* 31.

THE CARLYLE BIRTHDAY BOOK. Compiled, with the permission of Mr. Thomas Carlyle, by C. N. WILLIAMSON. Second Edition. Small fcap. 8vo, 3s.

*CHALDÆAN AND ASSYRIAN ART—*

A HISTORY OF ART IN CHALDÆA AND ASSYRIA. By GEORGES PERROT and CHARLES CHIPIEZ. Translated by WALTER ARMSTRONG, B.A., Oxon. With 452 Illustrations. 2 vols. Imperial 8vo, 42s.

*CHURCH (PROFESSOR A. H.), M.A., Oxon.—*

FOOD GRAINS QF INDIA. With numerous Woodcuts. Small 4to, 6s.

ENGLISH PORCELAIN. A Handbook to the China made in England during the Eighteenth Century, as illustrated by Specimens chiefly in the National Collection. With numerous Woodcuts. Large crown 8vo, 3s.

ENGLISH EARTHENWARE. A Handbook to the Wares made in England during the 17th and 18th Centuries, as illustrated by Specimens in the National Collections. With numerous Woodcuts. Large crown 8vo, 3s.

PLAIN WORDS ABOUT WATER. Illustrated. Crown 8vo, sewed, 6d.

FOOD: Some Account of its Sources, Constituents, and Uses. Sixth Thousand. Large Crown 8vo, cloth, 3s.

PRECIOUS STONES: considered in their Scientific and Artistic Relations. With a Catalogue of the Townsend Collection of Gems in the South Kensington Museum. With a Coloured Plate and Woodcuts. Large crown 8vo, 2s. 6d.

*CLINTON (R. H.)—*

A COMPENDIUM OF ENGLISH HISTORY, from the Earliest Times to A.D. 1872. With Copious Quotations on the Leading Events and the Constitutional History, together with Appendices. Post 8vo, 7s. 6d.

COBDEN, RICHARD, LIFE OF. By the R!GHT HON. JOHN MORLEY, M.P. With Portrait. Fourth Thousand. 2 vols. Demy 8vo, 32s.
New Edition, with Portrait. Crown 8vo, 7s. 6d.
Popular Edition, with Portrait, 4to, sewed, 1s.; cloth, 2s.

**CHAPMAN & HALL'S ONE SHILLING SERIES OF BOOKS.**
*Crown 8vo, sewed.*
MEMOIRS OF A STOMACH. Written by Himself, that all who eat may read.
FAST AND LOOSE. By ARTHUR GRIFFITHS, Author of "The Chronicles of Newgate."
A SINGER'S STORY, related by the Author of "Flitters, Tatters, and the Counsellor."
NUMBER NINETY-NINE. By ARTHUR GRIFFITHS.
THE CASE OF REUBEN MALACHI. By H. SUTHERLAND EDWARDS.
SARTOR RESARTUS. By THOMAS CARLYLE. Crown 8vo, sewed.
THE WEAR AND TEAR OF LONDON LIFE. By ROBSON ROOSE, M.D, F.C.S.

**CHAPMAN & HALL'S SERIES OF POPULAR NOVELS.**
*New and Cheaper Editions of Popular Novels. Crown 8vo.*
KARMA. By A. P. SINNETT. 3s. 6d.
MOLOCH. A Story of Sacrifice. By MRS. CAMPBELL PRAED, Author of "Nadine." 6s.
FAUCIT OF BALLIOL. By HERMAN MERIVALE. 6s.
AN AUSTRALIAN HEROINE. By MRS. CAMPBELL PRAED. 6s.
STORY OF AN AFRICAN FARM. By RALPH IRON. 5s.
TO LEEWARD. By F. MARION CRAWFORD. New Edition. 5s.
AN AMERICAN POLITICIAN. By F. MARION CRAWFORD. 5s.
TIE AND TRICK. By HAWLEY SMART. 6s.

*COOKERY—*
THE PYTCHLEY BOOK OF REFINED COOKERY AND BILLS OF FARE. By MAJOR L——. Second Edition. Large crown 8vo, 8s.
BREAKFASTS, LUNCHEONS, AND BALL SUPPERS. By MAJOR L——. Crown 8vo.
OFFICIAL HANDBOOK FOR THE NATIONAL TRAINING SCHOOL FOR COOKERY. Containing Lessons on Cookery; forming the Course of Instruction in the School. Compiled by "R. O. C." Fourteenth Thousand. Large crown 8vo, 8s.
BREAKFAST AND SAVOURY DISHES. By "R. O. C." Seventh Thousand. Crown 8vo, 1s.
HOW TO COOK FISH. A Series of Lessons in Cookery, from the Official Handbook to the National Training School for Cookery, South Kensington. Compiled by "R. O. C." Crown 8vo, sewed, 3d.
SICK-ROOM COOKERY. From the Official Handbook to the National School for Cookery, South Kensington. Compiled by "R. O. C." Crown 8vo, sewed, 6d.
THE ROYAL CONFECTIONER: English and Foreign. A Practical Treatise. By C. E. FRANCATELLI. Fourth Thousand. With numerous Illustrations. Crown 8vo, 5s.
THE KINGSWOOD COOKERY BOOK. By H. F. WICKEN. Crown 8vo, 2s.

*COURTNEY (W. L.), LL.D.—*

CONSTRUCTIVE ETHICS: A Review of Modern Philo-
sophy and its Three Stages of Interpretation, Criticism, and Reconstruction.
Demy 8vo, 12s.

*CRAIK (GEORGE LILLIE)—*

ENGLISH OF SHAKESPEARE. Illustrated in a Philo-
logical Commentary on his "Julius Cæsar." Seventh Edition. Post 8vo, cloth, 5s.

OUTLINES OF THE HISTORY OF THE ENGLISH
LANGUAGE. Tenth Edition. Post 8vo, cloth, 2s. 6d.

*CRAWFORD (F. MARION)—*

TO LEEWARD. Crown 8vo, 5s.

AN AMERICAN POLITICIAN. Crown 8vo, 5s.

*CRIPPS (WILFRED JOSEPH), M.A., F.S.A.—*

COLLEGE AND CORPORATION PLATE. A Hand-
book for the Reproduction of Silver Plate. [*In the South Kensington Museum,
from celebrated English collections.*] With numerous Illustrations. Large crown
8vo, cloth, 2s. 6d.

*DAIRY FARMING—*

DAIRY FARMING. To which is added a Description of
the Chief Continental Systems. By James Long. With numerous Illustrations.
Crown 8vo, 9s.

DAIRY FARMING, MANAGEMENT OF COWS, &c.
By Arthur Roland. Edited by William Ablett. Crown 8vo, 5s.

*DAUBOURG (E.)—*

INTERIOR ARCHITECTURE. Doors, Vestibules, Stair-
cases, Anterooms, Drawing, Dining, and Bed Rooms, Libraries, Bank and Newspaper Offices, Shop Fronts and Interiors. Half-imperial, cloth, £2 12s. 6d.

*DAUGLISH (M. G.) and BARKER (G. F. RUSSELL), of Lincoln's Inn,
Barristers-at-Law—*

HISTORICAL AND POLITICAL HANDBOOK. Crown
8vo, 6s.

*DAVIDSON (ELLIS A.)—*

PRETTY ARTS FOR THE EMPLOYMENT OF
LEISURE HOURS. A Book for Ladies. With Illustrations. Demy 8vo, 6s.

*DAVITT (MICHAEL)—*

LEAVES FROM A PRISON DIARY; or, Lectures
to a Solitary Audience. 2 vols. Crown 8vo, 21s.

In one vol. Crown 8vo, cloth, 6s.

Cheap Edition. Ninth Thousand. Crown 8vo, sewed, 1s. 6d.

*DAY (WILLIAM)—*

## THE RACEHORSE IN TRAINING, with Hints on
Racing and Racing Reform, to which is added a Chapter on Shoeing. Fifth Edition. Demy 8vo, 9s.

*DE CHAMPEAUX (ALFRED)—*

## TAPESTRY. With numerous Woodcuts. Cloth, 2s. 6d.

*D'HAUSSONVILLE (VICOMTE)—*

## SALON OF MADAME NECKER. Translated by H. M.
TROLLOPE. 2 vols. Crown 8vo, 18s.

*DE KONINCK (L. L.) and DIETZ (E.)—*

## PRACTICAL MANUAL OF CHEMICAL ASSAYING,
as applied to the Manufacture of Iron. Edited, with notes, by ROBERT MALLET. Post 8vo, cloth, 6s.

## DE LISLE (MEMOIR OF LIEUTENANT RUDOLPH),
R.N., of the Naval Brigade. By the Rev. H. N. OXENHAM, M.A. Second Edition. Crown 8vo, 7s. 6d.

*DICKENS (CHARLES), WORKS BY—See pages 32—39.*

## THE LETTERS OF CHARLES DICKENS. Edited
by his Sister-in-Law and his Eldest Daughter. Two vols. uniform with "The Charles Dickens Edition" of his Works. Crown 8vo, 8s.

## THE LIFE OF CHARLES DICKENS—*See "Forster."*

## THE CHARLES DICKENS BIRTHDAY BOOK.
Compiled and Edited by his Eldest Daughter. With Five Illustrations by his Youngest Daughter. In a handsome fcap. 4to volume, 12s.

## THE HUMOUR AND PATHOS OF CHARLES
DICKENS : With Illustrations of his Mastery of the Terrible and Picturesque. By CHARLES KENT. With Portrait. Crown 8vo, 6s.

*DRAGE GEOFFREY—*

## CRIMINAL CODE OF THE GERMAN EMPIRE.
Translated with Prolegomena, and a Commentary, by G. DRAGE. Crown 8vo, 8s.

*DRAYSON (MAJOR-GENERAL A. W.), Late R.A., F.R.A.S.—*

## EXPERIENCES OF A WOOLWICH PROFESSOR
during Fifteen Years at the Royal Military Academy. Demy 8vo, 8s.

## THE CAUSE OF THE SUPPOSED PROPER MOTION
OF THE FIXED STARS. Demy 8vo, cloth, 10s.

## PRACTICAL MILITARY SURVEYING AND
SKETCHING. Fifth Edition. Post 8vo, cloth, 4s. 6d.

## DREAMS BY A FRENCH FIRESIDE. Translated from the
German by MARY O'CALLAGHAN. Illustrated by Fred Roe. Crown 8vo, 7s. 6d.

*DUFFY (SIR CHARLES GAVAN), K.C.M.G.—*
### THE LEAGUE OF NORTH AND SOUTH. An Episode
in Irish History, 1850–1854. Crown 8vo, 8s.

### DUPANLOUP, MONSEIGNEUR (BISHOP OF ORLEANS),
LIFE OF. By Abbé F. Lagrange. Translated from the French by Lady Herbert. With Two Portraits. 2 vols. 8vo, 32s.

### DYCE'S COLLECTION. A Catalogue of Printed Books and
Manuscripts bequeathed by the Rev. Alexander Dyce to the South Kensington Museum. 2 vols. Royal 8vo, half-morocco, 14s.

### A Collection of Paintings, Miniatures, Drawings, Engravings,
Rings, and Miscellaneous Objects, bequeathed by the Rev. Alexander Dyce to the South Kensington Museum. Royal 8vo, half-morocco, 6s. 6d.

*DYCE (WILLIAM), R.A.—*
### DRAWING-BOOK OF THE GOVERNMENT SCHOOL
OF DESIGN; OR, ELEMENTARY OUTLINES OF ORNAMENT. Fifty selected Plates. Folio, sewed, 5s.; mounted, 18s.
Text to Ditto. Sewed, 6d.

*EDWARDS, H. SUTHERLAND—*
### FAMOUS FIRST REPRESENTATIONS. Crown 8vo,
6s.

### THE CASE OF REUBEN MALACHI. Crown 8vo,
sewed, 1s.

*EGYPTIAN ART—*
### A HISTORY OF ART IN ANCIENT EGYPT. By
G. Perrot and C. Chipiez. Translated by Walter Armstrong. With over 600 Illustrations. 2 vols. Imperial 8vo, £2 2s.

*ELLIS (A. B., Major 1st West India Regiment)—*
### WEST AFRICAN ISLANDS. Demy 8vo. 14s.

### THE HISTORY OF THE WEST INDIA REGI-
MENT. With Maps and Coloured Frontispiece and Title-page. Demy 8vo. 18s.

### THE LAND OF FETISH. Demy 8vo. 12s.

*ENGEL (CARL)—*
### A DESCRIPTIVE AND ILLUSTRATED CATALOGUE
OF THE MUSICAL INSTRUMENTS in the SOUTH KENSINGTON MUSEUM, preceded by an Essay on the History of Musical Instruments. Second Edition. Royal 8vo, half-morocco, 12s.

### MUSICAL INSTRUMENTS. With numerous Woodcuts.
Large crown 8vo, cloth, 2s. 6d.

*ESCOTT (T. H. S.)—*
### POLITICS AND LETTERS. Demy 8vo, 9s.

### ENGLAND. ITS PEOPLE, POLITY, AND PURSUITS.
New and Revised Edition. Sixth Thousand. 8vo, 8s.

### PILLARS OF THE EMPIRE : Short Biographical
Sketches. 8vo, 10s. 6d.

*EWALD (ALEXANDER CHARLES), F.S.A.—*
REPRESENTATIVE STATESMEN : Political Studies.
2 vols. Large crown 8vo, £1 4s.
SIR ROBERT WALPOLE. A Political Biography,
1676-1745. Demy 8vo, 18s.

*FANE (VIOLET)—*
QUEEN OF THE FAIRIES (A Village Story), and other
Poems. Crown 8vo, 6s.
ANTHONY BABINGTON : a Drama. Crown 8vo, 6s.

*FLEMING (GEORGE), F.R.C.S.—*
ANIMAL PLAGUES : THEIR HISTORY, NATURE,
AND PREVENTION. 8vo, cloth, 15s.
PRACTICAL HORSE-SHOEING. With 37 Illustrations.
Fifth Edition, enlarged. 8vo, sewed, 2s.
RABIES AND HYDROPHOBIA : THEIR HISTORY,
NATURE, CAUSES, SYMPTOMS, AND PREVENTION. With 8 Illustra-
tions. 8vo, cloth, 15s.

*FORSTER (JOHN), M.P. for Berwick—*
THE CHRONICLE OF JAMES I., KING OF ARAGON,
SURNAMED THE CONQUEROR. Written by Himself. Translated from
the Catalan by the late JOHN FORSTER, M.P. for Berwick. With an Historical
Introduction by DON PASCUAL DE GAYANGOS. 2 vols. Royal 8vo, 28s.

*FORSTER (JOHN)—*
THE LIFE OF CHARLES DICKENS. With Portraits
and other Illustrations. 3 vols. 8vo, cloth, £2 2s.
THE LIFE OF CHARLES DICKENS. Uniform with
the Illustrated Library Edition of Dickens's Works. 2 vols. Demy 8vo, £1 8s.
THE LIFE OF CHARLES DICKENS. Uniform with
the Library Edition. Post 8vo, 10s. 6d.
THE LIFE OF CHARLES DICKENS. Uniform with
the "C. D." Edition. With Numerous Illustrations. 2 vols. 7s.
THE LIFE OF CHARLES DICKENS. Uniform with
the Household Edition. With Illustrations by F. BARNARD. Crown 4to, cloth, 5s.
WALTER SAVAGE LANDOR : a Biography, 1775-1864.
With Portrait. A New and Revised Edition. Demy 8vo, 12s.

*FORTESCUE (THE HON. JOHN)—*
RECORDS OF STAG-HUNTING ON EXMOOR. With
Illustrations by EDGAR GIBERNE. Large crown 8vo.

*FORTNIGHTLY REVIEW—*
FORTNIGHTLY REVIEW.—First Series, May, 1865, to
Dec. 1866. 6 vols. Cloth, 13s. each.
New Series, 1867 to 1872. In Half-yearly Volumes. Cloth,
13s. each.
From January, 1873, to the present time, in Half-yearly
Volumes. Cloth, 16s. each.
CONTENTS OF FORTNIGHTLY REVIEW. From
the commencement to end of 1878. Sewed, 2s.

*FORTNUM (C. D. E.), F.S.A.—*

A DESCRIPTIVE AND ILLUSTRATED CATALOGUE
OF THE BRONZES OF EUROPEAN ORIGIN in the SOUTH KEN-
SINGTON MUSEUM, with an Introductory Notice.   Royal 8vo, half-morocco,
£1 10s.

A DESCRIPTIVE AND ILLUSTRATED CATALOGUE
OF MAIOLICA, HISPANO-MORESCO, PERSIAN, DAMASCUS, AND
RHODIAN WARES in the SOUTH KENSINGTON MUSEUM. Royal
8vo, half-morocco, £2.

MAIOLICA.   With   numerous   Woodcuts.   Large   crown
8vo, cloth, 2s. 6d.

BRONZES.   With   numerous   Woodcuts.   Large   crown
8vo, cloth, 2s. 6d.

*FRANCATELLI (C. E.)—*

THE ROYAL CONFECTIONER : English and Foreign.
A Practical Treatise.   Fourth Edition.   With Illustrations.   Crown 8vo, 5s.

*FRANKS (A. W.)—*

JAPANESE POTTERY.   Being a Native Report, with an
Introduction and Catalogue.   With numerous Illustrations and Marks.   Large
crown 8vo, cloth, 2s. 6d.

*GALLENGA (ANTONIO)—*

ITALY : PRESENT AND FUTURE.   2 vols.   Demy 8vo.

EPISODES OF MY SECOND LIFE.   2 vols.   Demy 8vo,
28s.

IBERIAN REMINISCENCES.   Fifteen Years' Travelling
Impressions of Spain and Portugal.   With a Map.   2 vols.   Demy 8vo, 32s.

*GASNAULT (PAUL) and GARNIER (ED.)—*

FRENCH POTTERY.   With Illustrations and   Marks.
Large crown 8vo, 3s.

*GILLMORE (PARKER)—*

THE HUNTER'S ARCADIA.   With numerous Illustrations.   Demy 8vo.

*GORDON (GENERAL)—*

LETTERS FROM THE CRIMEA, THE DANUBE,
AND ARMENIA.   Edited by DEMETRIUS C. BOULGER.   Second Edition:
Crown 8vo, 5s.

*GORST (SIR J. E.), Q.C., M.P.—*

An ELECTION MANUAL.   Containing the Parliamentary
Elections (Corrupt and Illegal Practices) Act, 1883, with Notes.   Third Edition.
Crown 8vo, 1s. 6d.

*GRESWELL (WILLIAM), M.A., F.R.C.I.—*

OUR SOUTH AFRICAN EMPIRE.   With Map.   2 vols.
Crown 8vo, 21s.

*GREVILLE (LADY VIOLET)—*

MONTROSE. With an Introduction by the EARL OF
ASHBURNHAM. With Portrait. Large crown 8vo.

*GRIFFIN (SIR LEPEL HENRY), K.C.S.I.—*

THE GREAT REPUBLIC. Second Edition. Crown 8vo,
4s. 6d.

*GRIFFITHS (MAJOR ARTHUR), H.M. Inspector of Prisons—*

CHRONICLES OF NEWGATE. Illustrated. New
Edition. Demy 8vo, 16s.

MEMORIALS OF MILLBANK : or, Chapters in Prison
History. With Illustrations by R. Goff and Author. New Edition. Demy 8vo,
12s.

FAST AND LOOSE. A Novel. Crown 8vo, sewed, 1s.

NUMBER NINETY-NINE. A Novel. Crown 8vo,
sewed, 1s.

*GRIMBLE (AUGUSTUS)—*

DEER-STALKING. With 6 Full-page Illustrations. Large
crown 8vo, 6s.

*HALL (SIDNEY)—*

A TRAVELLING ATLAS OF THE ENGLISH COUN-
TIES. Fifty Maps, coloured. New Edition, including the Railways, corrected
up to the present date. Demy 8vo, in roan tuck, 10s. 6d.

*HARDY (LADY DUFFUS)—*

DOWN SOUTH. Demy 8vo. 14s.

THROUGH CITIES AND PRAIRIE LANDS. Sketches
of an American Tour. Demy 8vo, 14s.

*HATTON (JOSEPH) and HARVEY (REV. M.)—*

NEWFOUNDLAND. The Oldest British Colony. Its
History, Past and Present, and its Prospects in the Future. Illustrated from
Photographs and Sketches specially made for this work. Demy 8vo, 18s.

*HAWKINS (FREDERICK)—*

ANNALS OF THE FRENCH STAGE : FROM ITS
ORIGIN TO THE DEATH OF RACINE. 4 Portraits. 2 vols. Demy 8vo,
28s.

*HILDEBRAND (HANS), Royal Antiquary of Sweden—*

INDUSTRIAL ARTS OF SCANDINAVIA IN THE
PAGAN TIME. With numerous Woodcuts. Large crown 8vo, 2s. 6d.

*HILL (MISS G.)—*

## THE PLEASURES AND PROFITS OF OUR LITTLE
POULTRY FARM. Small 8vo, 3s.

*HOLBEIN—*

## TWELVE HEADS AFTER HOLBEIN. Selected from
Drawings in Her Majesty's Collection at Windsor. Reproduced in Autotype, in portfolio. £1 16s.

*HOLLINGSHEAD (JOHN)—*

## FOOTLIGHTS. Crown 8vo. 7s. 6d.

*HOVELACQUE (ABEL)—*

## THE SCIENCE OF LANGUAGE: LINGUISTICS,
PHILOLOGY, AND ETYMOLOGY. With Maps. Large crown 8vo, cloth, 5s.

*HUMPHRIS (H. D.)—*

## PRINCIPLES OF PERSPECTIVE. Illustrated in a
Series of Examples. Oblong folio, half-bound, and Text 8vo, cloth, £1 1s.

## INDUSTRIAL ARTS: Historical Sketches. With numerous
Illustrations. Large crown 8vo, 3s.

## INTERNATIONAL POLICY : Essay on the Foreign Relations
of England. By FREDERIC HARRISON, PROF. BEESLEY, RICHARD CONGREVE, and others. New Edition. Crown 8vo, 2s. 6d.

*IRON (RALPH)—*

## THE STORY OF AN AFRICAN FARM. New Edition.
Crown 8vo, 5s.

*JARRY (GENERAL)—*

## OUTPOST DUTY. Translated, with TREATISES ON
MILITARY RECONNAISSANCE AND ON ROAD-MAKING. By Major-Gen. W. C. E. NAPIER. Third Edition. Crown 8vo, 5s.

*JEANS (W. T.)—*

## CREATORS OF THE AGE OF STEEL. Memoirs of
Sir W. Siemens, Sir H. Bessemer, Sir J. Whitworth, Sir J. Brown, and other Inventors. Second Edition. Crown 8vo, 7s. 6d.

*JOHNSON (DR. SAMUEL)—*

## LIFE AND CONVERSATIONS OF DR. SAMUEL
JOHNSON. By A. MAIN. Crown 8vo, 10s. 6d.

*JONES (CAPTAIN DOUGLAS), R.A.—*

## NOTES ON MILITARY LAW. Crown 8vo, 4s.

## JONES COLLECTION (HANDBOOK OF THE) IN THE
SOUTH KENSINGTON MUSEUM. With Portrait and Woodcuts. Large crown 8vo, 2s. 6d.

*KEMPIS (THOMAS A)—*

## OF THE IMITATION OF CHRIST. Four Books.
Beautifully Illustrated Edition. Demy 8vo, 16s.

*KENNARD (MRS. EDWARD)—*

## TWILIGHT TALES. Illustrated by EDITH ELLISON.
Crown 8vo, 7s. 6d.

*KENT (CHARLES)—*

## HUMOUR AND PATHOS OF CHARLES DICKENS,
WITH ILLUSTRATIONS OF HIS MASTERY OF THE TERRIBLE
AND PICTURESQUE. Portrait. Crown 8vo, 6s.

*KINGSTON (W. BEATTY)—*

## MUSIC AND MANNERS. 2 vols. Crown 8vo.

*KING (MAJOR COOPER)—*

## GEORGE WASHINGTON. Crown 8vo.

*KLACZKO (M. JULIAN) —*

## TWO CHANCELLORS : PRINCE GORTCHAKOF AND
PRINCE BISMARCK. Translated by Mrs. TAIT. New and cheaper Edition, 6s.

## LACORDAIRE'S JESUS CHRIST; GOD; AND GOD AND
MAN. Conferences delivered at Notre Dame in Paris. New Edition in 1 vol.
Crown 8vo, 6s.

*LAING (S.)—*

## MODERN SCIENCE AND MODERN THOUGHT.
Third and Cheaper Edition. With a Supplementary Chapter on Gla lstone's "Dawn
of Creation" and Drummond's "Natural Law in the Spiritual World." Demy
8vo, 7s. 6d.

*LAVELEYE (ÉMILE DE)—*

## THE ELEMENTS OF POLITICAL ECONOMY.
Translated by W. POLLARD, B.A., St. John's College, Oxford. Crown 8vo, 6s.

*LANDOR (W. S.)—*

## LIFE AND WORKS. 8 vols.
VOL. 1. WALTER SAVAGE LANDOR. A Biography in Eight Books. By
JOHN FORSTER. Demy 8vo, 12s.

VOL. 2. Out of print.

VOL. 3. CONVERSATIONS OF SOVEREIGNS AND STATESMEN, AND
FIVE DIALOGUES OF BOCCACCIO AND PETRARCA.
Demy 8vo, 14s.

VOL. 4. DIALOGUES OF LITERARY MEN. Demy 8vo, 14s.

VOL. 5. DIALOGUES OF LITERARY MEN (*continued*). FAMOUS
WOMEN. LETTERS OF PERICLES AND ASPASIA. And
Minor Prose Pieces. Demy 8vo, 14s.

VOL. 6. MISCELLANEOUS CONVERSATIONS. Demy 8vo, 14s.

VOL. 7. GEBIR, ACTS AND SCENES AND HELLENICS. Poems
Demy 8vo, 14s.

VOL. 8. MISCELLANEOUS POEMS AND CRITICISMS ON THEO-
CRITUS, CATULLUS, AND PETRARCH. Demy 8vo, 14s.

*LEFÈVRE (ANDRÉ)—*

PHILOSOPHY, Historical and Critical. Translated, with
an Introduction, by A. W. KEANE, B.A. Large crown 8vo, 7s. 6d.

*LESLIE (R. C.)—*

A SEA PAINTER'S LOG. With 12 Full-page Illustrations
by the Author. Large crown 8vo, 12s.

*LETOURNEAU (DR. CHARLES)—*

SOCIOLOGY. Based upon Ethnology. Translated by
HENRY M. TROLLOPE. Large crown 8vo, 10s.

BIOLOGY. Translated by WILLIAM MacCALL. With Illustrations. Large crown 8vo, 6s.

*LILLY (W. S.)—*

CHAPTERS ON EUROPEAN HISTORY. With an
Introductory Dialogue on the Philosophy of History. 2 vols. Demy 8vo, 21s.

ANCIENT RELIGION AND MODERN THOUGHT.
Third Edition, revised, with additions. Demy 8vo, 12s.

*LLOYD (MAJOR E. M.), R.E., late Professor of Fortification at the Royal
Military Academy, Woolwich—*

VAUBAN, MONTALEMBERT, CARNOT : ENGINEER
STUDIES. With Portraits. Crown 8vo.

*LONG (JAMES)—*

DAIRY FARMING. To which is added a Description of
the Chief Continental Systems. With numerous Illustrations. Crown 8vo, 9s.

*LOW (C. R.)—*

SOLDIERS OF THE VICTORIAN AGE. 2 vols. Demy
8vo, £1 10s.

*LYTTON (ROBERT, EARL)—*

POETICAL WORKS—

FABLES IN SONG. 2 vols. Fcap 8vo, 12s.
THE WANDERER. Fcap. 8vo, 6s.
POEMS, HISTORICAL AND CHARACTERISTIC. Fcap. 6s.

*MALLET (ROBERT)—*

PRACTICAL MANUAL OF CHEMICAL ASSAYING,
as applied to the Manufacture of Iron. By L. L. DE KONINCK and E. DIETZ.
Edited, with notes, by ROBERT MALLET. Post 8vo, cloth, 6s.

*MASKELL (ALFRED)*—

## RUSSIAN ART AND ART OBJECTS IN RUSSIA.

A Handbook to the Reproduction of Goldsmiths' Work and other Art Treasures from that Country, in the SOUTH KENSINGTON MUSEUM. With Illustrations. Large Crown 8vo, 4s. 6d.

*MASKELL (WILLIAM)*—

## A DESCRIPTION OF THE IVORIES, ANCIENT AND

MEDIÆVAL, in the SOUTH KENSINGTON MUSEUM, with a Preface. With numerous Photographs and Woodcuts. Royal 8vo, half-morocco, £1 1s.

## IVORIES: ANCIENT AND MEDIÆVAL. With nume-

rous Woodcuts. Large crown 8vo, cloth, 2s. 6d.

## HANDBOOK TO THE DYCE AND FORSTER COL-

LECTIONS. With Illustrations. Large crown 8vo, cloth, 2s. 6d.

## MEMOIRS OF A STOMACH. Written by himself, that all

who eat may read. Crown 8vo, sewed, 1s.

---

# GEORGE MEREDITH'S WORKS.

## MODERN LOVE AND POEMS OF THE ENGLISH

ROADSIDE, WITH POEMS AND BALLADS. Fcap. cloth, 6s.

*A New and Uniform Edition. In Six-Shilling Volumes. Crown 8vo:*

## DIANA OF THE CROSSWAYS.

## EVAN HARRINGTON.

## THE ORDEAL OF RICHARD FEVEREL.

## THE ADVENTURES OF HARRY RICHMOND.

## SANDRA BELLONI. Originally EMILIA IN ENGLAND.

## VITTORIA.

## RHODA FLEMING.

## BEAUCHAMP'S CAREER.

## THE EGOIST.

## THE SHAVING OF SHAGPAT. [In the Press.

*MERIVALE (HERMAN CHARLES)*—

## BINKO'S BLUES. A Tale for Children of all Growths.

Illustrated by EDGAR GIBERNE. Small crown 8vo, 5s.

## THE WHITE PILGRIM, and other Poems. Crown 8vo, 9s.

## FAUCIT OF BALLIOL. Crown 8vo, 6s.

B

## MILITARY BIOGRAPHIES—

FREDERICK THE GREAT. By Col. C. B. Brackenbury; with Maps and Portrait. Large crown 8vo, 4s.

LOUDON. A Sketch of the Military Life of Gideon Ernest, Freicherr von Loudon, sometime Generalissimo of the Austrian Forces. By Col. G. B. MALLESON, C.S.I. With Portrait and Maps. Large crown 8vo, 4s.

TURENNE. By H. M. Hozier. With Portrait and Two Maps. Large crown 8vo, 4s.

PARLIAMENTARY GENERALS OF THE GREAT CIVIL WAR. By Major Walford, R.A. With Maps. Large crown 8vo, 4s.

*MOLESWORTH (W. NASSAU)—*

HISTORY OF ENGLAND FROM THE YEAR 1830 TO THE RESIGNATION OF THE GLADSTONE MINISTRY, 1874. Twelfth Thousand. 3 vols. Crown 8vo, 18s.

ABRIDGED EDITION. Large crown, 7s. 6d.

*MOLTKE (FIELD-MARSHAL COUNT VON)—*

POLAND: AN HISTORICAL SKETCH. An Authorised Translation, with Biographical Notice by E. S. Buchheim. Crown 8vo, 4s. 6d.

*MORLEY (HENRY)—*

TABLES OF ENGLISH LITERATURE. Containing 20 Charts. Second Edition, with Index. Royal 4to, cloth, 12s.
    In Three Parts. Parts I. and II., containing Three Charts, each 1s. 6d.
    Part III. in Sections, 1, 2, and 5, 1s. 6d. each; 3 and 4 together, 3s.
    *₊* The Charts sold separately.

*MORLEY (THE RIGHT HON. JOHN), M.P.—*

LIFE AND CORRESPONDENCE OF RICHARD COBDEN. Fourth Thousand. 2 vols. Demy 8vo £1 12s.

Crown 8vo Edition, with Portrait, 7s. 6d.

Popular Edition. With Portrait. 4to, sewed, 1s. Bound in cloth, 2s.

*MUNTZ (EUGENE), From the French of—*

RAPHAEL: HIS LIFE, WORKS, AND TIMES. Edited by W: Armstrong. With 155 Wood Engravings and 41 Full-page Plates. Imperial 8vo, 36s.

*MURPHY (J. M.)—*

RAMBLES IN NORTH-WEST AMERICA. With Frontispiece and Map. 8vo, 16s.

*MURRAY (ANDREW), F.L.S.—*

ECONOMIC ENTOMOLOGY. Aptera. With numerous Illustrations. Large crown 8vo, 7s. 6d.

*NAPIER (MAJ.-GEN. W. C. E.)*

## TRANSLATION OF GEN. JARRY'S OUTPOST DUTY.
With TREATISES ON MILITARY RECONNAISSANCE AND ON ROAD-MAKING. Third Edition. Crown 8vo, 5s.

NAPOLEON. A Selection from the Letters and Despatches of the First Napoleon. With Explanatory Notes by Captain the Hon. D. BINGHAM. 3 vols. Demy 8vo, £2 2s.

*NECKER (MADAME)—*

## THE SALON OF MADAME NECKER. By VICOMTE
D'HAUSSONVILLE. Translated by H. M. TROLLOPE. 2 vols. Crown 8vo 18s.

*NESBITT (ALEXANDER)—*

## GLASS. With numerous Woodcuts. Large crown 8vo,
cloth, 2s. 6d.

*NEVINSON (HENRY)*

## A SKETCH OF HERDER AND HIS TIMES. With
a Portrait. Demy 8vo, 14s.

*NEWTON (E. TULLEY), F.G.S.*

## THE TYPICAL PARTS IN THE SKELETONS OF
A CAT, DUCK, AND CODFISH, being a Catalogue with Comparative Description arranged in a Tabular form. Demy 8vo, cloth, 3s.

*NORMAN (C. B.), late of the 90th Light Infantry and Bengal Staff Corps—*

## TONKIN; OR, FRANCE IN THE FAR EAST. With
Maps. Demy 8vo, 14s.

*O'GRADY (STANDISH)*

## TORYISM AND THE TORY DEMOCRACY. Crown
8vo, 5s.

*OLIVER (PROFESSOR), F.R.S., &c.—*

## ILLUSTRATIONS OF THE PRINCIPAL NATURAL
ORDERS OF THE VEGETABLE KINGDOM, PREPARED FOR THE SCIENCE AND ART DEPARTMENT, SOUTH KENSINGTON. With 109 Plates. Oblong 8vo, plain, 16s.; coloured, £1 6s.

*"ONE OF THE CROWD"—*

## A WORKING MAN'S PHILOSOPHY. Crown 8vo, 3s.

*OXENHAM (REV. H. N.)—*

## MEMOIR OF LIEUTENANT RUDOLPH DE LISLE,
R.N., OF THE NAVAL BRIGADE. Second Edition, with Illustrations. Crown 8vo, 7s. 6d.

## SHORT STUDIES, ETHICAL AND RELIGIOUS.
Demy 8vo. 12s.

## SHORT STUDIES IN ECCLESIASTICAL HISTORY
AND BIOGRAPHY. Demy 8vo, 12s.

*PERROT (GEORGES) and CHIPIEZ (CHARLES)—*

## A HISTORY OF ANCIENT ART IN PHŒNICIA

AND ITS DEPENDENCIES. Translated from the French by WALTER ARMSTRONG. B.A. Oxon. Containing 644 Illustrations in the text, and 10 Steel and Coloured Plates. 2 vols. Imperial 8vo, 42s.

## A HISTORY OF ART IN CHALDÆA AND ASSYRIA.

Translated by WALTER ARMSTRONG, B.A. Oxon. With 452 Illustrations. 2 vols. Imperial 8vo, 42s.

## A HISTORY OF ART IN ANCIENT EGYPT. Trans-

lated from the French by W. ARMSTRONG, B A. Oxon. With over 600 Illustrations. 2 vols. Imperial 8vo, 42s.

*PHŒNICIAN ART—*

## A HISTORY OF ANCIENT ART IN PHŒNICIA

AND ITS DEPENDENCIES. By GEORGES PERROT and CHARLES CHIPIEZ. Translated from the French by WALTER ARMSTRONG, B.A., Oxon. Containing 644 Illustrations in the text, and 10 Steel and Coloured Plates. 2 vols. Imperial 8vo, 42s.

*PIASSETSKY (P.)—*

## RUSSIAN TRAVELLERS IN MONGOLIA AND

CHINA. Translated by GORDON-CUMMING. With 75 Illustrations. 2 vols. Crown 8vo, 24s.

*PILLING (WILLIAM)—*

## ORDER FROM CHAOS : a Treatise on Land Tenure.

Large Crown 8vo. 2s. 6d.

*PITT TAYLOR (FRANK)—*

## THE CANTERBURY TALES. Selections from the Tales

of GEOFFREY CHAUCER rendered into Modern English, with close adherence to the language of the Poet. With Frontispiece. Crown 8vo, 6s.

*POLLEN (J. H.)—*

## ANCIENT AND MODERN FURNITURE AND

WOODWORK IN THE SOUTH KENSINGTON MUSEUM. With an Introduction, and Illustrated with numerous Coloured Photographs and Woodcuts. Royal 8vo, half-morocco, £1 1s.

## GOLD AND SILVER SMITH'S WORK. With nume-

rous Woodcuts. Large crown 8vo, cloth, 2s. 6d.

## ANCIENT AND MODERN FURNITURE AND

WOODWORK. With numerous Woodcuts. Large crown 8vo, cloth, 2s. 6d.

*POOLE (STANLEY LANE), B.A., M.R.A.S., Hon. Member of the Egyptian Commission for the Preservation of the Monuments of Cairo—*

## THE ART OF THE SARACENS IN EGYPT. Pub-

lished for the Committee of Council on Education. With 108 Woodcuts. Demy 8vo, 12s.

*\*₊\* A few copies of the large-paper edition printed on hand-made paper are still to be had, price 31s. 6d.*

*POYNTER (E. J.), R.A.—*

TEN LECTURES ON ART. Third Edition. Large
crown 8vo, 9s.

*PRAED (MRS. CAMPBELL)—*

AUSTRALIAN LIFE: Black and White. With Illustration. Crown 8vo, 8s.

AN AUSTRALIAN HEROINE. Crown 8vo, 6s.

MOLOCH. A Story of Sacrifice. Crown 8vo, 6s.

*PRINSEP (VAL), A.R.A.—*

IMPERIAL INDIA. Containing numerous Illustrations
and Maps. Second Edition. Demy 8vo, £1 1s.

RADICAL PROGRAMME, THE. From the *Fortnightly
Review*, with additions. With a Preface by the RIGHT HON. J. CHAMBERLAIN,
M.P. Thirteenth Thousand. Crown 8vo, 2s. 6d.

*RAMSDEN (LADY GWENDOLEN)—*

A BIRTHDAY BOOK. Illustrated. Containing 46 Illustra-
tions from Original Drawings, and numerous other Illustrations. Royal 8vo, 21s.

*REDGRAVE (GILBERT)—*

OUTLINES OF HISTORIC ORNAMENT. Translated
from the German. Edited by GILBERT REDGRAVE. With numerous Illustrations.
Crown 8vo, 4s.

*REDGRAVE (GILBERT R.)—*

MANUAL OF DESIGN, compiled from the Writings and
Addresses of RICHARD REDGRAVE, R.A. With Woodcuts. Large crown 8vo, cloth,
2s. 6d.

*REDGRAVE (RICHARD)—*

ELEMENTARY MANUAL OF COLOUR, with a
Catechism on Colour. 24mo, cloth, 9d.

*REDGRAVE (SAMUEL)—*

A DESCRIPTIVE CATALOGUE OF THE HIS-
TORICAL COLLECTION OF WATER-COLOUR PAINTINGS IN THE
SOUTH KENSINGTON MUSEUM. With numerous Chromo-lithographs and
other Illustrations. Royal 8vo, £1 1s.

*RENAN (ERNEST)—*

## RECOLLECTIONS OF MY YOUTH. Translated from
the original French, and revised by MADAME RENAN. Crown 8vo, 8s.

*REYNARDSON (C. T. S. BIRCH)—*

## SPORTS AND ANECDOTES OF BYGONE DAYS
In England, Scotland, Ireland, Italy, and the Sunny South. With numerou Illustrations in Colour. Demy 8vo.

*RIANO (JUAN F.)—*

## THE INDUSTRIAL ARTS IN SPAIN. With numerous
Woodcuts. Large crown 8vo, cloth, 4s.

*RIBTON-TURNER (C. J.)—*

## A HISTORY OF VAGRANTS AND VAGRANCY AND
BEGGARS AND BEGGING. Demy 8vo.

*ROBINSON (JAMES F.)—*

## BRITISH BEE FARMING. Its Profits and Pleasures.
Large crown 8vo, 5s.

*ROBINSON (J. C.)—*

## ITALIAN SCULPTURE OF THE MIDDLE AGES
AND PERIOD OF THE REVIVAL OF ART. With 20 Engravings. Royal 8vo, cloth, 7s. 6d.

*ROBSON (GEORGE)—*

## ELEMENTARY BUILDING CONSTRUCTION. Illus-
trated by a Design for an Entrance Lodge and Gate. 15 Plates. Oblong folio, sewed, 8s.

*ROBSON (REV. J. H.), M.A., LL.M.—*

## AN ELEMENTARY TREATISE ON ALGEBRA.
Post 8vo, 6s.

*ROCK (THE VERY REV. CANON), D.D.—*

## ON TEXTILE FABRICS. A Descriptive and Illustrated
Catalogue of the Collection of Church Vestments, Dresses, Silk Stuffs, Needlework, and Tapestries in the South Kensington Museum. Royal 8vo, half-morocco, £1 11s. 6d.

## TEXTILE FABRICS. With numerous Woodcuts. Large
Crown 8vo, cloth, 2s. 6d.

*ROOSE (ROBSON), M.D., F.C.S.—*

## THE WEAR AND TEAR OF LONDON LIFE.
Crown 8vo, sewed, 1s.

*ROLAND (ARTHUR)—*

## FARMING FOR PLEASURE AND PROFIT. Edited
by WILLIAM ABLETT. 8 vols. Crown 8vo, 5s. each.

DAIRY-FARMING, MANAGEMENT OF COWS, &c.

POULTRY-KEEPING.

TREE-PLANTING, FOR ORNAMENTATION OR PROFIT.

STOCK-KEEPING AND CATTLE-REARING.

DRAINAGE OF LAND, IRRIGATION, MANURES, &c.

ROOT-GROWING, HOPS, &c.

MANAGEMENT OF GRASS LANDS, LAYING DOWN GRASS, ARTIFICIAL GRASSES, &c.

MARKET GARDENING, HUSBANDRY FOR FARMERS AND GENERAL CULTIVATORS.

*RUSDEN (G. W.), for many years Clerk of the Parliament in Victoria—*

## A HISTORY OF AUSTRALIA. With a Coloured Map.
3 vols. Demy 8vo, 50s.

## A HISTORY OF NEW ZEALAND. With Maps. 3 vols.
Demy 8vo, 50s.

*SCOTT (A. DE C., MAJOR-GENERAL, late Royal Engineers)—*

## LONDON WATER : a Review of the Present Condition and
Suggested Improvements of the Metropolitan Water Supply. Crown 8vo, sewed, 2s.

*SCOTT-STEVENSON (MRS.)—*

## ON SUMMER SEAS. Including the Mediterranean, the
Ægean, the Ionian, and the Euxine, and a voyage down the Danube. With a Map. Demy 8vo, 16s.

## OUR HOME IN CYPRUS. With a Map and Illustra-
tions. Third Edition. Demy 8vo, 14s.

## OUR RIDE THROUGH ASIA MINOR. With Map.
Demy 8vo, 18s.

*SHEPHERD (MAJOR), R.E.—*

## PRAIRIE EXPERIENCES IN HANDLING CATTLE
AND SHEEP. With Illustrations and Map. Demy 8vo, 10s. 6d.

*SHIRREFF (MISS)—*

## HOME EDUCATION IN RELATION TO THE
KINDERGARTEN. Two Lectures. Crown 8vo, 1s. 6d.

*SHORE (ARABELLA)—*

## DANTE FOR BEGINNERS : a Sketch of the " Divina
Commedia." With Translations, Biographical and Critical Notices, and Illustrations. With Portrait. Crown 8vo, 6s.

*SIMMONDS (T. L.)—*

### ANIMAL PRODUCTS: their Preparation, Commercial
Uses, and Value. With numerous Illustrations. Large crown 8vo, 7s. 6d.

### SINGER'S STORY, A. Related by the Author of "Flitters,
Tatters, and the Counsellor." Crown 8vo, sewed, 1s.

*SINNETT (A. P.)—*

### ESOTERIC BUDDHISM. Annotated and enlarged by
the Author. Fifth Edition. Crown 8vo, 6s.

### KARMA. A Novel. New Edition. Crown 8vo, 3s. 6d.

*SINNETT (MRS.)—*

### THE PURPOSE OF THEOSOPHY. Crown 8vo, 3s.

*SMART (HAWLEY)—*

### TIE AND TRICK. Crown 8vo, 6s.

*SMITH (MAJOR R. MURDOCK), R.E.—*

### PERSIAN ART. Second Edition, with Map and Woodcuts.
Large crown 8vo, 2s.

*STORY (W. W.)—*

### ROBA DI ROMA. Seventh Edition, with Additions and
Portrait. Crown 8vo, cloth, 10s. 6d.

### CASTLE ST. ANGELO. With Illustrations. Crown
8vo, 10s. 6d.

*SUTCLIFFE (JOHN)—*

### THE SCULPTOR AND ART STUDENT'S GUIDE
to the Proportions of the Human Form, with Measurements in feet and inches of
Full-Grown Figures of Both Sexes and of Various Ages. By Dr. G. SCHADOW,
Member of the Academies, Stockholm, Dresden, Rome, &c. &c. Translated by
J. J. WRIGHT. Plates reproduced by J. SUTCLIFFE. Oblong folio, 31s. 6d.

*TAINE (H. A.)—*

### NOTES ON ENGLAND. Translated, with Introduction,
by W. FRASER RAE. Eighth Edition. With Portrait. Crown 8vo, 5s.

*TANNER (PROFESSOR), F.C.S.—*

### HOLT CASTLE; or, Threefold Interest in Land. Crown
8vo, 4s. 6d.

### JACK'S EDUCATION; OR, HOW HE LEARNT
FARMING. Second Edition. Crown 8vo, 3s. 6d.

TEMPLE (SIR RICHARD), BART., M.P., G.C.S.I.—
COSMOPOLITAN ESSAYS. With Maps. Demy 8vo, 16s.

TOPINARD (DR. PAUL)—
ANTHROPOLOGY. With a Preface by Professor PAUL
BROCA. With numerous Illustrations. Large crown 8vo, 7s. 6d.

TOVEY (LIEUT.-COL., R.E.)—
MARTIAL LAW AND CUSTOM OF WAR; or, Military
Law and Jurisdiction in Troublous Times. Crown 8vo, 6s.

TRAILL (H. D.)—
THE NEW LUCIAN. Being a Series of Dialogues of the
Dead. Demy 8vo, 12s.

TROLLOPE (ANTHONY)—
AYALA'S ANGEL. Crown 8vo. 6s.
LIFE OF CICERO. 2 vols. 8vo. £1 4s.
THE CHRONICLES OF BARSETSHIRE. A Uniform
Edition, in 8 vols., large crown 8vo, handsomely printed, each vol. containing
Frontispiece. 6s. each.

| | |
|---|---|
| THE WARDEN and BAR-CHESTER TOWERS. 2 vols. | THE SMALL HOUSE AT ALLINGTON. 2 vols. |
| DR. THORNE. | LAST CHRONICLE OF |
| FRAMLEY PARSONAGE. | BARSET. 2 vols. |

UNIVERSAL CATALOGUE OF BOOKS ON ART. Com-
piled for the use of the National Art Library, and the Schools of Art in the
United Kingdom. In 2 vols. Crown 4to, half-morocco, £2 2s.
Supplemental Volume to Ditto. Crown 8vo, 8s. nett.

VERON (EUGENE)—
ÆSTHETICS. Translated by W. H. ARMSTRONG. Large
crown 8vo, 7s. 6d.

WALE (REV. HENRY JOHN), M.A.—
MY GRANDFATHER'S POCKET BOOK, from 1701 to
1796. Author of "Sword and Surplice." Demy 8vo, 12s.

WALKER (MRS.)—
EASTERN LIFE AND SCENERY, with Excursions to
Asia Minor, Mitylene, Crete, and Roumania. 2 vols., with Frontispiece to each
vol. Crown 8vo, 21s.

*WESTWOOD (J. O.), M.A., F.L.S., &c.—*

## CATALOGUE OF THE FICTILE IVORIES IN THE
SOUTH KENSINGTON MUSEUM. With an Account of the Continental Collections of Classical and Mediæval Ivories. Royal 8vo, half-morocco, £1 4s.

## WHIST HANDBOOKS. By AQUARIUS—

### THE HANDS AT WHIST. 32mo, cloth gilt, 1s.

### EASY WHIST. 32mo, cloth gilt, 1s.

### ADVANCED WHIST. 32mo, cloth gilt, 1s.

*WHITE (WALTER)—*

## A MONTH IN YORKSHIRE. With a Map. Fifth
Edition. Post 8vo, 4s.

## A LONDONER'S WALK TO THE LAND'S END, AND
A TRIP TO THE SCILLY ISLES. With 4 Maps. Third Edition. Post 8vo, 4s.

## WILL-O'-THE-WISPS, THE. Translated from the German
of Marie Petersen by CHARLOTTE J. HART. With Illustrations. Crown 8vo, 7s. 6d.

## WORKING MAN'S PHILOSOPHY, A. By "ONE OF THE
CROWD." Crown 8vo, 3s.

*WORNUM (R. N.)—*

## ANALYSIS OF ORNAMENT: THE CHARACTER-
ISTICS OF STYLES. An Introduction to the History of Ornamental Art. With many Illustrations. Ninth Edition. Royal 8vo, cloth, 8s.

*WORSAAE (J. J. A.)—*

## INDUSTRIAL ARTS OF DENMARK, FROM THE
EARLIEST TIMES TO THE DANISH CONQUEST OF ENGLAND. With Maps and Woodcuts. Large crown 8vo, 3s. 6d.

*YEO (DR. J. BURNEY)—*

## CLIMATE AND HEALTH RESORTS. New Edition.
Crown 8vo, 10s. 6d.

*YOUNGE (C. D.)—*

## PARALLEL LIVES OF ANCIENT AND MODERN
HEROES. New Edition. 12mo, cloth, 4s. 6d.

## SOUTH KENSINGTON MUSEUM
## DESCRIPTIVE AND ILLUSTRATED CATALOGUES.
*Royal 8vo, half-bound.*

BRONZES OF EUROPEAN ORIGIN. By C. D. E. FORTNUM.
£1 10s.

DYCE'S COLLECTION OF PRINTED BOOKS AND MANUSCRIPTS. 2 vols. 14s.

DYCE'S COLLECTION OF PAINTINGS, ENGRAVINGS, &c. 6s. 6d.

FURNITURE AND WOODWORK, ANCIENT AND MODERN. By J. H. POLLEN. £1 1s.

GLASS VESSELS. By A. NESBITT. 18s.

GOLD AND SILVER SMITH'S WORK. By J. G. POLLEN. £1 6s.

IVORIES, ANCIENT AND MEDIÆVAL. By W. MASKELL. 21s.

IVORIES, FICTILE. By J. O. WESTWOOD. £1 4s.

MAIOLICA, HISPANO-MORESCO, PERSIAN, DAMAS- CUS AND RHODIAN WARES. By C. D. E. FORTNUM. £2.

MUSICAL INSTRUMENTS. By C. ENGEL. 12s.

SCULPTURE, ITALIAN SCULPTURE OF THE MIDDLE AGES. By J. C. ROBINSON. Cloth, 7s. 6d.

SWISS COINS. By R. S. POOLE. £2 10s.

TEXTILE FABRICS. By Rev. D. ROCK. £1 11s. 6d.

WATER-COLOUR PAINTING. By S. REDGRAVE. £1 1s.

UNIVERSAL CATALOGUE OF BOOKS ON ART. 2 vols. Small 4to, £1 1s. each.

UNIVERSAL CATALOGUE OF BOOKS ON ART. Supple- mentary vol. 8s. nett.

# SOUTH KENSINGTON MUSEUM SCIENCE AND ART HANDBOOKS.

## Handsomely printed in large crown 8vo.

*Published for the Committee of the Council on Education.*

**FOOD GRAINS OF INDIA.** By Prof. A. H. Church, M.A., F.C.S., F.I.C. With Numerous Woodcuts. Small 4to. 6s.

**THE ART OF THE SARACENS IN EGYPT.** By Stanley Lane Poole B A., M.A.R.S. With 108 Woodcuts. Demy 8vo, 12s.

**ENGLISH PORCELAIN:** A Handbook to the China made in England during the 18th Century, as illustrated by Specimens chiefly in the National Collections. By Prof. A. H. Church, M.A. With numerous Woodcuts. 3s.

**RUSSIAN ART AND ART OBJECTS IN RUSSIA:** A Handbook to the reproduction of Goldsmiths' work and other Art Treasures from that country in the South Kensington Museum. By Alfred Maskell. With Illustrations. 4s. 6d.

**FRENCH POTTERY.** By Paul Gasnault and Edouard Garnier. With Illustrations and marks. 3s.

**ENGLISH EARTHENWARE:** A Handbook to the Wares made in England during the 17th and 18th Centuries, as illustrated by Specimens in the National Collection. By Prof. A. H. Church, M.A. With numerous Woodcuts. 3s.

**INDUSTRIAL ARTS OF DENMARK.** From the Earliest Times to the Danish Conquest of England. By J. J. A. Worsaae, Hon. F.S.A., &c. &c. With Map and Woodcuts. 3s. 6d.

**INDUSTRIAL ARTS OF SCANDINAVIA IN THE PAGAN TIME.** By Hans Hildebrand, Royal Antiquary of Sweden. With numerous Woodcuts. 2s. 6d.

**PRECIOUS STONES:** Considered in their Scientific and Artistic relations, with a Catalogue of the Townsend Collection of Gems in the South Kensington Museum. By Prof. A. H. Church, M.A. With a Coloured Plate and Woodcuts. 2s. 6d.

**INDUSTRIAL ARTS OF INDIA.** By Sir George C. M. Birdwood, C.S.I., &c. With Map and Woodcuts. Demy 8vo, 14s.

**HANDBOOK TO THE DYCE AND FORSTER COLLEC-**TIONS in the South Kensington Museum. With Portraits and Facsimilies. 2s. 6d.

**INDUSTRIAL ARTS IN SPAIN.** By Juan F. Riaño. With numerous Woodcuts. 4s.

**GLASS.** By Alexander Nesbitt. With numerous Woodcuts. 2s. 6d.

**GOLD AND SILVER SMITHS' WORK.** By John Hunger-ford Pollen, M.A. With numerous Woodcuts. 2s. 6d.

**TAPESTRY.** By Alfred de Champeaux. With Woodcuts. 2s. 6d.

**BRONZES.** By C. Drury E. Fortnum, F.S.A. With numerous Woodcuts. 2s. 6d.

SOUTH KENSINGTON MUSEUM SCIENCE & ART HANDBOOKS—*Continued.*

**PLAIN WORDS ABOUT WATER.** By A. H. CHURCH, M.A. Oxon. With Illustrations. Sewed, 6d.

**ANIMAL PRODUCTS:** their Preparation, Commercial Uses, and Value. By T. L. SIMMONDS. With Illustrations. 7s. 6d.

**FOOD:** Some Account of its Sources, Constituents, and Uses. By PROFESSOR A. H. CHURCH, M.A. Oxon. Sixth Thousand. 3s.

**ECONOMIC ENTOMOLOGY.** By ANDREW MURRAY, F.L.S. APTERA. With Illustrations. 7s. 6d.

**JAPANESE POTTERY.** Being a Native Report. With an Introduction and Catalogue by A. W. FRANKS, M.A., F.R.S., F.S.A. With Illustrations and Marks. 2s. 6d.

**HANDBOOK TO THE SPECIAL LOAN COLLECTION** of Scientific Apparatus. 3s.

**INDUSTRIAL ARTS:** Historical Sketches. With Numerous Illustrations. 3s.

**TEXTILE FABRICS.** By the Very Rev. DANIEL ROCK, D.D. With numerous Woodcuts. 2s. 6d.

**JONES COLLECTION IN THE SOUTH KENSINGTON MUSEUM.** With Portrait and Woodcuts. 2s. 6d.

**COLLEGE AND CORPORATION PLATE.** A Handbook to the Reproductions of Silver Plate in the South Kensigton Museum from Celebrated English Collections. By WILFRED JOSEPH CRIPPS, M.A., F.S.A. With Illustrations. 2s. 6d.

**IVORIES: ANCIENT AND MEDIÆVAL.** By WILLIAM MASKELL. With numerous Woodcuts. 2s. 6d.

**ANCIENT AND MODERN FURNITURE AND WOOD-WORK.** By JOHN HUNGERFORD POLLEN, M.A. With numerous Woodcuts. 2s. 6d.

**MAIOLICA.** By C. DRURY E. FORTNUM, F.S.A. With numerous Woodcuts. 2s. 6d.

**THE CHEMISTRY OF FOODS.** With Microscopic Illustrations. By JAMES BELL, Ph.D., &c., Principal of the Somerset House Laboratory. Part I.—Tea, Coffee, Cocoa, Sugar, &c. 2s. 6d. Part II.—Milk, Butter, Cheese, Cereals, Prepared Starches, &c. 3s.

**MUSICAL INSTRUMENTS.** By CARL ENGEL. With numerous Woodcuts. 2s. 6d.

**MANUAL OF DESIGN,** compiled from the Writings and Addresses of RICHARD REDGRAVE, R.A. By GILBERT R. REDGRAVE. With Woodcuts. 2s. 6d.

**PERSIAN ART.** By MAJOR R. MURDOCK SMITH, R.E. With Map and Woodcuts. Second Edition, enlarged. 2s.

# CARLYLE'S (THOMAS) WORKS.

## THE ASHBURTON EDITION.

An entirely New Edition of the Writings of Mr. CARLYLE, to be completed in Seventeen Volumes, demy 8vo, is now publishing. For Particulars see page 2.

### CHEAP AND UNIFORM EDITION.

*23 vols., Crown 8vo, cloth, £7 5s.*

THE FRENCH REVOLUTION.: A History. 2 vols., 12s.

OLIVER CROMWELL'S LETTERS AND SPEECHES, with Elucidations, &c. 3 vols., 18s.

LIVES OF SCHILLER AND JOHN STERLING. 1 vol., 6s.

CRITICAL AND MISCELLANEOUS ESSAYS. 4 vols., £1 4s.

SARTOR RESARTUS AND LECTURES ON HEROES. 1 vol., 6s.

LATTER-DAY PAMPHLETS. 1 vol., 6s.

CHARTISM AND PAST AND PRESENT. 1 vol., 6s.

TRANSLATIONS FROM THE GERMAN OF MUSÆUS, TIECK, AND RICHTER. 1 vol., 6s.

WILHELM MEISTER, by Göethe. A Translation. 2 vols., 12s.

HISTORY OF FRIEDRICH THE SECOND, called Frederick the Great. 7 vols., £2 9s.

### LIBRARY EDITION COMPLETE.

Handsomely printed in 34 vols., demy 8vo, cloth, £15 3s.

SARTOR RESARTUS. With a Portrait, 7s. 6d.

THE FRENCH REVOLUTION. A History. 3 vols., each 9s.

LIFE OF FREDERICK SCHILLER AND EXAMINATION OF HIS WORKS. With Supplement of 1872. Portrait and Plates, 9s.

CRITICAL AND MISCELLANEOUS ESSAYS. With Portrait. 6 vols., each 9s.

ON HEROES, HERO WORSHIP, AND THE HEROIC IN HISTORY. 7s. 6d.

PAST AND PRESENT. 9s.

CARLYLE'S (THOMAS) WORKS.—LIBRARY EDITION—*Continued.*

## OLIVER CROMWELL'S LETTERS AND SPEECHES. With
Portraits. 5 vols., each 9s.

## LATTER-DAY PAMPHLETS. 9s.

## LIFE OF JOHN STERLING. With Portrait, 9s.

## HISTORY OF FREDERICK THE SECOND. 10 vols.,
each 9s.

## TRANSLATIONS FROM THE GERMAN. 3 vols., each 9s.

## EARLY KINGS OF NORWAY; ESSAY ON THE POR-
TRAITS OF JOHN KNOX; AND GENERAL INDEX. With Portrait
Illustrations. 8vo, cloth, 9s.

---

### PEOPLE'S EDITION.

*37 vols., small 8vo, 2s. each vol.; or in sets, 37 vols. in 19, cloth gilt, £3 14s.*

SARTOR RESARTUS.

FRENCH REVOLUTION. 3 vols.

LIFE OF JOHN STERLING.

OLIVER CROMWELL'S LET-
TERS AND SPEECHES. 5 vols.

ON HEROES AND HERO
WORSHIP.

PAST AND PRESENT.

CRITICAL AND MISCELLA-
NEOUS ESSAYS. 7 vols.

LATTER-DAY PAMPHLETS.

LIFE OF SCHILLER.

FREDERICK THE GREAT.
10 vols.

WILHELM MEISTER. 3 vols.

TRANSLATIONS FROM MU-
SÆUS, TIECK, AND RICHTER.
2 vols.

THE EARLY KINGS OF NOR-
WAY; Essay on the Portraits of Knox;
and General Index.

---

SARTOR RESARTUS. Cheap Edition, crown 8vo, sewed, 1s.

---

### SIXPENNY EDITION.
*4to, sewed.*

SARTOR RESARTUS. Eightieth Thousand.

HEROES AND HERO WORSHIP.

ESSAYS: BURNS, JOHNSON, SCOTT, THE DIAMOND NECKLACE.
*The above in 1 vol., cloth, 2s. 6d.*

# DICKENS'S (CHARLES) WORKS.

## ORIGINAL EDITIONS.

### *In demy 8vo.*

THE MYSTERY OF EDWIN DROOD. With Illustrations
by S. L. Fildes, and a Portrait engraved by Baker. Cloth, 7s. 6d.

OUR MUTUAL FRIEND. With Forty Illustrations by Marcus
Stone. Cloth, £1 1s.

THE PICKWICK PAPERS. With Forty-three Illustrations
by Seymour and Phiz. Cloth, £1 1s.

NICHOLAS NICKLEBY. With Forty Illustrations by Phiz.
Cloth, £1 1s.

SKETCHES BY "BOZ." With Forty Illustrations by George
Cruikshank. Cloth, £1 1s.

MARTIN CHUZZLEWIT. With Forty Illustrations by Phiz.
Cloth, £1 1s.

DOMBEY AND SON. With Forty Illustrations by Phiz.
Cloth, £1 1s.

DAVID COPPERFIELD. With Forty Illustrations by Phiz.
Cloth, £1 1s.

BLEAK HOUSE. With Forty Illustrations by Phiz. Cloth,
£1 1s.

LITTLE DORRIT. With Forty Illustrations by Phiz. Cloth,
£1 1s.

THE OLD CURIOSITY SHOP. With Seventy-five Illus-
trations by George Cattermole and H. K. Browne. A New Edition. Uniform with
the other volumes, £1 1s.

BARNABY RUDGE: a Tale of the Riots of 'Eighty. With
Seventy-eight Illustrations by George Cattermole and H. K. Browne. Uniform with
the other volumes, £1 1s.

CHRISTMAS BOOKS: Containing—The Christmas Carol;
The Cricket on the Hearth; The Chimes; The Battle of Life; The Haunted House.
With all the original Illustrations. Cloth, 12s.

OLIVER TWIST and TALE OF TWO CITIES. In one
volume. Cloth, £1 1s.

OLIVER TWIST. Separately. With Twenty-four Illustrations
by George Cruikshank Cloth, 11s.

A TALE OF TWO CITIES. Separately. With Sixteen Illustrations by Phiz. Cloth, 9s.

\*\* *The remainder of Dickens's Works were not originally printed in demy 8vo.*

## DICKENS'S (CHARLES) WORKS.—*Continued.*

### LIBRARY EDITION.

*In post 8vo. With the Original Illustrations, 30 vols., cloth, £12.*

| | | | | s. | d. |
|---|---|---|---|---|---|
| PICKWICK PAPERS ... ... | ... 43 | Illustrns., | 2 vols. | 16 | 0 |
| NICHOLAS NICKLEBY ... | ... 39 | ,, | 2 vols. | 16 | 0 |
| MARTIN CHUZZLEWIT ... ... ... | ... 40 | ,, | 2 vols. | 16 | 0 |
| OLD CURIOSITY SHOP & REPRINTED PIECES | 36 | ,, | 2 vols. | 16 | 0 |
| BARNABY RUDGE and HARD TIMES ... | ... 36 | ,, | 2 vols. | 16 | 0 |
| BLEAK HOUSE ... | ... 40 | ,, | 2 vols. | 16 | 0 |
| LITTLE DORRIT | ... 40 | ,, | 2 vols. | 16 | 0 |
| DOMBEY AND SON ... | ... 38 | ,, | 2 vols. | 16 | 0 |
| DAVID COPPERFIELD | ... 38 | ,, | 2 vols. | 16 | 0 |
| OUR MUTUAL FRIEND | ... 40 | ,, | 2 vols. | 16 | 0 |
| SKETCHES BY "BOZ" | ... 39 | ,, | 1 vol. | 8 | 0 |
| OLIVER TWIST | ... 24 | ,, | 1 vol. | 8 | 0 |
| CHRISTMAS BOOKS ... | ... 17 | ,, | 1 vol. | 8 | 0 |
| A TALE OF TWO CITIES ... | ... 16 | ,, | 1 vol. | 8 | 0 |
| GREAT EXPECTATIONS ... ... ... | ... 8 | ,, | 1 vol. | 8 | 0 |
| PICTURES FROM ITALY & AMERICAN NOTES | 8 | ,, | 1 vol. | 8 | 0 |
| UNCOMMERCIAL TRAVELLER ... | .. 8 | ,, | 1 vol. | 8 | 0 |
| CHILD'S HISTORY OF ENGLAND ... | ... 8 | ,, | 1 vol. | 8 | 0 |
| EDWIN DROOD and MISCELLANIES ... | ... 12 | ,, | 1 vol. | 8 | 0 |
| CHRISTMAS STORIES from "Household Words," &c. | 14 | ,, | 1 vol. | 8 | 0 |

THE LIFE OF CHARLES DICKENS. By JOHN FORSTER. With Illustrations. Uniform with this Edition. 10s. 6d.

**A NEW EDITION OF ABOVE, WITH THE ORIGINAL ILLUSTRATIONS, IN CROWN 8vo, 30 VOLS. IN SETS ONLY.**

## DICKENS'S (CHARLES) WORKS.—*Continued.*

### THE "CHARLES DICKENS" EDITION.

*In Crown 8vo. In 21 vols., cloth, with Illustrations, £3 16s.*

| | | s. | d. |
|---|---|---|---|
| PICKWICK PAPERS | 8 Illustrations | 4 | 0 |
| MARTIN CHUZZLEWIT | 8 ,, | 4 | 0 |
| DOMBEY AND SON | 8 ,, | 4 | 0 |
| NICHOLAS NICKLEBY | 8 ,, | 4 | 0 |
| DAVID COPPERFIELD | 8 ,, | 4 | 0 |
| BLEAK HOUSE | 8 ,, | 4 | 0 |
| LITTLE DORRIT | 8 ,, | 4 | 0 |
| OUR MUTUAL FRIEND | 8 ,, | 4 | 0 |
| BARNABY RUDGE | 8 ,, | 3 | 6 |
| OLD CURIOSITY SHOP | 8 ,, | 3 | 6 |
| A CHILD'S HISTORY OF ENGLAND | 4 ,, | 3 | 6 |
| EDWIN DROOD and OTHER STORIES | 8 ,, | 3 | 6 |
| CHRISTMAS STORIES, from "Household Words" | 8 ,, | 3 | 6 |
| SKETCHES BY "BOZ" | 8 ,, | 3 | 6 |
| AMERICAN NOTES and REPRINTED PIECES | 8 ,, | 3 | 6 |
| CHRISTMAS BOOKS | 8 ,, | 3 | 6 |
| OLIVER TWIST | 8 ,, | 3 | 6 |
| GREAT EXPECTATIONS | 8 ,, | 3 | 6 |
| TALE OF TWO CITIES | 8 ,, | 3 | 0 |
| HARD TIMES and PICTURES FROM ITALY | 8 ,, | 3 | 0 |
| UNCOMMERCIAL TRAVELLER | 4 ,, | 3 | 0 |
| THE LIFE OF CHARLES DICKENS. Numerous Illustrations. | 2 vols. | 7 | 0 |
| THE LETTERS OF CHARLES DICKENS. | 2 vols. | 8 | 0 |

## DICKENS'S (CHARLES) WORKS.—*Continued.*

# THE ILLUSTRATED LIBRARY EDITION.

*Complete in 30 Volumes. Demy 8vo, 10s. each; or set, £15.*

This Edition is printed on a finer paper and in a larger type than has been employed in any previous edition. The type has been cast especially for it, and the page is of a size to admit of the introduction of all the original illustrations.

No such attractive issue has been made of the writings of Mr. Dickens, which, various as have been the forms of publication adapted to the demands of an ever widely-increasing popularity, have never yet been worthily presented in a really handsome library form.

The collection comprises all the minor writings it was Mr. Dickens's wish to preserve.

SKETCHES BY "BOZ." With 40 Illustrations by George Cruikshank.

PICKWICK PAPERS. 2 vols. With 42 Illustrations by Phiz.

OLIVER TWIST. With 24 Illustrations by Cruikshank.

NICHOLAS NICKLEBY. 2 vols. With 40 Illustrations by Phiz.

OLD CURIOSITY SHOP and REPRINTED PIECES. 2 vols. With Illustrations by Cattermole, &c.

BARNABY RUDGE and HARD TIMES. 2 vols. With Illustrations by Cattermole, &c.

MARTIN CHUZZLEWIT. 2 vols. With 40 Illustrations by Phiz.

AMERICAN NOTES and PICTURES FROM ITALY. 1 vol. With 8 Illustrations.

DOMBEY AND SON. 2 vols. With 40 Illustrations by Phiz.

DAVID COPPERFIELD. 2 vols. With 40 Illustrations by Phiz.

BLEAK HOUSE. 2 vols. With 40 Illustrations by Phiz.

LITTLE DORRIT. 2 vols. With 40 Illustrations by Phiz.

A TALE OF TWO CITIES. With 16 Illustrations by Phiz.

THE UNCOMMERCIAL TRAVELLER. With 8 Illustrations by Marcus Stone.

GREAT EXPECTATIONS. With 8 Illustrations by Marcus Stone.

OUR MUTUAL FRIEND. 2 vols. With 40 Illustrations by Marcus Stone.

CHRISTMAS BOOKS. With 17 Illustrations by Sir Edwin Landseer, R.A., Maclise, R.A., &c. &c.

HISTORY OF ENGLAND. With 8 Illustrations by Marcus Stone.

CHRISTMAS STORIES. (From "Household Words" and "All the Year Round.") With 14 Illustrations.

EDWIN DROOD AND OTHER STORIES. With 12 Illustrations by S. L. Fildes.

DICKENS'S (CHARLES) WORKS.—*Continued.*

# THE POPULAR LIBRARY EDITION
OF THE WORKS OF

# CHARLES DICKENS,

. *In* 30 *Vols., large crown 8vo, price £6; separate Vols.* 4s. *each.*

An Edition printed on good paper, each volume containing 16 full-page Illustrations, selected from the Household Edition, on Plate Paper.

SKETCHES BY "BOZ."
PICKWICK.   2 vols.
OLIVER TWIST.
NICHOLAS NICKLEBY.   2 vols.
MARTIN CHUZZLEWIT.   2 vols.
DOMBEY AND SON.   2 vols.
DAVID COPPERFIELD.   2 vols.
CHRISTMAS BOOKS.
OUR MUTUAL FRIEND.   2 vols.
CHRISTMAS STORIES.
BLEAK HOUSE.   2 vols.
LITTLE DORRIT.   2 vols.
OLD CURIOSITY SHOP AND REPRINTED PIECES.   2 vols.
BARNABY RUDGE.   2 vols.
UNCOMMERCIAL TRAVELLER.
GREAT EXPECTATIONS.
TALE OF TWO CITIES.
CHILD'S HISTORY OF ENGLAND.
EDWIN DROOD AND MISCELLANIES.
PICTURES FROM ITALY AND AMERICAN NOTES.

# DICKENS'S (CHARLES) WORKS.—*Continued.*

## HOUSEHOLD EDITION.

*In 22 Volumes. Crown 4to, cloth, £4 8s. 6d.*

MARTIN CHUZZLEWIT, with 59 Illustrations, cloth, 5s.

DAVID COPPERFIELD, with 60 Illustrations and a Portrait, cloth, 5s.

BLEAK HOUSE, with 61 Illustrations, cloth, 5s.

LITTLE DORRIT, with 58 Illustrations, cloth, 5s.

PICKWICK PAPERS, with 56 Illustrations, cloth, 5s.

OUR MUTUAL FRIEND, with 58 Illustrations, cloth, 5s.

NICHOLAS NICKLEBY, with 59 Illustrations, cloth, 5s.

DOMBEY AND SON, with 61 Illustrations, cloth, 5s.

EDWIN DROOD; REPRINTED PIECES; and other Stories, with 30 Illustrations, cloth, 5s.

THE LIFE OF DICKENS. BY JOHN FORSTER. With 40 Illustrations. Cloth, 5s.

BARNABY RUDGE, with 46 Illustrations, cloth, 4s.

OLD CURIOSITY SHOP, with 32 Illustrations, cloth, 4s.

CHRISTMAS STORIES, with 23 Illustrations, cloth, 4s.

OLIVER TWIST, with 28 Illustrations, cloth, 3s.

GREAT EXPECTATIONS, with 26 Illustrations, cloth, 3s.

SKETCHES BY "BOZ," with 36 Illustrations, cloth, 3s.

UNCOMMERCIAL TRAVELLER, with 26 Illustrations, cloth, 3s.

CHRISTMAS BOOKS, with 28 Illustrations, cloth, 3s.

THE HISTORY OF ENGLAND, with 15 Illustrations, cloth, 3s.

AMERICAN NOTES and PICTURES FROM ITALY, with 18 Illustrations, cloth, 3s.

A TALE OF TWO CITIES, with 25 Illustrations, cloth, 3s.

HARD TIMES, with 20 Illustrations, cloth, 2s. 6d.

DICKENS'S (CHARLES) WORKS.—*Continued.*

# THE CABINET EDITION.
*Now Publishing.*

To be completed in 30 vols. small fcap. 8vo, Marble Paper Sides, Cloth Backs, with uncut edges, price Eighteenpence each.

A Complete Work will be Published every Month, and *each Volume* will contain *Eight Illustrations reproduced from the Originals.*

CHRISTMAS BOOKS, One Vol.,

MARTIN CHUZZLEWIT, Two Vols.

DAVID COPPERFIELD, Two Vols.,

OLIVER TWIST, One Vol.,

GREAT EXPECTATIONS, One Vol.,

NICHOLAS NICKLEBY, Two Vols.,

SKETCHES BY BOZ, One Vol.,  [*November.*

CHRISTMAS STORIES, One Vol.  [*December.*

### MR. DICKENS'S READINGS.
*Fcap. 8vo, sewed.*

CHRISTMAS CAROL IN PROSE. 1s.
CRICKET ON THE HEARTH. 1s.
CHIMES: A GOBLIN STORY. 1s.

STORY OF LITTLE DOMBEY. 1s.
POOR TRAVELLER, BOOTS AT THE HOLLY-TREE INN, and MRS. GAMP. 1s.

A CHRISTMAS CAROL, with the Original Coloured Plates, being a reprint of the Original Edition. Small 8vo, red cloth, gilt edges, 5s.

### REPRINTED FROM THE ORIGINAL PLATES.

A CHRISTMAS CAROL. Fcap. cloth, 1s.

THE CHIMES: A Goblin Story. Fcap. cloth, 1s.

THE CRICKET ON THE HEARTH: A Fairy Tale of Home. Fcap. cloth, 1s.

THE BATTLE OF LIFE. A Love Story. Fcap. cloth, 1s.

THE HAUNTED MAN AND THE GHOST'S STORY. Fcap. cloth, 1s

DICKENS'S (CHARLES) WORKS.—*Continued.*

*The Cheapest and Handiest Edition of*

# THE WORKS OF CHARLES DICKENS.

The Pocket-Volume Edition of Charles Dickens's Works.

*In 30 Vols. small fcap. 8vo, £2 5s.*

## SIXPENNY REPRINTS:

(I.)

### READINGS FROM THE WORKS OF CHARLES DICKENS.

As selected and read by himself and now published for the first time.   Illustrated.

(II.)

### A CHRISTMAS CAROL AND THE HAUNTED MAN.

By CHARLES DICKENS.   Illustrated.

(III.)

### THE CHIMES: A GOBLIN STORY, AND THE CRICKET ON THE HEARTH.   Illustrated.

(IV.)

### THE BATTLE OF LIFE: A LOVE STORY, HUNTED DOWN, AND A HOLIDAY ROMANCE.   Illustrated.

**The last Three Volumes as Christmas Works,**
In One Volume, red cloth, 2s. 6d.

# THE FORTNIGHTLY REVIEW.

### Edited by FRANK HARRIS.

THE FORTNIGHTLY REVIEW is published on the 1st of every month, and a Volume is completed every Six Months.

*The following are among the Contributors:—*

GRANT ALLEN.
SIR RUTHERFORD ALCOCK.
MATHEW ARNOLD.
PROFESSOR BAIN.
SIR SAMUEL BAKER.
PROFESSOR BEESLY.
PAUL BERT.
BARON GEORGETON BUNSEN.
DR. BRIDGES.
HON. GEORGE C. BRODRICK.
JAMES BRYCE, M.P.
THOMAS BURT, M.P.
SIR GEORGE CAMPBELL, M.P.
THE EARL OF CARNARVON.
EMILIO CASTELAR.
RT. HON. J. CHAMBERLAIN, M.P.
PROFESSOR SIDNEY COLVIN.
MONTAGUE COOKSON, Q.C.
L. H. COURTNEY, M.P.
G. H. DARWIN.
SIR GEORGE W. DASENT.
PROFESSOR A. V. DICEY.
M. E. GRANT DUFF, M.P.
T. H. S. ESCOTT.
RIGHT HON. H. FAWCETT, M.P.
EDWARD A. FREEMAN.
J. A. FROUDE.
MRS. GARRET-ANDERSON.
J. W. L. GLAISHER, F.R.S.
SIR J. E. GORST, Q.C., M.P.
THOMAS HARE.
F. HARRISON.
LORD HOUGHTON.
PROFESSOR HUXLEY.
PROFESSOR R. C. JEBB.
PROFESSOR JEVONS.
ANDREW LANG.
EMILE DE LAVELEYE.

T. E. CLIFFE LESLIE.
MARQUIS OF LORNE.
SIR JOHN LUBBOCK, Bart., M.P.
THE EARL LYTTON.
SIR H. S. MAINE.
DR. MAUDSLEY.
PROFESSOR MAX MÜLLER.
GEORGE MEREDITH.
G. OSBORNE MORGAN, Q.C., M.P.
PROFESSOR HENRY MORLEY.
RT. HON. JOHN MORLEY, M.P.
WILLIAM MORRIS.
PROFESSOR H. N. MOSELEY.
F. W. H. MYERS.
F. W. NEWMAN.
PROFESSOR JOHN NICHOL.
W. G. PALGRAVE.
WALTER H. PATER.
RT. HON. LYON PLAYFAIR, M.P.
LORD SHERBROOKE.
PROFESSOR SIDGWICK.
HERBERT SPENCER.
HON. E. L. STANLEY.
SIR J. FITZJAMES STEPHEN, Q.C.
LESLIE STEPHEN.
J. HUTCHISON STIRLING.
A. C. SWINBURNE.
DR. VON SYBEL.
J. A. SYMONDS.
THE REV. EDWARD F. TALBOT
(Warden of Keble College).
SIR RICHARD TEMPLE, Bart.
W. T. THORNTON
HON. LIONEL A. TOLLEMACHE.
H. D. TRAILL.
PROFESSOR TYNDALL.
A. J. WILSON.
THE EDITOR.

&c. &c. &c.

THE FORTNIGHTLY REVIEW *is published at* 2s. 6d.